BAD LAWS

Philip Johnston

To my parents

Constable & Robinson Ltd
3 The Lanchesters
162 Fulham Palace Road
London W6 9ER
www.constablerobinson.com

Published in the UK by Constable,
an imprint of Constable & Robinson Ltd, 2010

A copy of the British Library Cataloguing in Publication Data
is available from the British Library

ISBN 978-1-8490-1010-8

Printed and bound in the EU

3 5 7 9 10 8 6 4 2

CONTENTS

ACKNOWLEDGEMENTS

I would like to thank Andreas Campomar and Rob Blackhurst at Constable for putting the idea for *Bad Laws* to me after reading my 'Home Front' columns in the *Daily Telegraph*; Martin Newland, the former *Daily Telegraph* editor, for giving me the column in the first place in 2003; my sons Nick and Alexander for their encouragement and help; Dr Caroline Shenton, Clerk of the Records, for kindly showing me around the Parliamentary Archives; Howard Watson for helping to knock the book into shape; and my wife Juliet for her unstinting support and for putting up with the interrupted holidays and weekends.

INTRODUCTION: SOMETHING IS ROTTEN IN THE STATE OF BRITAIN

Although I worked as a political correspondent for many years I had never before seen the real treasures of the Palace of Westminster. They live in the Victoria Tower at the south-western end of Sir Charles Barrie's Gothic masterpiece, a few hundred yards from its better known counterpart Clock Tower, which houses Big Ben. Here can be found the archives containing more than 1.5 million Acts of Parliament passed since 1497. They include some of the seminal laws of the land, the very essence of nationhood: the Petition of Right 1628, the Habeas Corpus Act 1679, the Bill of Rights 1689, the Slave Trade Acts of 1807 and 1833, the Great Reform Act of 1832 and the Parliament Acts of 1911 and 1949. They also contain a few best forgotten: the Dangerous Dogs Act 1991, the ID Card Act 2006, the Safeguarding Vulnerable Groups Act 2006, umpteen Criminal Justice Acts, the Licensing Act 2005 and a welter of legislation to restrict, rather than enhance, our freedoms, such as the ban on smoking or on making hostile comments about religion.

If there is a fundamental difference between the laws passed today and those of yore, this is it: for hundreds of years the fight, both literally and metaphorically, was to advance the cause of personal liberty and to reduce the power of the state; in recent times, the reverse has happened. Parliament, which is meant to defend the citizen from the executive, has connived in allowing the government to encroach once more on our rights. The means of doing so has been through increasingly intrusive and restrictive legislation that is introduced ostensibly for our own good by a state that seeks to control more and more aspects of our lives.

This not an anti-government point; nor is this an anti-government book. It is about the limits that should properly be put on government. Its contention is that government has overstepped the line in a significant way in recent years and especially since 1997 when Labour came to power, sporting a sneer for the nation's institutions and a swaggering determination to smash them. However, this is not meant to be an anti-Labour book, though no doubt it will feel like one to that party's supporters. If a new government of a different stripe continues the trend of the last decade or so, it will be equally deserving of criticism. Yet despite its claim to represent the British people, New Labour actually felt like an alien interloper in an ancient land, preaching the fetish of modernism and despising tradition. It evinced a predisposition to micromanage individual behaviour and ride roughshod over liberties, both of which are very non-British traits.

We have had over a dozen years of pointless, often harmful, legislative tinkering. This is not to say that new laws are always bad; nor is it to aver that all government action is flawed. This is clearly preposterous. But it is to say that it has not been necessary to have had dozens of laws whose lack of efficacy has been apparent from the outset, which were introduced simply to make a political point and not to make anyone's life better or simpler or freer. Scores of criminal justice measures were promulgated so that ministers could say they were doing something, not because they made any difference. We have had a permanent revolution in schools that has failed to improve standards; an axe has been taken to the nation's constitutional edifice which was so painstakingly put together, albeit haphazardly, over the centuries; the database state has burgeoned to the detriment of personal privacy; CCTV cameras festoon our cities; and millions of adults are treated as though they are potential child molesters when all they seek to do is to offer their time to help others.

We are living in a looking-glass world where everything is back to front, where the owner of a Shetland pony has to obtain an ID card for the animal, but claiming more than £100,000 of taxpayers' money by abusing parliamentary expenses rules is OK providing the culprit (in this case the former home secretary) apologizes.

People often talk about big government in a theoretical way but these are its practical consequences. Big government is emphatically not, as some would have us believe, the new centre ground in British politics, a consensus around which we can all happily gather. It is not about running the NHS or the police, or the Army or care homes; it is about interfering in our lives to an extent that is neither healthy nor wanted. We are snooped on, harried, pestered and made to feel like criminals by a regime ruled by targets and tick-box craziness.

And what have our legislators been doing while all this has been going on? They have spent too much of their time thinking up ever more imaginative ways to claim their generous allowances and have given up their primary task: they are there to hold the government to account but have allowed a torrent of legislation to pour forth. There has been a frenzy of law-making that has changed the character of the nation in a way that many of us neither expected nor wanted – even those who voted Labour (especially those who voted Labour, perhaps).

The great expenses crisis of 2009 merely brought all this to the surface: resentment against a government that raised taxes after promising not to and then wasted billions of pounds on failed IT systems and top-heavy administration; incredulity over ministerial claims that crime has fallen when we can see with our own eyes that it hasn't; frustration at the inane regulations, the unjustified use of fines and charges, the bloody-minded parking restrictions, unreasonable European directives, multiculturalist busybodies, and the vast, overpaid and largely useless quango-cracy disconnected from the rest of us. It has all gone on for too long and the people to blame are those who failed to put a stop to it: our MPs. Yet having said that, real freedom resides in the power of parliament to hold the executive in check. Only here can the balance be restored and the essential elements of British commonsense reinstated in our national life. Despite the expenses scandal and the demoralization of MPs, it is to a renewed House of Commons that we must look to get a grip on this and restore some sanity.

Something was already rotten in the state of Britain, but this is not a rotten country: those archives in Victoria Tower are testament to its greatness. Older Acts, written on vellum (as they still are), are rolled up and stored while more recent documents are kept in file boxes, some so large that they cannot easily be held together. Once upon a time we had even more laws passed each year. Then, however, Acts took up just a page or two; today many are longer than a nineteenth-century Russian novel.

It is true that we live in a more complex world but modern government seems to regard its primary task to make it even more onerous and complicated rather than less. This is not confined to central government; local councils, the government that most people come into contact with on a day-to-day basis, also feel it necessary to make our lives more difficult, often in order to justify their own existence. It is particularly true of that least accountable institution of all, the European Union (EU), which is responsible for probably half our laws but which for reasons of space cannot be dealt with here, even if its presence pervades much of the legislative narrative of the past quarter of a century.

Instead, this book lays out the mind-boggling problems that the British government and legislature have brought upon their own people. The book opens with a broad sweep highlighting where government has stepped in and commonsense has been pushed aside, and then focuses more specifically on the major problems caused by bad laws in the areas of criminal justice, licensing, ID cards, education and childcare, smoking, the DNA database, counter-terrorism, and health and safety.

This book is not intended to be a libertarian tract, nor does it seek to rail against the state in all its forms. I acknowledge a role for government that is irreversibly greater than previous generations could possibly have imagined outside wartime. But we all know that something has gone wrong in recent years; we all recognize that there has been a significant, even profound, shift in the relationship between the citizen and the state that is distinctly unsettling – and, indeed, un-British. This can be rectified without great constitutional upheaval. It simply requires politicians to trust people to make their own decisions and run their own lives with minimum interference from the centre; they should give a helping hand when it is needed and wanted. Above all, this means that the government, whichever party is in power, should simply stop meddling.

CHAPTER I

THE THEFT OF COMMONSENSE

This is a story about a theft. Our commonsense has been stolen. In its place we have been given new laws, dozens of them, hundreds of them, thousands of them. A long tradition of pragmatism has been replaced by a legalistic approach to everything. Where common law once provided the glue to our society, statute has taken its place. It has restricted the scope for discretion and for latitude; and this inflexibility has made us angry, not least when we discovered that the very people who were supposed to be keeping an eye on this – our MPs – were spending their time obsessing about their expenses in order to live a grand life on our money.

When I was growing up there were two common phrases that you hardly ever hear today. One was 'It's a free country.' The other was 'There should be a law against it.' They tended to be uttered by people older than my parents who had probably been born not long after the First World War and may well have fought in the Second. These phrases captured the very essence of Britishness and why those wars were fought. We were, or imagined ourselves to be, 'a free country' in a way that most European countries were not and had never been. That notion of being a free country defined us. We were not people subject to arbitrary state power and we both knew it and could say it. Perhaps this first phrase was used ironically at times; but when I heard it as a young boy it had a sense of certainty and permanence about it. What are we? A free country.

The second phrase also says much about the sort of country we were, and are no longer. There were, obviously, lots of laws, but they were less obviously restrictive of individual activity. They set parameters within which the 'free' bit could be exercised and were largely governed by common law precedents handed down over the centuries. We had liberty; we did not have licence. Yet there were clearly things of which many people, especially older ones, disapproved and that they sometimes wished could be legislated away, such as the looser morals that were on show in the 1960s. You could imagine an old codger leering at a girl in her thigh-high mini-skirt in 1963 (when sexual intercourse began, according to the poet Philip Larkin) and saying: 'There should be a law against it.' And if the girl had overheard, she would have replied: 'It's a free country, grandad. Mind your own business.'

However, neither of these phrases applies today. We are no longer a free country, not in the sense that previous generations would have understood the phrase; and, whatever it is, there almost certainly already is a law against it. The point is that the two go together. Liberty is freedom from the arbitrary exercise of the law, even if the people applying it believe they are doing it for your own good. There is nothing worse than a paternalistic government that believes it has the right to interfere in most aspects of our personal lives and justifies doing so on altruistic grounds. At least with despotisms you know where you stand: despots are seeking to exercise power over the individual and have few philanthropic reasons for doing so. It is far easier to rail against them, if more dangerous. However, the insidious accretion of power to a benign and democratic state through the increasing use of the legislative process to restrict what we do and shape who we are – sometimes literally – is more destructive in the long run because it creates a society of pliant individuals who are forever looking for someone else to help them out. Personal responsibility is destroyed and gives way to a notion that the state or one of its many agencies will provide everything. We become dependent upon others rather than on ourselves; we become supplicants and clients of the state.

How did this come about? For an answer we must look to an unusual set of circumstances that came together with the election of New Labour in 1997. This brought into office a fundamentally different administration from any seen since the early twentieth century. Because Labour had been out of office for so long, none of the senior cabinet posts was occupied by anyone with experience of governing. Tony Blair announced himself the leader of 'the political arm of none other than the British people as a whole'[1], even though the majorities in 1997 and 2001 of 170 or thereabouts were secured with a smaller proportion of the votes than Harold Wilson took when losing to Ted Heath in 1970. At the 2005 election, the 'political arm of the British people as a whole' took just over 36 per cent of the vote, the lowest share of any government since the Second World War. Since the turnout was just 61 per cent, that means Labour had the support, at the ballot box, of only 23 per cent of the electorate.

Inexperience linked to a disproportionately large parliamentary majority was a dangerous concoction. Labour set about undermining another bulwark of the system, the Civil Service. After 18 years of brooding resentment at its treatment at the hands of what it considered to be a predominantly Tory-supporting media, Labour also believed that Whitehall was stuffed full of conservatives, both with a small and large 'C', who would resist the 'reforms' they wanted to push through. This involved the introduction on an industrial scale of management consultants to provide advice once given by civil servants. A baleful consequence of this was the imposition of a target culture that stifled local decision-making, removed discretion, cost the earth and suffocated commonsense. This machinery has been presided over by Gordon Brown, a chancellor-cum-prime minister so convinced of his own rectitude that he considered himself entitled to waste vast sums of our money and then to suggest that we thank him for doing so.

It was a toxic mix. We knew and felt it happening but were powerless to do anything about it, a bit like Howard Beale, the fictional newsreader in *Network*, a satirical film set in the newsroom of an American TV company that cynically exploits the deranged ravings of their top anchorman. Beale becomes so frustrated at the refusal of anyone to listen to reason that he invited viewers to open their windows and yell into the streets: 'I am as mad as hell and I am not going to take it any more.' Maybe such conspicuous expressions of indignation are more acceptable in the United States than they are here. When we are as mad as hell, the most forceful manifestation of our emotions has tended to be a resigned shrug or a heavy sigh. Understatement is one of our endearing national characteristics; but it also means we can more easily be taken for a ride. Our predisposition to react benignly to developments that would have other people taking to the streets is to be applauded. However, this quintessential mildness relies on governments, local councils and others who can interfere in our lives to do so only when it is absolutely necessary, and then in a fair and balanced way. In its years in office, the Labour government patently failed to identify this fulcrum. It introduced legislation because it believed that its very function was to pour forth a cascade of new laws each year, even when there was no demand for them.

Labour is not unique in this regard, though the past decade has almost certainly been the worst in modern peacetime history for government interference in people's lives and the encroachment of the state on individual liberties. Depressingly, it is by no means certain that matters will improve under any other government. Suggest to a minister of any political stripe that they might try to get through the parliamentary session without legislating and they will look at you as if you are crazy. Propose that existing laws should take effect before new ones are introduced and expect a blank stare. Urge that for every new law an old one should be repealed and wait for the snort of derision. After all, what are politicians for if not to bring in laws? 'We legislate therefore we are' should be written on the gates of the Palace of Westminster. I once asked a cabinet minister at a news conference if, in view of the large amount of criminal justice legislation that was being introduced, there would be a moratorium on future laws while the new ones took effect. 'But what would we do with our lives?' was the response, only half in jest.

Every year, there are 20 or 30 major Acts of Parliament. That is up to 350 substantial pieces of legislation over the past 12 years, each spawning dozens of secondary regulations. Since 1997, the Home Office alone has introduced 60 Bills, launched more than 100 consultation papers, made at least 350 regulations and created an astonishing 271 new offences. In his ten years as prime minister, Tony Blair presided over more than 3,000 new laws, more than 1,000 of which carried jail terms. Gordon Brown added hundreds more. To call this a frenzy would be to do an injustice to sharks in a blood-filled ocean. Labour created new offences at twice the rate of the previous Tory administration, which had been bad enough in this regard.

Whereas many governments might feel it necessary to have an opening blitz of law-making to get its pet ideas onto the statute book, Labour started off slow and then picked up speed. In 1998, Labour's first full year in power, 160 new offences passed into legislation, rising to 346 in 2000 and 527 in 2005. And what was the result of this? Nick Clegg, the Liberal Democrat leader, observed: 'A country less free than before, and a marked erosion of the trust which should exist between the Government and the governed. Weighing down the statute book with new laws was no substitute for good government.'[2]

Then again, many of these new laws were actually directives laid down by the European Union about which Mr Clegg and his party are so enthusiastic. Yet while the influence of the EU has been considerable, that does not explain how so many areas outside the EU's competence, such as criminal justice policy, have seen so many new laws.

The Home Office's 60 Bills in 10 years have caused confusion in the criminal justice system, inviting the opprobrium of judges while achieving little that has obviously made the country a safer place. The Department for Environment, Food and Rural Affairs brought in 640 new offences, the vast majority through secondary legislation, and the Department for Trade and Industry produced another 592. Even the Foreign Office brought in more than 250. Each addition swelled the enormous number of offences already on the statute book.

Much of this legislation has been an attempt to change the way people are rather than to deal with the consequences of their misbehaviour. Ministers, too many of them with too much time on their hands, believed that any crisis, any perceived social ill, should invite legislation. Rather than take a deep breath, they greeted every moral panic with new laws. Being seen to have 'done something' required a statute where a press release might have sufficed.

New criminal offences can symbolize many things: they can reflect changing cultural sensibilities or they can be a response to technological or economic developments. In Labour's case they exposed both the government's strength and weakness: it had the strength through its parliamentary majority to push legislation through parliament and control the political process; its weakness was an inability to do anything about the things that matter, like crime, much of which has remained almost untouched. Anti-Social Behaviour Orders (Asbos), introduced in the Crime and Disorder Act, one of New Labour's first major pieces of legislation, may have made ministers feel better and might have given some sort of redress to people whose lives have been made miserable by the behaviour of others. However, Asbos have done nothing to repair the social malfunction of the communities on which they are imposed. What happened to 'tough on the causes of crime'?

will it all end? When we get in, says the opposition,
will be such a mess that we will need more laws to undo
last lot. Will any politicians really, truly commit themselves
to stop frustrating the activities and livelihoods of Her Majesty's
law-abiding subjects with unwarranted interference, intrusiveness and incompetence?

How did we get to this point? What is that drives the legislative mania of modern governments? Have they no sense of
history, no philosophical framework within which they can
understand the point at which government activity must end
and the private citizen begins? They have lost all concept
of the impact of excessive law-making on the freedom of the
individual. Perhaps they have never read the wise words of
John Stuart Mill, whose powerful assertion of the individual's
right to resist the blandishments of society and to be free, by
and large, from interference by the state was contained in his
short treatise *On Liberty*, published in 1859. He did not take an
ultra-libertarian approach, that all state interference and laws
circumscribing actions were wrong; but he believed he could
devise a principle enabling us to decide the point at which
legislation impairs the spirit of liberty:

> The only purpose for which power can rightfully be exer-
> cised over any member of a civilized community, against
> his will, is to prevent harm to others. His own good,
> either physical or moral, is not a sufficient warrant. . . It is
> important to give the freest scope possible to uncustomary
> things in order that it may in time appear which of these
> are fit to be converted into customs.[3]

This analysis is even more valid today, given the encroachment
of the state on the lives of its citizens to a far greater degree
than could have been imagined by Mill.

State interference on its own is not incompatible with liberty;
it can, indeed, be its protector. The state clearly needs to keep

law and order, fight wars, provide strategic infrastructure and defend minorities from the tyranny of the majority. It is the extent of its intrusiveness that is at issue here, a gradual arrogation of the power to interfere so that increasingly people feel powerless to resist. The question is to what extent are those in a position of superiority justified in disciplining and constraining the behaviour of others for their own good?

In *1984*, George Orwell recognized that the greatest infringement of liberty was not incarceration or torture by the state but to make a man think as the state decreed. That is why the novel is the ultimate extension of the illiberal propensities of state power, why we are both right and wrong to describe modern society as Orwellian: wrong because it is nowhere near as bad, despite some sinister similarities (like cameras in the street); but right because it is the direction of travel.

The principal justification for state interference is that it saves the individual from being interfered with by other individuals who are more powerful than themselves. In many ways, this should be the only justification. However, the twentieth century saw a gradual acceptance of the view that the state is entitled to interfere in order to protect the individual from his own actions. Licensing laws which were introduced during the First World War because munitions workers were getting drunk were practical, not moral.

Now we have laws on drinking that are designed quite specifically to stop people getting drunk even if they are not going to pose a threat to others, for their own good. We have allowed the state to interfere in our lives to stop us smoking, eating the wrong food, taking drugs, driving without a seat belt or riding without a crash helmet even though these are only for the protection of individuals who should be free to make up their own minds. There are, of course, aspects of all these activities in which the state as the representative of society has an interest. The cost to the NHS and the taxpayer of treating alcohol- and smoking-related diseases, the victims of car and motorbike crashes, drug addiction and obesity evidently gives the state a say in these matters.

The ban on smoking in some public places was ostensibly created to prevent staff in pubs and clubs being affected by passive smoking. It has been justified because it has encouraged people to give up for their own good. However, the ban on foxhunting was an unjustifiable interference on human liberties because some people did not like what a minority of people did. It was pure class spite and falls perfectly into what Mill would have considered excessive intrusion, by a party whose members have never liked foxhunters as a group. Where a political party has a huge parliamentary majority, it becomes difficult if not impossible to defend the freedom of the individual or small groups of people against the arbitrary power of an executive able to demand total loyalty from most of its legislators. Even sizeable rebellions by party members fail to dent such majorities. MPs become insouciant to the defence of liberty, believing it is pointless to confront a majority that will inevitably push the legislation through.

Opponents become isolated and regarded as trouble-makers when all they are doing is fighting for their liberties. There has been too much legislation in recent years that has penalized legitimate minority pastimes. Mill's principle that 'the only purpose for which power can rightfully be exercised over any member of a civilized community, against his will, is to prevent harm to others' disappeared a long time ago. We now have too many laws introduced for the wrong reasons and for no obvious benefit. Worse, they circumscribe freedom and privacy, which should not happen without good cause.

This book will explore some of the more egregious examples of pernicious intrusion into all our lives, from the database society and the forests of CCTV cameras watching our every move to the nitpicking laws that have simply served to make life more difficult. In addition are those laws that have curtailed free speech, allowed strangers access to our homes, entitled the state to purloin our property, stopped activities that have been legal for centuries and banned lawful protest. In large part, I have ignored all the bad financial laws – the tax changes and plugged loopholes that probably cause more people greater angst than almost anything else.

The problem with so much regulation and social policing is that, when a law is proposed that may well be a proper response to a real problem, it just seems like another wretched addition to the dismally long list of things we can do no longer. Why are so many laws introduced that merely inconvenience the respectable and law-abiding majority, while almost daily, it seems, there is a horror story telling the dreadful consequences that have arisen because someone in authority has failed to keep real criminals in jail for the duration of their sentence? Employees of government agencies, from social services to the police, are so laden with statutory requirements and targets that they are no longer able to exercise discretion and commonsense. Would not the great efforts of government (and I include Brussels) to bury us under an avalanche of laws and regulations be put to better purpose if they were properly directed?

Can any of this be stopped? One answer would be to take a leaf out of the book of Zaleucus, the lawgiver, who ruled at Locri Epizefiri, one of the earliest Greek colonies in Italy, at around 660 BC. According to the historian Edward Gibbon: 'A Locrian who proposed any new law stood forth in the assembly of the people with a cord around his neck and if the law was rejected the innovator was instantly strangled.'[4] If we introduced that at Westminster we might be better governed – and have fewer MPs.

But what constitutes a bad law? One that circumscribes or prohibits what was once a perfectly acceptable form of behaviour could qualify, though that is not of itself bad. For instance, requiring people to wear a seatbelt is a restriction on what was once a legal and harmless activity, namely travelling in a car without restraint. However, there was potential risk to the individual driver or passenger and the law was devised in order to reduce that risk. Road accident statistics suggest it has succeeded in that end, as has the law requiring a motorcyclist to wear a crash helmet. It is not, then, a necessary condition of a bad law that it stops people doing something they should be allowed to do in any free society, provided the restriction on liberty is proportionate and the law achieves its intended aim. However, many of the laws introduced in recent years are either disproportionate or they fail to do what the government said they would do. The worst laws, as we shall see, fail both tests. It is said, though less often now than it used to be, that the basis of our liberty is the rule of law, under which everything is allowed unless specifically prohibited.

According to A.V. Dicey, the nineteenth-century constitutionalist, this was one of the features that distinguished England from its continental counterparts, where people were subject to the exercise of arbitrary power and were proscribed from actions that were not specifically authorized.[5] Effectively, this principle limited the scope of the state to intervene in people's lives. Law set the boundaries of personal action but did not dictate the course of such action. Some limitations on personal freedom are introduced ostensibly for our own good, but since 1997 the pace of proscription has grown alarmingly.

On July 1, 2007, it became a criminal offence throughout the United Kingdom not merely to smoke a cigarette in a public place, but in your own car if other people share it to travel to work or if it is used for work purposes. It is also an offence to smoke in a room in your own home if it doubles as a workplace. It is now a crime, punishable by up to five years in prison, to smack your own child if a visible mark is left as a result. It is also an offence to mount a horse and ride off in pursuit of a fox. Since 1997, it has been a crime to possess any handgun, even a .22 calibre, for sporting purposes. An individual whose most aggressive instinct is to fire at a target can no longer do so in this country, even under licence, though special dispensation has been given to the British team for the 2012 Olympics in London. Since 2003, it has been illegal to own a horse, donkey or a Shetland pony without obtaining an identity card for the animal to ensure it does not poison anyone who eats it. At the same time, a thief who steals goods worth £200 or less from a shop is no longer arrested and taken to the police station but handed an £80 fixed-penalty notice, without any criminal record provided it is paid on time.

Even teenage 'canoodling' is now criminalized under the Sexual Offences Act 2003, which forbids under-16s from engaging in any sexual activity. One solicitor told how he had to deal with the case of two teenagers arrested on suspicion of mutual indecent assault, following a complaint by social workers. The case was dropped, though the children had to spend time in custody late at night.

It is now an offence, punishable by a £5,000 fine or six months in jail, to set off a firework after 11 p.m., an objectionable and anti-social thing to do, but one that has not been a crime until recently. Under new EU proposals, it will be an offence to deny that the genocide of the Jews in Europe or of the Tutsi in Rwanda happened. Now, it may be especially obnoxious and somewhat loopy to hold such views but here we really are entering the realms of 'thoughtcrime'.

The state has taken other powers, justified under cover of the war on terrorism but which in the wrong hands could prove sinister indeed. The Civil Contingencies Act, introduced in 2004, significantly extended the arbitrary powers of ministers, once again (and this is characteristic of many of these developments) with little public or parliamentary debate. This measure would allow a minister to suspend sittings of parliament if necessary and to declare a bank holiday to shut down businesses. Any panic or disorder could result in armed troops being placed on the streets. By executive decree, property could be destroyed or requisitioned, assemblies banned, the Armed Forces mobilized and special courts set up to deal with suspects if it was felt another atrocity was planned. Only retrospectively would ministers need to get the endorsement of parliament that they were right to use these powers.

As the government correctly points out, there have always been powers – for example, the Defence of the Realm Act – that can be wielded by the executive in times of national emergency, such as an imminent invasion. However, this new Act (which is less about defending the country and more about dealing with contingencies whose severity will be for the state agencies to determine) does not make clear the precise circumstances in which the powers would be used, other than that they must be 'grave and serious' and pose a threat to the security and economic wellbeing of the nation, or part of it. The potential for the misuse of this legislation by a malign administration in more unsettled times is enormous.

We know, too, that given powers to restrict individual freedom, the police may use them in ways that were not intended, or certainly not understood by parliament when they were passed. Section 44 of the Terrorism Act 2000 has given the police carte blanche to stop anyone and to question them within certain designated areas; it is no longer a requirement that reasonable suspicion that a crime has been committed must be present. It was under this provision that Walter Wolfgang, the octogenarian Labour activist later elected to the party's national executive, was held after being ejected from a conference for having the temerity to heckle Jack Straw, the then foreign secretary. Section 44 was also the reason given to a trio of bemused trainspotters detained and questioned by anti-terror police over what they were doing on a railway platform at a station through which politicians were expected to travel. This power has been used hundreds of times in ways that it should not have been, a fact acknowledged by both the government and the police.

Another aspect of liberty is privacy. It may be hard to believe in a world where people crave televised notoriety that there are still many who cherish anonymity. In a truly free society it should be possible for someone who does not wish to come to the attention of the state to remain unnoticed provided he breaks no laws. As A.J.P. Taylor observed, before the First World War, the average citizen's interaction with the government was largely limited to paying tax.

> Until August 1914 a sensible, law-abiding Englishman could pass through life and hardly notice the existence of the state, beyond the post office and the policeman. He could live where he liked and as he liked. He had no official number or identity card. He could travel abroad or leave his country for ever without a passport or any sort of official permission. He could exchange his money for any other currency without restriction or limit. He could buy goods from any country in the world on the same terms as he bought goods at home.[6]

Of one thing he could be certain: the inviolability of his home. However, recent research has uncovered 266 separate powers under which the police and other state agents can enter your home, often using force to do so. As Harry Snook, who conducted the study for the Centre for Policy Studies, said: 'The growth in powers of entry should be seen in context as a symptom of the expanding role of the state in the lives of citizens.'[7]

The proliferation of state databases, again very much a recent occurrence, has also rendered the concept of the private individual a thing of the past. ContactPoint, the children's database, will contain confidential details on every child in the land, including a record of school achievements, police and social services records and home address. Each child will be assigned an identifying number so that the authorities can access his or her records.

This database is being developed ostensibly to curb child abuse, but it goes much further than the Child Protection

Register, which held information about children considered to be 'at risk'. One reason all children are to be included is to avoid 'stigmatization'. Only gradually have people become aware of the existence of this database, but they have every reason to be interested. As the joint parliamentary select committee on human rights pointed out:

> The information which may be included on the database about a child goes beyond purely objective facts about a child, such as name, address and date of birth. It includes information, such as contact details of persons providing services including health services, which may reveal very sensitive information, such as the fact that a 17-year-old girl has been referred to family planning services.[8]

It also includes 'the existence of any cause for concern' about a child, 'an extremely subjective and open-ended phrase which is almost bound to include very sensitive information'.[9] How long will this information remain on the state database? It is supposed to be erased when the children turn 24 but will some youthful, even childish, transgression return to haunt them in adulthood? We cannot be sure.

Meanwhile, the NHS is continuing to develop its database that will, for the first time, make all our medical records available electronically and centrally, rather than filed away in the surgeries of our family doctors. Medical records are, perhaps, the most sensitive that are kept and we are understandably reluctant that anyone should see them except those that must. Supporters of the idea say a centralized electronic system will stop records going missing (will it?) and ensure instant access to the records of patients if they are taken ill away from home.

However, many GPs are distinctly uncomfortable with this plan and are concerned that comments they include on a patient's record will fall into the wrong hands because the scheme allows for 'summary information captured during a GP consultation [to] be automatically extracted and transferred to a nationally accessible spine'.[10] Would it not be better – and more in keeping with the concept of privacy – if everyone could keep their own records on a health card rather than place them on a multibillion pound national database that will be vulnerable to hacking or crashing? There is, of course, one group that will always be able to access all the information with one click, and that is the state and its agencies.

Ministers have always promised to keep the information separate, yet they have proposed that details held by one department should be available to another, though the legislation to make this possible was withdrawn from the Coroners and Justice Bill, where it had no reason to be, in the spring of 2009. Furthermore, given the welter of anecdotal evidence from those wrongly identified as miscreants by the Criminal Records Bureau or the innocent people whose details are now on the world's largest criminal DNA database, does anyone trust that the information held about us will be accurate or consider that the technology is foolproof?

Link all these databases together and you have something that is awesomely intrusive, whatever the justification that can be advanced in favour of each. We have, almost without realizing it, become the most snooped-on nation on earth, electronically tracked from cot to coffin. Our most personal details will be stored forever, all in the name of modernization and, we are told, for our own good.

But we have not yet got to the main event, the ultimate weapon of state control: the national identity system. This is something that the state has long sought to introduce. When it comes to softening up the country for an ID card, the Home Office has been prepared to play a very long game. Every home secretary for the last 50 years has been presented with a proposal drafted by officials for an ID scheme.

It is this extension of state control through the unfettered and unthinking deployment of modern surveillance technology and databases for which the Labour years will most be remembered. Our children, millions of whom are now routinely fingerprinted without parental consent, will be perplexed as to why their forebears came so easily and with so little public debate to allow the state to manipulate their lives.

To make any of these points is to invite opprobrium from government ministers, who not only dispute the thesis but question the motives and the sanity of its promulgators. Before he left the Home Office, Charles Clarke loosed off a broadside against what he called 'a dangerous poison now slipping into some parts of the media view of the world'.[11] He added: 'In the absence of many of the genuinely dangerous and evil totalitarian dictatorships to fight – since they've gone – the media has [sic] steadily rhetorically transferred to some of the existing democracies, particularly the United States and the United Kingdom, some of the characteristics of those dictatorships.'

This was a classic Aunt Sally speech. Nobody sensible has called the British state totalitarian, nor compared it with Soviet Russia or Nazi Germany. The true benchmark for comparison is not Europe under fascism or communism but Britain as the doughty champion of individual freedoms that it once was; it is this instinct that has been eviscerated. Mr Clarke said those who denounce the government for its illiberalism are fantasists who do not understand, 'the balance of powers which currently exists in our society, whether legal or political'. Yet it is the government that has tilted this balance quite deliberately – in some cases properly, in others not – to exercise greater control over the citizen. There can be no other explanation for what has happened.

So why do we not care more? We have, apparently, been convinced by the government that the liberties we once cherished are worth trading for security. According to the British Social Attitudes Survey, there has been a marked decline in the 'British public's traditionally strong commitment to civil liberties'.[12] More people than ever are prepared to see freedoms that used to be taken for granted, such as free speech and the right to protest, dispensed with. A large majority sees some erosions of liberty as 'a price worth paying' to combat terrorism.

The survey even uncovered dwindling support for the fundamental principle of the criminal justice system, the presumption of innocence. People were asked whether they regarded an innocent person being convicted as a worse outcome to a trial than a guilty individual walking free. Whereas 20 years ago, nearly 70 per cent said they would be more perturbed to learn that an innocent person had been convicted, that has now fallen to 52 per cent. We have become inured to restrictions on liberty that few would have tolerated outside wartime a generation or two ago. However, are those of us who are deeply concerned about the illiberal tendencies of recent years guilty of hankering after a time that never existed, of perpetuating a false mythology around the notion of 'ancient liberties' for which we do not really care much?

Professor Conor Gearty of the London School of Economics, one of the compilers of the British Social Attitudes survey, says liberal values peaked in the late 1960s and early 1970s, and have since been assailed by 'folk devils and moral panics'. He added: 'The idea of political liberty needs to be argued afresh for generations unfamiliar with what it means to struggle for freedom: it is too good an idea to let go without a fight.'[13]

It would never have crossed the minds of an earlier generation that such a fight would even be necessary. The great danger is that those growing up now do not understand the importance of winning it.

CHAPTER 2

THERE IS JUST TOO MUCH LEGISLATION

Laws have always been needed to regulate relationships between people. Laws are the rules of life. When we lived in caves, there would have been codes governing who slept where and with whom, who got the first hunk of mammoth and who sat nearest the fire. These were hierarchical laws that relied on brute force for their implementation. Invariably, the caveman who benefited from these rules was the biggest and toughest in the tribe and got the best ribs and the woman with least facial hair.

Why do governments introduce laws? The answer may seem obvious: to control behaviour. Yet most of us are already circumscribed in the way we act by social constraints and by older laws of the land that can be traced back to time immemorial. Is it really necessary to keep passing new laws every year further to dictate the way people act? And sometimes what appears to be an altruistic motive can have perverse consequences. Successive governments, for instance, have thought that they should seek to manage the behaviour of individuals in order to save money, for instance by curbing smoking and thereby reducing the illnesses that cost the NHS a fortune to treat. Arguably, the economic justification is suspect since fewer smokers or drinkers results in less tax and less money to fund the NHS. It also means people live longer, which is another financial pressure on health and social care.

The desire of government to manipulate and determine personal behaviour is a fairly recent phenomenon. The state has always wanted people to pay taxes, to conform to the orthodoxies (either religious or political) of the day, to be loyal to their country and to observe certain standards of decorum that were expected by the society of the time. But that was about it. It was not really until the twentieth century, and especially after the Second World War, that governments began actively to intervene in people's lives specifically to transform society and mould it in the image it wanted. There is an academic discipline devoted to 'behaviouralism' that has influenced modern politicians in a way they are probably unaware of, though their officials would be well apprised of the science, if such it could be called. When an issue bursts into the news and a government minister comes under pressure, often from the media, to 'do something about it', the politician is immediately confronted with the problematic nature of people's behaviour.

For instance, if there is a newspaper campaign against prostitution, how do governments go about preventing women (or men) selling their bodies for sex; or how do they control demand for paid-for sex? More to the point, why should they? There might be a burst of moral indignation against activities of which the majority disapproves, but if two adults wish to engage in a financial transaction for sex who are the rest of us to stop them? The government might argue there are other matters at stake: there is the exploitation of women by pimps, though an answer to that would be to legalize prostitution. There is the seediness of areas associated with the sex trade, though a solution would be to have licensed red-light districts. There are the criminals and the drug traffickers drawn to the tawdry areas in which prostitutes operate. In which case make drugs legal. However, even though legalizing activities that many might find shocking or immoral might actually solve all the problems that governments find intractable, what they seek to do instead is to keep them unlawful but change the behaviour of the people in order to choke off demand. As we know, they invariably fail to do so.

The failure of legalism is becoming apparent to governments around the world. A few years ago, the Downing Street Strategy Unit carried out a study into how the state went about changing behaviour and whether it actually succeeded in doing so.[1] The report noted how much more compliant people had become over the past 30 or 40 years and readier to accept the strictures of the state:

> Attitudes to risk and responsibility can change dramatically over time. For example, the overwhelming public support for the compulsory wearing of seatbelts today is far removed from public resistance to their imposition in the 1970s. It was once unthinkable to ban smoking on aircraft; now it is almost unthinkable to allow it. Similarly, today's narrowly-balanced attitudes towards the state ban on prostitution reflect a steady softening in attitudes among the public over the past 20 years.

The study focused on the conundrum with which modern governments grapple: how far can they go before there is a backlash from a public that is simply sick to death of being hectored?

> Although there are areas where the public expects government to act (for example, drink driving) there are others where the public is less sure of the government's appropriate role (for example, banning smacking of children). On the one hand there is a desire for government not to interfere within people's personal lives and choices. On the other hand, there is also a growing awareness of causal responsibility and a desire for people to get the rewards (or suffer the consequences) of their own choices and decisions.

The report went on:

> Broadly, the public recognizes a legitimate role for the
> government to intervene where there are significant
> externalities to behaviour – i.e. individual behaviour
> creates costs or benefits for others. For example, rob-
> bery clearly creates significant negative externalities
> and government is expected to intervene to discourage
> that behaviour. Similarly, for behaviours which generate
> significant positive externalities – such as charitable giv-
> ing – government can legitimately act to encourage that
> behaviour.[2]

What is most interesting about this document is the somewhat
blasé assumption that it is the function of the state to interfere
in the lives of people up to a point at which they start to find
it intolerable. And, when that point is reached, governments
are then invited to consider how they might best break down
resistance in order to bring about the behaviour that they want
to see. At no stage is the question asked: should governments
be doing this at all? The report maintains that the principal
justification for the extraordinary amounts of legislation that we
see today is that the public wants government to achieve various
goals: a strong economy, better education, security, health and
so on. To achieve these, they must employ many tools, including
laws, punishments and regulations, taxes and subsidies, the provision of public services, information and persuasion. Of course
people want a strong economy and good health care: the point
here is whether achieving them should be the sole preserve of
the state or whether they can be obtained in some other way,
through greater private provision for instance. However, while
the public will clearly want many or all of these goals to be
achieved, they are persuaded and convinced that only the state
can deliver them.

WE HAVE TOO MANY MINISTERS

One reason why we have more laws than ever before is because we have more government ministers than ever before. They have to do something, and what better than pilot a new Bill through parliament? Private offices exist to get their minister something to do; civil servants are waiting around to facilitate the new legislation. Everything in government is set up to encourage the promulgation of more laws, not their removal. A junior minister who does not get their name in the paper is a junior minister going nowhere. With such a growth in government, there is a commensurate burgeoning of the stuff of government, which is no longer about running things efficiently but about finding new areas to get involved in. The trend was supposed to be the other way.

When the Thatcher government took office in 1979, the government ran the railways, the airlines, delivered water, electricity and gas, dug coal from the ground, made steel and operated the buses: the great postwar nationalizations meant the state was all pervasive. It needed a bureaucracy to manage it and ministers to guide the bureaucracy. It was by far the biggest employer in the land. Yet when all of these industries were privatized and the state's blue-collar staff was reduced almost to none, whereas the battalions of white-collar civil servants hung on in there. There are roughly the same number of employees in the Home Civil Service (about 480,000) today as there was in 1979, despite 30 years of supposed rationalization, value for money blitzes and efficiency drives. Post-Thatcher Britain was meant to have less government, yet we have more than ever, with extra tiers in Brussels, Scotland, Wales and London as well as dozens of central agencies, quangos and regional bodies. The cost is stupefying. In 2008, £1 billion was spent simply on the PR of state-run organizations.[3]

This expansion of governance is commensurate with the aggrandizement of the political classes. To cut the civil service it is first necessary to take an axe to the great thicket of ministers, special advisers and political researchers that it is required to sustain. In the nineteenth century, a sizeable chunk of the globe was ruled by a group of ministers and a civil service a fraction of the size it is today. Gordon Brown presided over the biggest cabinet in history: 23 full members, 6 others entitled to attend and 4 more who could attend if their business was being discussed. That is 50 per cent larger than the average cabinet over the past 100 years. In 1900, the government of Lord Salisbury had 19 cabinet ministers, 10 non-cabinet ministers and 31 junior ministers. That was 60 paid government posts. It took 60 years for that figure to rise by 20 and another 20 years for it to rise by a further 20, so by 1970 there were 102 total paid government posts. Today there are 106.

It is a law of politics that the size of the cabinet is in inverse proportion to the stature of the prime minister. Winston Churchill and David Lloyd George, who established the modern system, preferred smaller cabinets, averaging about 10 members, though that was partly because they were wartime leaders. Even in peacetime, Churchill had only 16 members in his 1951 cabinet. A big difference today is that many decisions are taken in smaller committees and rubber-stamped by the cabinet, which does not have the authority it once had.

The so-called payroll vote of ministers, whips and parliamentary aides who can be relied upon to support the government has ballooned in the past 25 years from just over 100 to more than 150. In 1983, there were 21 cabinet ministers, 32 ministers of state, 29 junior ministers and 20 whips. Now there are 23 cabinet ministers, 33 senior ministers, 38 juniors and 26 whips. There have been various attempts to arrest this trend, but the initiative, inevitably, always comes from the opposition, not least because the government needs to find jobs for its MPs to keep them sweet. The Norton Commission established by William Hague when he was Tory leader recommended capping the size of the cabinet at 20 and other ministers at 50. In addition, there would be only one parliamentary private secretary per department responsible to the cabinet minister. Then there is Parliament itself. David Cameron, the Conservative leader, has said the number of MPs could be cut by 10 per cent 'without any problem at all'.[4] The same could be said for local government and the EU, where bureaucracy exists for its own sake.

WE HAVE TOO MANY OFFICIALS

Big government seeks out responsibilities that it should never have in a democracy. It interferes where it is neither wanted nor needed because it must justify its existence. It places excessive bureaucratic burdens on businesses, and then over-taxes the populace in order to sustain itself. Members of an over-governed society come to rely upon those in power to control their lives, which reduces personal freedom and saps enterprise and initiative. Too much government is a bad thing; yet we seem unable to stop it growing. Appearing before the public administration committee of the House of Commons, Lord Jones of Birmingham, aka Digby Jones, the former director general of the CBI, said that in his year in the government as a so-called GOAT (a member of the Government Of All The Talents) he found the civil service to be 'honest, stuffed full of decent people who work hard'. But he added: 'Frankly the job could be done with half as many, it could be more productive, more efficient, it could deliver a lot more value for money for the taxpayer.'[5]

The state now employs more people than the population of Scotland, and the civil service is larger than the population of Sheffield; 1.2 million people – the size of Glasgow – are employed in 'Public Administration'; 2.9 million people – bigger than the population of Greater Manchester – work in local government. The size of the state is out of proportion to what it has to do, but an even bigger issue concerns the extent of its role: it is doing too much. The big question of politics in the next 20 years or so is can we define what the state should do and set limits upon its expansion or even curtail it?

There is a political consensus to which the post-Thatcherite political elites subscribe: an unwillingness to reconsider the roles government should perform. We still let the state intervene in areas that it first became involved in solely because of war. In a lecture given in 1950, the head of the civil service observed that, 'the arrangements now used for the direction of our economic affairs are in part derived from the wartime techniques of programmes and allocation of resources'.[6]

Lord Jones is right to want to see a cut in government but it has to be right across the board. This is about more than administrative incompetence. Big government seeks out responsibilities that it should never have in a democracy. It interferes where it is neither wanted nor needed because it must justify its existence. Too much government is a bad thing; yet we seem unable to stop it growing.

THINK OF THE POOR QUEEN

The head of state who nominally appoints this government has no control over what it does or how many laws it introduces. Queen Elizabeth II has made the short trip from Buckingham Palace to the Palace of Westminster for the State Opening of Parliament on more than 50 occasions during her reign, and each time her government has managed to conjure up enough legislation to make her trip along The Mall appear worthwhile. The Gracious Speech, aside from the usual niceties about state visits and the like, normally contains pledges for another 16 or so major Bills. In addition, MPs and peers are told that 'other measures will be laid before you'. It is hard to believe that Her Majesty has started into motion some 900 major pieces of legislation since 1953, and thousands more 'other measures'.

When the government changes and a new party takes office, it is understandable that it will want to legislate for the pet projects on which it has been elected and, occasionally, to unravel the efforts of previous administrations. However, when a party has been in office for 13 years and is in the final stages of its third parliament, you would have thought that it might just have got things right by now on most of the areas that matter. The problem is that New Labour, more so than its predecessors, used legislation to make statements that would have been infinitely cheaper to have delivered by way of a press release, and probably just as enduring. Labour took the view that to criticize its obsessive law-making was somehow to misunderstand the political process that legislation is necessary to change the country and to fulfil electoral promises, which indeed it is.

However, a great deal of this legislation was simply perverse because it reversed earlier decisions to overturn initiatives that had been made by the previous Tory administration. For instance, laws to inject competition into public services were brought in by Labour in 2005 even though it had spent years undoing those very market-orientated reforms – grant-maintained schools, fund-holding GPs, etc. – that the previous Tory government had introduced. When a government starts to bring forward legislation to unpick the damage its previous legislation caused it really is insane. Early on in Labour's term its excessive lawmaking became a bee in the bonnet of certain campaigners and journalists (such as your author). But as time has gone on many commentators have come to recognize that too many laws were being passed.

At the height of the expenses furore that rocked parliament in the early summer of 2009, Danny Finkelstein, the chief leader writer on *The Times* newspaper and former head of the Conservative research department, envisaged another scandal heading down the tracks towards the political classes:

> I used to have a little game. Rather unfair, but still fun. Dinners with MPs of all parties are frequently interrupted by

the division bell – that is, the alert for a Commons vote. And as they left I would ask: 'What are you voting on?' On a very large proportion of occasions, the MPs didn't have much of a clue. How long before someone mounts a proper survey of parliamentarians on their way to a vote? The moment that the slavish following of the whip becomes an issue, so will all the practices associated with it. What will people think of votes on major topics when the chamber is almost completely empty for the debate? What about the absence of MPs at the theatre when a controversy is being settled in Parliament? What about the way MPs just vote the line?[7]

Anyone who knows Westminster is aware that MPs are not simply passing bad laws with worrying regularity; they have hardly the barest knowledge about the content of the legislation they are enacting. They are there to follow the party line and they simply ask the whips which way they are supposed to vote: the legislation itself is of secondary importance. There is a story that a peer, whose presence in the Lords was less assiduous than the government whips would have liked it to be, was prevailed upon to turn up for a particular debate in order to maximize the party's vote in what was expected to be a close division. The peer arrived, listened to the debate – and duly voted for the opposition. When he was asked why he said he had listened to the arguments and had been convinced of the opposition's case.

You might have thought that was the purpose of parliament but you would be wrong. It is to put through the manifesto on which the government was elected. However, if this was all it did that, of itself, would not be a bad thing. In reality, parties often stray well beyond anything they put to the electorate. As Finkelstein observed:

MPs have long been aware that they are passing too many laws to be able to scrutinise them properly. They even passed a special Act to allow existing laws to be changed without having to go back before Parliament at all. The public is not aware of this. Most think laws still have to go through Parliament, however rigid whipping might be. How long before these arrangements to make laws by shortcut become a scandal?[8]

DOOMSDAY BILL

It should already be a scandal. The Act to which Finkelstein referred above was the Legislative and Regulatory Reform Act and its intention was to give the government the power to excise at the drop of a hat any legislation that it saw fit in order to undo all the damage it had caused by having so much legislation. It was like giving an alcoholic the key to the drinks cabinet. Had they got their way, the Bill would have empowered any minister to make provisions to amend, repeal or replace any legislation, primary or secondary, for any purpose, and to reform the common law in order to implement Law Commission recommendations.

The government said it needed this 'fast-track' method of repealing laws as part of its war on the red tape for which it was mostly responsible. Armed with such a weapon, it could scythe through the forests of regulations, many of them planted by the very same government, and relieve the £50 billion annual burden on hundreds of thousands of hard-pressed small businesses. It was a bit like handing out weapons to everyone in the land and then declaring martial law on the grounds that the streets have become too dangerous. Ministers just could not understand why so many people objected to this measure. They said: 'Trust us. We may be taking extraordinary powers that could, in the wrong hands, be misused. But we wouldn't dream of doing any such thing. This is Britain, for goodness sake.' They simply refused to get their heads around the possibility that benign governments of the sort we are used to might not always be the norm. Eventually, the Bill was watered down or it would have been thrown out by the Lords; but the problem it sought to address was a very real one and it was institutional, not legislative.

When it was first published, the Legislative and Regulatory Reform Bill was one of the most extraordinary measures to come before a democratic chamber in peacetime. The fact that it is not on the statute book in the form that ministers envisaged was purely because a coalition of concerned MPs, peers and civil liberties campaigners kicked up a sufficient stink to force ministers to rewrite the Bill and remove its more noxious provisions. Otherwise this measure would have given the executive power to rule almost by diktat. Yet during its committee stage in the Commons, members of the standing committee could be seen dealing with their correspondence and other paperwork, paying not a blind bit of notice to the proceedings. They were just there to vote the way the whips told them to. To be honest, that is true of most Bills. However, this was fundamentally different in scope and required the custodians of our democracy to pay more attention.

In the name of reducing the vast number of regulations, the government proposed giving itself the power to amend, replace or repeal any law without proper scrutiny. Sanity prevailed, and the Bill was changed to make clear that its powers may be deployed only in the cause of deregulation. Nevertheless, the measure made its way through parliament and is now the most powerful weapon in the government's armoury for attacking excessive bureaucracy. Instead of being the constitutional excrescence it began life as, ministers hailed it as 'a measure that promises to bring benefits to hundreds of thousands of businesses, charities and individuals'.

Before the government starts patting itself on the back for this magnanimous gesture toward democratic sensibilities, we need to ask why such a heavy-handed measure was needed at all. Have we become so mesmerized by the image of a British administration promulgating a law that would not have looked out of place in Eastern Europe 30 years ago that we have lost sight of the real problem, which is the sheer volume of unnecessary and often baleful regulation?

Every year thousands of laws are made by Statutory Instrument, with inadequate scrutiny. Take the Safeguarding Vulnerable Groups Act, about which a great deal will be heard in coming years (and which is looked at in more detail later). This is an apparently innocuous piece of legislation that, it turns out, will extend criminal-record checks to some nine million adults, a third of the working population. Yet this Bill was so badly drafted that 250 amendments needed to be made by the end of its parliamentary progress, almost certainly ensuring that it was not properly scrutinized.

There is simply too much primary legislation and not enough parliamentary time for it all to be properly debated. The 'guillotine' (a motion to allow only a fixed time for a Bill so that its stages are completed by a certain date or number of sittings) used to be a rare enough event to make it newsworthy; now virtually every Bill is on a timetable and sometimes key measures receive just cursory attention. Tony Blair and latterly Gordon Brown's administration have brought forward truckloads of legislation simply to send out signals, make a point or obtain a headline. That is not what it is for. Government should commit itself unequivocally to less legislation. What is needed is a change of culture throughout Whitehall, starting with ministers themselves.

In the 10 years Tony Blair was in power, there were 455 Acts of Parliament and more than 32,000 Statutory Instruments, which contain the regulations underpinning the primary legislation. There were 6 Acts on immigration, 7 on terrorism, 12 on education, 11 on health and social care, and 25 on criminal justice. Labour created new crimes at a rate of nearly one a day. Yet questioning this incontinence is derided as 'simplistic libertarianism' by Mr Brown.[9] He caricatured those who consider freedom to be synonymous with the absence of government from public life as akin to support for child labour in the nineteenth century.

However, it is possible to argue for less government and a smaller state without countenancing the dispatch of an eight-year-old up a chimney. It is also justifiable to maintain that there has been too much of the wrong legislation and not enough of the right. Where, for instance, were the great welfare reforms promised in 1997 and whose savings would both end the culture of state handouts and fund extra spending on health and education? True, many Labour MPs fought any reforms that seriously linked receipt of benefit to a willingness to work, but with majorities in excess of 150 they would have got through, not least with Tory support. However, they had a very powerful opponent, the then chancellor, one Gordon Brown. He decided to plough his own furrow, championing a centralist tax-credits system that both entrenched the dependency culture and was incompetently administered to boot at vast cost to the country.

What happened to the vaunted reforms of health and education to give us greater say and choice over schools and treatment? They have been introduced latterly with choice in schools and new NHS trusts; but for many years changes in these areas were so piecemeal, so limited in their ambition and so lacking in vision that we will all pay a heavy price. And who stopped the more fundamental reforms that were needed? Have a guess. Instead of grandstanding with dozens of criminal justice Acts, aimed principally at tomorrow's headlines rather than making the streets safe, the legislative effort should have been expended on proper, lasting and effective reforms of public services.

Brown fails to acknowledge not just that there is simply too much legislation but that most of it is useless. There have been measures introduced in the past 10 years that were repealed before they even came into force. There are others that were passed years ago and still have not been enacted. More than that, the root-and-branch reforms to the public services that were sorely needed never materialized. These were 13 wasted years.

EVENING, ALL. NOW WHERE DID I PUT THAT FORM?

New laws mean more regulations. More regulations mean those on the wrong end of them have to spend time responding to them in some way. They include the police who should be out and about but spend a lot of their time in their stations filling out forms. This was exposed by a police officer writing under the pseudonym David Copperfield in a 2006 book called *Wasting Police Time*, based on his online blog. He later revealed himself as PC Stuart Davidson, before leaving Britain to start a new life in Canada, also as a policeman. Davidson's book was the first full-scale work to lift the lid on the disenchantment within the service at the bureaucracy, the paperwork, the target mentality – everything, indeed, that the government now acknowledges has undermined good policing, but about which it has done absolutely nothing. Many other police officers substantiated Davidson's account, though it was denounced in the House of Commons by Tony McNulty, then the police minister, as 'more of a fiction than Dickens'.[10]

Since then, another book has emerged, this time penned by a higher ranking officer who disguised his identity as Inspector Gadget. It is also based on a blog that recounts his experiences with a shire constabulary: 'Rules and processes brought in to save time and money and make things fairer ended up costing time and money and hampering us in our attempts to fight crime. This is about well-meaning idiocy, the usurping of frontline professionals by managers and bureaucrats, and the law of unintended consequences.'[11]

One of those consequences is that the police are increasingly in conflict, not with crooks, but with law-abiding people who are being criminalized by the myriad new laws that now plague our lives. As Gadget said: 'I wrote this book because I am worried about the gulf that has opened up between us and our core supporters – law-abiding, tax-paying folk living ordinary lives ... This is important because ... without the support of the majority we are lost'.

Outside the *Daily Telegraph's* offices in central London, police officers patrol to assist council wardens ('the cigarette Nazis', as a colleague terms them) catch people throwing butts on the ground, a bad thing to do, but one that only happens because smokers are no longer able to light up indoors. It is hardly surprising that complaints about police rudeness and neglect of duty have risen sharply, as recent figures show. Ian Johnston, the leader of the Police Superintendents' Association, has acknowledged that public confidence in the police is fragile. He blamed the culture of chasing government performance targets.[12]

An inquiry by Sir Ronnie Flanagan, former HM chief inspector of constabulary, found that police have to deal with a 'staggering' amount of paperwork for even the most minor incident. Officers were spending up to 14 hours at a time filling in forms simply to allow them to keep tabs on known criminals. Strict rules governing surveillance operations mean that a police officer has to fill in a form to hide behind a wall to keep an eye on a car park where thieves operate. In one case, an officer seeking authorization for directed surveillance against a serial burglar had to complete 10 forms, including one that ran to 40 pages and required a full background briefing on the number of burglaries in the area. Police in one county had to fill in a 17-page form just to adjust the position of a CCTV camera. Police officers have hundreds of similar stories of spending hours filling in acres of paperwork just to make a straightforward arrest for criminal damage.[13]

There are many reasons for this, some of which have to do with targets and standards introduced by the government; others go back further to times when the police were a little less scrupulous with their note-taking than they are now. Officers have to provide information to the courts, the Crown Prosecution Service, central government, local and national auditors, various inspectorates (including Sir Ronnie's own), the Health and Safety Executive and the Office of Surveillance Commissioners. All want forms, sometimes in triplicate.

On top of that, the police say they have new duties more akin to social work that make old-fashioned policing difficult. Then there is the notorious 'stop' form which takes a police officer around seven minutes to fill in every time he stops someone. This was introduced after Sir William Macpherson's inquiry into the murder of Stephen Lawrence to monitor whether an 'institutionally racist' police force was discriminating against ethnic minorities. Ministers were told that it would be unreasonably burdensome, but the Home Secretary David Blunkett introduced it anyway.

Just filling in the 'stop' forms ties up the equivalent of 16 staff in one force for a whole year. Gordon Brown said that where stop and search was concerned, he was 'clear the current rules have to go'. This has generated headlines like 'Stop and Search returns',[14] but it never went away. Hundreds of thousands of suspects every year are searched, just as they have been for a long time. However, the big change in recent years is that the police have been circumscribed from carrying it out effectively in high crime areas because of a fear of being denounced as racist or triggering a backlash like that in Brixton in 1981.

After Lord Scarman's report into those riots, the Police and Criminal Evidence Act of 1984 codified the rules for stop and search – principally that 'reasonable suspicion' that a crime has been committed must be present – and that is where the law stands. Nothing has changed, least of all the amount of red tape which Flanagan wanted to see burned and for which Brown promised to provide the bonfire.

BLOGS TO THE LOT OF YOU

It is not just the police who are frustrated, demoralized and angry, and consequently expressing their views on the internet. We can all now share in the irritations of many on frontline public services through their blogs.

There is a theme here. Go to the blog site of the Army Rumour Service (which has the wonderful acronym ARRSE) or NHS sites like Blog Doc and Dr Rant or Frank Chalk's teaching blogs and the extent of the crisis in the public sector becomes apparent. These are anecdotal accounts, but they tell a story experienced by many. Thus Frank Chalk, a comprehensive school teacher, writing about Inspector Gadget: 'His revelations of how the police are made to concentrate on crimes that improve the force's figures and achieve Government targets, rather than those which you or I might consider important, are explosive and should be headline news . . . All this sounds just like what goes on in schools.' These blogs are a cry of frustration and some in government see them as a threat.

Of course, people working in the public sector have always complained about the inadequacies and incompetence of the system. Many years ago, when I 'worked' in a local council office I was staggered by the indolence, waste and devil-may-care attitudes. This was meant to have been eradicated when the disciplines of the private sector were imported into the public sector to make it leaner and fitter. This was why salaries went up dramatically at the top end: to attract or retain senior officials who might be lured into banking or business. They now get high salaries as well as the gold-plated pensions and security of tenure that once compensated them for low pay, while the services remain bloated with bureaucrats. More laws mean more people to enforce them, more regulators to oversee them and more inspectors to ensure they are adhered to.

Since Labour took office, the number of people working in the public sector has grown by more than 650,000. Figures released by the Office for National Statistics showed that while people are losing their jobs in the private sector, public-sector employment increased by 13,000 in the second quarter of 2008 to 5.771

million. Who are all these people? They are not all doctors, nurses, policemen or teachers. Mostly, they are administrators, pen-pushers, inspectors, quangocrats, outreach officers, box-tickers and busybodies: thousands upon thousands of them. They include the cigarette wardens that make smokers' lives a misery and the corporate-speak officialdom that has driven Inspector Gadget, PC Copperfield and the rest of us to distraction.

CIVIL CONTINGENCY – OR DRACONIAN POWER?

Of course, governments have to legislate where it is needed, though you would have thought that after a few centuries of parliamentary democracy it would have been possible by now to devise a criminal justice or education system that could last longer than a year or so. To expect ministers to spend a bit more time at home and leave things alone is probably too much to ask. Governments like to be seen to do something, even more so with a general election approaching. Laws for a parliamentary session are normally announced in the Queen's Speech which accompanies the State Opening in November or December, or straight after an election. But what we are told in the Gracious Speech often bears little resemblance to what we get.

In 2005, the queen said: 'The threat of international terrorism and a changing climate have led to a series of emergencies and heightened concerns for the future. My Government will introduce a Bill creating a long-term foundation for civil contingencies capable of meeting these challenges at a national and local level.' Nothing wrong with that, though there is already a system for dealing with civil defence matters, albeit many years old. But where did the speech say: 'My Government will take the most sweeping and draconian powers ever bestowed upon a British government in peacetime, reserving the right to suspend the foundations of our liberties, such as habeas corpus and the Bill of Rights, when it judges that an emergency has occurred'?

Yet, this is what the Civil Contingencies Act allows, and, as is often the case, its exceptional nature only really dawned upon parliament at a late stage, leading to a flurry of 11th-hour attempts to hose it down. Peers introduced what is known as a 'sunset' clause, whereby the measure would lapse after three years unless renewed. This was resisted by the government, though ministers in the end agreed that if the emergency powers were used, there would be an independent inquiry afterwards to see if they had been properly deployed.

One peculiarity of this Act passed largely unnoticed, though it was picked up by Lady Buscombe, the Tory spokesman in the Lords. Under the legislation, if there is an emergency – and we have to take the government's word for it that it would be of the utmost gravity – its powers would enable the government to order the requisitioning of private property and to tell people where to go, what to do and when to do it. Laws to do with criminal evidence, trials and freedom of expression could be suspended. MPs and peers could be prevented from attending parliament and it would be possible to take over the media, intern suspects and forcibly evacuate whole communities.

Other than ruling out conscription, there is one, and only one, exception in the legislation. The right to strike is specifically exempted from its scope. This seems bizarre. Since the powers are to be used only in the direst circumstances, surely the one thing that the country would not need is for key workers, such as train drivers or firemen, to be taking industrial action. The likelihood must be that they would do their jobs like everyone else when the security of the nation is at stake, but why exempt strikers?

The government said existing laws ensuring that industrial action did not endanger human life would hold good in these circumstances. It considered that the right to withdraw labour within the law was a fundamental liberty that should be protected, even during emergencies. Yet the same could be said about all the other laws that would be suspended, not least freedom of speech. Lady Buscombe could only imagine that this was a sop to the trade unions, which remain Labour's biggest source of income.

HIP HIP HOORAY!

Was there any new law that captured the essence of New Labour more than the home information pack or HIP? It will serve as a fitting memorial to Tony Blair's 10 years in office. It is pure, unadulterated, 24-carat New Labour: pointless, ill-conceived, spiteful, smug and incompetently delivered. HIPs were originally a Labour manifesto promise in 1997. There was a perception that the house-sales system needed to be stream-lined, but Labour, as it does all too often, chose instead the route of petty interference.

Then – and here is another New Labour hallmark – it took six years of consultations, Green Papers, White Papers, pilot schemes (which showed that the HIPs were flawed) and draft legislation before the idea was brought to parliament in the Housing Bill in 2004. HIPs went through with hardly a murmur of dissent. Only when they were actually about to be introduced, long after the legislation had been through parliament, did opponents wake up and gird their loins.

This lack of an opposing voice in parliament to controversial measures was a characteristic of Labour's period in office – especially Tony Blair's first two parliaments, when Labour had such huge majorities and the Tories were a busted flush. Then, just as they were about to be implemented, the shouting began, by which time it was often too late. Outside parliament, ministers were told many times that HIPs would not work, yet they simply refused to listen.

Anyway, what business is it of the state if two people wish to engage in a property deal? The chancellor obviously has a fiscal interest, since he is creaming off a large tax chunk through stamp duty, but no more than that. Why should the seller have to compile an information pack containing search details that are required anyway, with no guarantee that the home will be sold? Each year, 600,000 properties placed on the market go unsold, rendering the information invalid unless the property is re-marketed within a year. The government even abandoned the original intention of the packs, which was to include a home-condition report (as though any buyer would rely upon a survey produced by the vendor). It gave the scheme a spurious veneer of environmental legitimacy by insisting they contain information about energy-efficiency levels. This requires a visit from a so-called energy assessor, who gives the property an efficiency rating from A to G. How many people are happy to buy a house on that basis, as opposed to its location, number of bedrooms or the size of the garden? If you refuse to have one of these HIPs prepared, then you will be fined – yet another way in which perfectly law-abiding people can be criminalized as a result of this government's actions.

HIPs were opposed all along by estate agents, though in the end many looked to the marketing opportunities presented by including HIP preparation as part of the sales process. Consumer groups, whom the government initially cited as supporters, turned against them. Even surveyors, once the greatest champions of HIPs when it was intended they should contain a home-condition report, gave up on them, while a Lords committee said the scheme had faced more opposition than any other government proposal they had reviewed.[15]

Preparing the packs slows down the sale process and makes it more expensive, creating worry and red tape for estate agents and sellers at a time when rising interest rates could hit the housing market. The packs will also put an end to same-day sales or to speculative tests of the market. This interference is a serious matter for millions of owners who have a good deal of equity tied up in their homes, on which they will rely for survival in their dotage. As the property market nose-dived and the recession took a grip, however, far from abandoning the HIPs the government simply ploughed ahead with their introduction. Under new rules that took effect in April 2009, HIPs had to be made available on the day that a property is put up for sale, rather than after a 28-day grace period, as was the case. Sellers are also burdened with more red tape in the form of a new requirement to fill in a six-page Property Information Questionnaire. There was something almost wilful in the government's refusal to accept that it might have been wrong to bring in HIPs and to persevere with them when the property market faltered.

ON THE PATH TO INJUSTICE

Modern government not only thinks it can interfere in what were once lawful transactions between mature adults; it can also take away your property without compensation. The Marine and Coastal Access Act 2009 introduced a 4-metre-wide 'corridor' around the entire English coastline to which everyone would have access, whether or not the owner wished it. Land is to be made available for open-air recreation – or 'spreading room' – for public use. The government is adamant that no compensation will be paid to landowners whose property is contained within the corridor.

At present, 70 per cent of the English coast is accessible (Scotland already has a continuous path) but it is broken up by pockets of private land. The proposed corridor will go through privately owned beaches, golf courses and farms, but the owners, while being consulted over the route, will have no right of appeal. It has been decreed that this would be 'inappropriate' and that a consultation carried out by Natural England, the quango in charge, will suffice. It will be for the environment secretary to make the final decision about the route and the extent of the 'spreading room'. At the time the Bill was going through parliament, this happened to be

Hilary Benn, whose own family owns a beach-side property on the Blackwater estuary on the Essex coast. A sea-wall runs at the end of the garden, yet no one is allowed to walk along it. As a result, it is one of only a handful of sites between the Thames and the Wash where the coastal path is broken. The Benns, understandably, want some privacy and this is almost certainly guaranteed because the Act excepts private gardens from its provisions and the sea-wall could be designated part of the garden. This is as it should be, otherwise tens of thousands of seaside properties could be affected. But why does Mr Benn, in the spirit of Labour's great vision of an unbroken coast path, not open up this part of the path voluntarily – or is it a case of do as I say and not as I do?

While private gardens are exempt, bigger estates are considered fair game. So, too, are hotels, caravan parks, golf courses and letting agencies that own private beaches. The Country Land & Business Association says there are hundreds of residences and businesses around the country for whom the Act will have significant financial implications. Even before the recent collapse in prices, estate agents estimated some affected properties could lose as much as 20 per cent of their value.

Needless to say, the Ramblers' Association, which has been the principal champion of the coastal corridor, refuses to believe this and says similar claims made when the right to roam was introduced in 2000 have proved to be unfounded. However, that legislation was amended to meet most of the objections and to stop walkers going where they pleased; and original plans to allow unlimited access to the coast have also now been modified.

A coastal corridor, however, can follow only one route; so why is it necessary to have a corridor rather than just a footpath, since this will stop some farmers ploughing the land close to cliff edges and has the potential to cause confrontation and acrimony? Furthermore, if there is any financial loss, how in all justice can there be no compensation, nor even an independent appeals process? When an earlier environment secretary,

David Miliband, mooted the idea of an unbroken coast path, he said: 'We are an island nation. The coast is our birthright and everyone should be able to enjoy it.' But another of our birthrights is, or used to be, a belief in justice and fair play. You can also be sure that if the land is owned by the government, especially the Ministry of Defence, no one will be allowed near it. The way this law was enacted was criticized by the Parliamentary Joint Committee on Human Rights.[16]

IT'S NONE OF YOUR BUSINESS

The Sexual Orientation Regulations, introduced at the EU's insistence through the Equality Act 2006, make it an offence for anyone providing goods, services, facilities, education or public functions to discriminate on the grounds that someone is heterosexual, homosexual or bisexual. And nor should they, I hear you say. But what happens when one person's liberty not to be discriminated against conflicts with another's to express a contrary opinion that is profoundly held and religious in origin? Take the case of Stephen Green, the head of a Christian lobby group accused of breaching public order at a gay festival. He was charged by South Wales police (the case was later dropped) for handing out leaflets entitled *Same-Sex Love, Same-Sex Sex: What Does The Bible Say*? Now, you may or may not agree with Mr Green's stance on this matter, but it hardly warranted detaining him for four hours or charging him with 'threatening behaviour'. Who was he threatening? Indeed, Mr Green could argue that, as a Christian who believes that homosexuality is wrong, he should be allowed to exercise his rights to say so, even at the risk of offending people. After all, the Equality Act also outlaws discrimination on the grounds of religion or belief.

One of the most breathtaking examples of the pernicious use of so-called hate-crime legislation concerned Mrs Pauline Howe, 67, a grandmother and a committed Christian living in

Norwich. In the summer of 2009, she wrote to the city council complaining about its decision to allow a gay-rights march in the city centre in July, at which she claims she was verbally abused. In the letter, she wrote, 'It is shameful that this small, but vociferous lobby should be allowed such a display unwarranted by the minimal number of homosexuals.' Mrs Howe referred to homosexuals as 'sodomites' and blamed 'their perverted sexual practice' for sexually transmitting diseases as well as the 'downfall of every Empire'. Whatever her views, they were being vouchsafed only to the council; she was not publicly trying to whip up animosity towards homosexuals. But you can guess what happened next.

Bridget Buttinger, deputy chief executive at the council, replied to Mrs Howe, warning that she could face being charged with a criminal offence for expressing such views:

> As a local authority we have a duty along with other public bodies to eliminate discrimination of all kinds. A hate incident is any incident that is perceived by the victim or any other person as being motivated by prejudice or hatred. A hate crime is any hate incident that constitutes a criminal offence. The content of your letter has been assessed as potentially being hate related because of the views you expressed towards people of a certain sexual orientation. Your details and details of the content of your letter have been recorded as such and passed to the police.

Two officers from Norfolk constabulary questioned Mrs Howe in her home and told her that her opinions were regarded as a hate incident and had caused offence. However, although they decided that no crime had been committed their presence frightened Mrs Howe: 'I've never been in any kind of trouble before so I was stunned to have two police officers knocking at my door. Their presence in my home made me feel threatened. It was a very unpleasant experience.'[17]

It gets more complicated with the new Sexual Orientation Regulations 2009. Faith groups say they will face prosecution if they fail to promote or encourage homosexual practices. For instance, teachers may fall foul of the law if they do not give homosexuality equal prominence with heterosexuality in sex education lessons. A Muslim printer could be charged for declining to publish a flyer for a gay pride march. An IT consultant with strong Christian convictions may be prosecuted for refusing to build a website designed for same-sex dating. It could be illegal for Christian conference and retreat centres to refuse bookings from gay and lesbian groups, or for Christian hostels to refuse beds to same-sex couples. It is tempting to say that they will all just have to adapt to the new world order, as did those who once considered it perfectly acceptable to refuse to let black people stay in their guest houses. But there is a difference. Discriminating on the grounds of race is pure bigotry. Doing so by declining to promote homosexuality is an article of faith for many millions of people, even though there are obvious disagreements on this within religions.

Where all this can lead became clear to a group of pensioners living at a home for the elderly in Brighton. As part of its 'fair access and diversity' policy, Brighton council started to ask sexual orientation questions of groups in receipt of council money, including this home. The charity running the home declined to do this and also refused to use images of elderly homosexuals, lesbians, bisexuals and transgender people in its leaflets. As a consequence, the council accused the charity of 'institutional discrimination' and withdrew its £13,000 grant. A spokesman said the charity had made 'limited progress' in ensuring the home was 'accessible' to homosexuals. However, this was a Christian charity and the residents are also Christians. It is their faith that defines them, not their sexuality. Some have been missionaries or in a ministry and they chose the scheme – part of the Pilgrim Homes network – because of its Christian ethos. Since the home had never asked impertinent and intrusive questions about their sexuality how was it possible to know how many homosexuals had actually stayed there in order to show if there was discrimination; and why should anyone care? As Phil Wainwright of Pilgrim Homes said: 'We have every reason to believe that we have given places to gay Christians, and no questions were ever asked.'[18]

So who was being discriminatory here: the home against homosexuals or the council against Christians? Would a Muslim charity have been treated in the same way? Can you imagine one being required to ask the same questions? Well, if it is providing services, like care for the elderly, it might well be because that is what the Equality Act (Sexual Orientation) Regulations 2007 say should happen. Although the questions do not have to be answered, an unwillingness to ask them could be construed, as it was in Brighton, as a sign of hostility to homosexuals, rather than simply of indifference.

It is only 40 years since homosexuality was made legal and overt discrimination of the sort depicted in Quentin Crisp's *The Naked Civil Servant* remained rife for many years after. That can hardly be said to apply any longer when so many gay people are now part of our national life and accepted as such. Most of us, naively, thought that a tolerant and civilized attitude had been reached whereby it simply did not matter any more. However, to be confronted with a questionnaire asking about what are, especially for older generations, private matters is outrageous. This issue goes far beyond the over-zealous application of the law by a single council which has the highest proportion of homosexual residents in the country.

The Office for National Statistics (ONS) now routinely asks people about their 'sexual identity' in every household survey it conducts. There had been a plan to include a question about sexuality in the 2011 Census, but this was dropped because officials recognized what a fearful row there would be. Instead, ONS surveys include the question 'to allow for more accurate baseline estimates, of the size and characteristics of the lesbian, gay and bisexual population in the UK'. Karen Dunnell, the National Statistician, said: 'ONS puts great emphasis on maintaining confidentiality of data. In this case, special show cards are used to ensure that even someone in the same room as the respondent at the time of the interview cannot know how they have answered.' That may be so, but why on earth should any of this be necessary? According to the ONS it is a requirement of the Equality Act in order that public policy and money can be properly targeted on needy groups. Yet we discover from the Brighton example that the opposite is true: it is so that funding can be withheld from organizations that do not subscribe to the intrusive demands of another madcap law.

This development is of a piece with many other attempts to gather more and more information about the population. Gay rights groups have long battled to get a sexual orientation question included on national surveys; but they should be careful what they wish for. The time may come when information like this is used against them, just as refusing to take part is now being used against a Christian charity. Even if the law expects those providing services to produce evidence that they are not discriminating against homosexuals, why should the rest of us be asked to declare our sexuality? The ONS survey question asks people to choose from the categories 'Heterosexual/straight', 'Gay/Lesbian', 'Bisexual' and 'Other', although they will also be allowed to decline to answer. The ONS said: 'The category "other" has been included (because) a very small group of people find that the answer categories provided do not describe themselves and that they would prefer to use another term.' Well, there is a much larger group of people who would like the opportunity to give one further answer. It is this: Mind your own business.

LET THERE BE LIGHT

For the greatest part of human existence, we have lived our

nights in almost total darkness, brightened occasionally by a full moon or the glow of a fire. We came to fear and distrust the dark and the dangers it shrouded: bandits or wild animals in the countryside; robbers in the towns. Only in the past 200 years have our cities been properly lit, from the introduction of gas lamps to London in 1807 through to the all-encompassing glare that can now be seen from miles away. Those of us who live in big towns rarely see the night sky anymore, but its disappearance was a trade-off for safety and ease of movement. Over many years, astronomers and groups such as the Campaign for Dark Skies have agitated against this 'light pollution', at which our forefathers would have marvelled, and have pressed for new legislation to stop it. Light pollution in 2005 became a statutory nuisance for the first time and refusal to obey an order to dim an offending illumination is now a criminal offence, punishable by a fine of up to £50,000. Now, I have a good deal of sympathy with the arguments about light pollution, not merely because it is such a shock to see the glory of the night sky when out of the city, but also because it represents such a colossal waste of energy. It is often public buildings that are the greatest offenders, both in having too many lights and in leaving them on too long, not least because those in charge of them do not have to foot the bill. The rest of us are encouraged to switch off a few more lights when the electricity demand comes in; for the public sector it is merely another cost to pass on to the taxpayer.

The councils who police the regulations say they do so with a 'light touch', no pun intended. In the first instance, complainants are encouraged to record the problem with a detailed note of times and dates of nuisance and, preferably, to take some photographs for evidence. Then, they are advised to speak to the light-owner and see if a compromise can be reached. If this fails, a complaint can be made to the environmental health officers, who will then take a decision as to whether the lighting is in fact a nuisance and, if so, request that it is abated. If the order is ignored, the local authority may begin legal action. No doubt for people irritated beyond measure by the incessant glare of a neighbour's lights, this law is a blessed relief, though they might be better advised to invest in a set of thick curtains first before starting proceedings that could prove costly and time-consuming.

The reason why this law just does not feel right is that it represents yet another incursion into our daily lives. You just know that, for all the talk of turning the cities into a star-gazer's paradise, it will inevitably be used to stop people having too many Christmas-tree lights, or to intercede in a row between neighbours over excessive security lighting, or to put an end to late-night floodlit tennis. Meanwhile, many of the worst light pollutants are exempt from the law: airports, bus stations, road and rail transport facilities and (sensible one, this) lighthouses are not covered by the new proscription. The campaigners' first target was not Heathrow Terminal Five, which lights up the horizon for about 20 miles around, but the floodlamps used to illuminate Nelson's Column in Trafalgar Square.

The danger with so much regulation and policing is that, when a law is proposed that may well be a proper response to a real problem, it just seems like another wretched addition to the dismally long list of things we could do even as recently as 1997, but can no longer.

At the same time as new laws were introduced to curb light pollution, the European Commission pushed forward with a directive whereby drivers have to keep their headlamps on at all times, day or night, with a £50 fine if they do not. The European Commission directive 2008/89/EC entered into force on 15 October 2008, although countries will have had a few years to adapt before everyone moves to the new 'daytime running lights' (DRLs) on all types of motor vehicles. These lights are automatically switched on when the engine starts. All new types of passenger cars and small delivery vans have to be equipped with DRLs from 2011 and trucks and buses will also be equipped with them from 2012.

This measure will place a further burden on UK manufacturers but will add nothing to road safety and may even be detrimental to it. Motorcyclists who use DRLs to differentiate themselves from other vehicles fear they will have more accidents as a result. Furthermore, according to the Society of Motor Manufacturers and traders: 'There is a small risk that some drivers will forget to switch on their headlights [rather than just using the DRLs] at night. We think there could also be confusion among road users between these lights and front fog lamps.' This law aims to increase road safety but it might increase risks for road users and environment. According to Eurobusiness, the mandatory requirement of DRLs is expected to raise car prices by around €150 and also cause a rise in petrol consumption.

On top of this, from 1 September 2009 old-fashioned incandescent light bulbs of the sort most people use have no longer been manufactured in an effort to persuade us all to switch to the alternative compact fluorescent lamps (CFLs) to save energy under another EU directive. The directive, as usual, was not carefully thought through as it made no mention of what is to be done about speciality incandescent lamps such as fireglows, nightlights, cooker hood lamps, fridge lights or oven and appliance lamps which cannot be replaced with CFLs.

I KNOW: LET'S HAVE A SUMMIT

You can always tell when a government is in trouble and does not really know what to do: it arranges a Downing Street summit. Over the years there have been more summits about crime in Number 10 than there are peaks in the Himalayas. Summits can be presented by ministers as a demonstration of activity when they are, in reality, a reflection of desperation.

This has never been truer than with the various summits over the years about knife crime. Usually, they result in two outcomes: the promise of an amnesty and the prospect of yet more laws, even though we already have a truckload of legislation designed to stop people carrying knives as offensive weapons. A summit is held in order to persuade an increasingly angry public that a government is getting to grips with the scourge of inner-city stabbings that have claimed dozens of young lives in recent years. One proposal that emerged from a summit in 2008 is to end the practice of just cautioning children aged 16 and 17 if they are found carrying a knife. Gordon Brown said: 'We have to send out a message and reinforce it with immediate action. It is completely unacceptable to carry a knife.'

This was hardly a new message. It has, after all, been illegal to possess an offensive weapon in a public place for more than 50 years. Controls on knives were introduced in 1953, after a spate of gangland stabbings, just as the Teddy Boys were beginning to strut the streets. The Prevention of Crime Act made it unlawful to have an offensive weapon in public. In 1959, the Restriction of Offensive Weapons Act banned the carrying, manufacture, sale, purchase, hire or lending of flick-knives and 'gravity knives'. The Criminal Justice Act 1988 contained a list of prohibited martial arts-style weapons and made it an offence to carry an article with a blade or sharp point in a public place. The Offensive Weapons Act 1996, brought in after the murder of Philip Lawrence, the London headmaster, made it illegal to sell knives to children under 16. The Knives Act 1997 prohibited the marketing of combat knives. The Violent Crime Reduction Bill 2006 banned the sale of knives to anyone under 18 and increased the penalty for possession of a knife with intent to cause harm from two years to four years.

There are, then, plenty of laws already. The issue is about enforcing them. Furthermore, the key here is 'offensive' weapon. There are obvious dangers of injustice in having catch-all presumptions of guilt for possessing what someone might legitimately be carrying for fishing or model-making. What is needed is not more laws but – as a few chief constables have conceded – a return of commonsense policing. Officers should be able to stop and search those youngsters they have good reason to believe may be carrying weapons in order to use them. They should be able to do this without being required to fill in a form or to be concerned about getting the right ethnic balance. There should be enough patrol officers in the inner cities where this is a problem to make vulnerable children feel less threatened by gangs so that they do not feel it necessary to carry a knife, too. Police should retain some discretion to issue warnings and a dressing down to children under 18 who do not pose a threat to others but are just scared – without having all the bureaucratic rigmarole of arrests, form-filling, court appearances and the like. A legalistic approach to this problem will simply keep officers tied up in police stations when what is needed is far more straightforward: the return of order and authority to the streets in those areas where it has clearly broken down.

Order on the streets – enforced by police, not gang leaders – would obviate the need for many children to hang around with habitual offenders for what they think is their own protection. Yet the promises of getting more bobbies on the beat are never carried through. Policy on youth crime is all over the place. One moment governments reach for the judicial stick of tougher punishments, the next for the welfare carrot of education and intervention. Sight has been lost of the fundamental need to ensure that, first and foremost, the inner cities are properly policed. Lawlessness and yobbish behaviour flourishes when order and authority is absent. Summits, pointless amnesties and fatuous campaigns to challenge the 'glamour' of knife-carrying will have no impact while the thugs continue to rule the streets. And all the laws that we have seen over the past 13 years have done nothing to stop them.

THE RISE OF THE SI

Most new laws nowadays are not promulgated by Acts of Parliament but by secondary legislation known as a Statutory Instrument (SI). Powers for these are often taken by ministers through primary legislation and then used to change the law, often without the same sort of scrutiny that accompanies an Act of Parliament.

Indeed, the trend in the number of Acts that are passed has declined over the last 30–40 years. However, the number of Statutory Instruments has seen a sharp increase from around 2,000 a year until the late 1980s to nearly double that now. However, even though there have been fewer Acts they have been much bigger and more all-embracing than was once the case.

Table I New Legislation Passed 1950–2008

Year	Acts of Parliament	Statutory Instruments
1950	50	2,144
1960	66	2,495
1970	58	2,044
1980	68	2,051
1990	46	2,667
1998	49	3,321
1999	35	3,491
2000	45	3,412
2001	25	4,150
2002	44	3,279
2003	45	3,367
2004	38	3,459
2005	24	3,601
2006	55	3,511
2007	31	3,662
2008	33	3,327

Total of new Statutory Instruments 1998–2008: 35,580 (9.6 per day)
Source: Office of Public Sector Information.

Table 2 Pages of Acts and Statutory Instruments 1911–2006

Year	Acts of Parliament	Statutory Instruments
1911	430	330
1921	420	1,080
1931	280	1,050
1940	370	1,970
1950	720	2,970
1955	540	2,340
1960	850	3,020
1965	1,340	4,730
1970	1,110	4,880
1975	2,060	6,210
1980	2,110	5,440
1985	2,380	4,760
1990	2,390	6,550
1995	3,000	9,690
1996	3,150	10,230
1997	2,060	8,660
1998	2,490	7,480
1999	2,096	10,760
2000	3,865	8,770
2001	1,605	10,830
2002	2,868	9,070
2003	4,073	8,942
2004	3,470	10,236
2005	2,712	11,868
2006	4,609	n/a

Source: House of Commons Library.

CHAPTER 3

JERKING THE KNEE – LAWS THAT WERE MADE IN HASTE AND REPENTED AT LEISURE

Some laws become exemplars of how not to make them: they are knee-jerk responses to perceived ills that are repented at leisure; they are inherently unjust; or they visit upon totally innocent people restrictions on their way of life, when the reasons for bringing about the law in the first place had nothing to do with them.

THE DANGEROUS DOGS ACT 1991

It began with a spate of dog attacks in 1991. On 16 January, 6-year-old Rachel Hetherington was mauled by a friend's pet lurcher near her Birmingham home. She received 26 stitches. On 18 February, William Roach, aged 38, was savaged to death by his Alsatian at his home in Rusholme, Manchester, as his wife tried to rescue him. On 22 March, baby Steven Berry was mauled in his pushchair by a bull terrier at a Sheffield bus stop. On 7 May, 5-year-old Michael Parkinson was savaged by two Rottweilers near his Bradford home. He received 80 stitches. By now, newspapers had discerned a pattern and were calling for action. In parliament, an early-day motion was tabled calling attention to the need for the control of dangerous dogs.

The attacks continued. On 8 May, 3-year-old Natasha Thorpe's nose was almost bitten off when she was attacked by a collie at a neighbour's house at Craigmillar in Edinburgh. She received 40 stitches. On 8 May, Frank Tempest, aged 54, had his nose and ear ripped off by two pit bull terriers as he walked home from work in a Lincoln suburb. He needed microsurgery. On 10 May, Karen Jowett, aged 21, was attacked by a Doberman in Westgate in Peterborough, Cambridgeshire. She needed more than 100 stitches. On 13 May, 2-year-old Paula Holmes was mauled by her grandmother's American pit bull terrier at her Bolton home. She suffered a broken nose and needed stitches for facial injuries. On 15 May, Pat Lord, aged 39, underwent microsurgery after her right arm was chewed to the bone and broken by her pet Rottweiler. On 17 May, police constable John Cooper was savaged by a pit bull terrier in Newcastle. He received stitches in a throat wound.

By now the press was in a frenzy of outrage at the apparent inability of our elected representatives to do anything about this. Every dog bite was front-page news and it reached its apogee with an attack in Bradford on a little girl called Rukhsana Khan. The *Bradford Telegraph and Argus* reported what happened:

> Rukhsana was tossed about like a rag doll by the ferocious dog for 15 minutes while onlookers struggled to free her from its vice-like grip. The six-year-old from Springfield Street, Manningham, Bradford, suffered 23 dog bites to her back and three deep bites to the left hand side of her chest where the dog gripped on for dear life. She has five other bites to her chest and lost two teeth in the attack.

The media were demanding that Something Must Be Done. The government, which until now had resisted, caved in and introduced emergency legislation. The Dangerous Dogs Act

(DDA) is often cited as the classic example of a bad law, a media-driven, knee-jerk reaction to a horrifying incident. For as long as people live near dogs, some will be bitten. If people have large and violent dogs in their homes with babies and young children, they are risking an attack. Can this be legislated away? The Tories in 1991 hoped something could be, preferably all the bad headlines. Kenneth Baker, who was home secretary, came to the Commons on 10 June armed with some hastily drafted ideas. As he observed, three of the most vicious attacks, including that on Rucksana Khan were carried out by pit bull terriers, a cross-breed fighting dog with few saving graces. Baker said:

> As has been tragically shown, it is capable of vicious and sustained assault without warning or provocation. Once a pit bull terrier has started an attack, it has been shown to be impossible for full-grown adults to prevent the dog from causing horrific injuries. The public are increasingly concerned about attacks by those vicious dogs and are entitled to look to the Government to take action to tackle the problem. I have therefore decided to bring before the House as soon as possible this Session legislation which will ban the breeding and ownership of pit bull terriers and other dogs bred especially for fighting. Also included in the ban will be the Japanese Tosa, a dog bred for fighting which, apparently, can weigh up to 17 stone.[1]

At the time, there was only one Tosa dog in the UK, whose owner threatened to emigrate if her animal was taken away. It is essential to rid the country of the danger from such dogs, said Baker. They have no place in our homes. Owners of those fighting dogs may be able to return them to their country of origin. The problem was that most dog attacks were not carried out by the breeds identified by Baker but by Alsatians, Rottweilers, terriers and collies. There were so many of these, however, that putting them down would have provoked insurrection. So the government focused on the owners and proposed a tougher criminal offence to penalize dog-owners, of whatever the breed, who fail to keep their dogs safely under control in public, as well as a power to allow a court to specify the control of a particular dog of any type. That could include muzzling.

When the emergency Bill came to the Commons for a Second Reading, Baker was already aware of the impending backlash:

> Since I announced my intention to introduce this legislation, some have suggested that the Government were over-reacting to the problem, that eliminating the fighting dogs is not the answer and that there is no such thing as a bad dog, only a bad owner. But there is clear evidence that these dogs are a danger and a menace and are a type to be set apart from other dogs. I understand that that view is shared by those on the Opposition Front Bench. That is why we acted to ban the import of these dogs and other fighting dogs last month and that is why we have introduced the Bill as an urgent response to this problem.[2]

Baker proposed that the pit bulls should be put down with compensation of £50, or that the owners could keep them provided they were neutered. There were two problems: identifying the owners and being sure that the breed was a pit bull and not some other terrier. Just as the press could demand action against dangerous dogs, so it could easily switch to a tear-jerking story of a six-year-old girl whose precious Staffie had just been killed. Three other breeds were specifically named in the Act: the aforementioned Japanese Tosa, the Dogo Argentino and the Fila Brasileiro. It became illegal to own these types unless exempted by neutering, microchipping, insurance and registration. Once the Index of Exempted Dogs closed in March 1992, any dogs not included on it and deemed to be of 'pit bull type' by a court were automatically ordered to be destroyed.

However, the legislation did not only cover the dogs named in the Act and the definition of 'type' proved problematic in law. When cases began to go through the courts it fell to the presiding judge to determine whether any dog was 'of type' and to define the meaning of the word. In 1993, the Appeal Court decided that 'a dog of the type known as a Pit Bull Terrier is an animal approximately amounting to, near to, having a substantial number of characteristics of the Pit Bull Terrier'.

This definition meant that any dog, regardless of the breed or cross-breed, with a 'substantial number of characteristics of a Pit Bull Terrier' risked being caught up in the ban, among them types of Staffordshire bull terriers. The emphasis in that Act was entirely on breed rather than behaviour, which should be no basis for legislation. The law also had another peculiarity: the burden of proof was reversed. It was up to the defendant to prove their dog was not of the 'type' covered by the law.

In 1997 the DDA was amended to remove mandatory destruction of dogs brought before a court. It stated that if a dog was deemed to be pit bull type but the owner could show they were a responsible owner and the dog posed no danger to the public, the judge could order the dog to be registered with the Index and not be destroyed. Efforts to unpick the Act continue. In the Lords in 2009, a Private Member's Bill was introduced by Lord Redesdale, with the support of the Kennel Club, to make a number of key changes. The law would no longer be breed-specific; there would be greater emphasis on dealing with the owner, not the dog, and dog-attacks on private property would become a criminal offence.

What has the result of this law been? The idea behind the Act was that with all the pit bull type dogs being neutered they would die out. Eighteen years on, the Act has clearly failed to achieve this goal. Today, more dodgy-looking young men than ever can be seen out on the streets with fighting dogs, which are a must-have accessory in some inner-city communities.

Fatalities caused by dog attacks continue and the number of dog 'bites or strikes' continues to rise. According to the campaign group DDAWatch: 'The Act has proven to be unworkable whilst creating huge welfare implications for those dogs unfortunate enough to be caught up in it. It wrongly focused on certain breeds or types of dogs instead of placing the emphasis on responsibility on the owners of dogs.'[3]

When commenting on Lord Redesdale's proposed Bill, Caroline Kisko, Kennel Club Communications Director, said: 'The current legislation is draconian and severely flawed, and does little to protect the public. We have long been saying that any dog can be dangerous in the wrong hands and we hope that this Bill will go some way to combat the growing culture of using dogs as weapons.'[4]

And what of the little girl who started it all? Rukhsana Khan, by now 21, told the *Bradford Telegraph and Argus* in 2006:

> I still have nightmares about the attack and I am still terrified of dogs to this day. When I see a dog I freeze. I don't think that will ever change. The law was changed because of an attack on me 15 years ago, but today these attacks are still taking place and people are suffering terrible injuries. I have to live with the memory of the attack and the scars for the rest of my life. I do not want another child to have to go through what I did. The Government must prevent another attack by updating the law to make it tougher.

Lord Redesdale told peers in the debate on his Bill:

> The Dangerous Dogs Act was a piece of knee-jerk-reaction legislation to deal with pit bull terriers . . . It was meant to lead to the extinction of pit bull terriers as a breed in this country. If it had been successful, there would be no or only very elderly micro-chipped pit bull terriers alive today. However, research by the RSPCA shows that there are now more pit bull terriers in the country than there were when the Act was passed.

Because it is extremely difficult to define a pit bull terrier, there have been a great number of cases in which police officers have tried to say that a dog is a pit bull terrier and an enormous amount of legal confusion has ensued. Indeed, the cost implications of the legislation are quite severe. The cost to the Metropolitan Police last year of kennelling dogs that are considered to be pit bull terriers stood at £1.3 million, and that is just the kennelling cost and does not include policing or court fees.[5]

The Dangerous Dogs Act failed to achieve anything beyond securing a few favourable headlines to help the government during a difficult time when it was getting it in the neck. In the end, it became synonymous with hasty and ill-thought-out legislation. It was regarded as the ultimate bad law, though its promulgators, Lord Baker among them, to this day maintain that it was not as bad as all that. And, to be fair, compared to many laws that have come since and which are documented in this book, it was a legislative paragon.

THE WAR CRIMES ACT 1991

The War Crimes Act was passed in 1991, the same year as the Dangerous Dogs Act, which makes it a vintage year for bad laws; but in reality it had been brought forward some time before, when Margaret Thatcher was still prime minister. Its enactment was delayed by an almighty tussle between the House of Commons and the House of Lords that necessitated the lower chamber to invoke the Parliament Acts, for the first time since 1949, to get its way. It began life as a Private Member's Bill with a powerful motivation: to bring to justice those people living in this country who were responsible for the deaths of hundreds if not thousands of people in the Nazi death camps during the Second World War. What could possibly be bad about a law that sought to achieve such an end?

We can see the answer, today, almost 20 years later. Even though some 400 suspects were investigated, only two people were prosecuted and only one was convicted of any offence. The first person to be prosecuted for war crimes was Szymon Serafinowicz. He was charged in July 1995, when he was already 85. It was not until January 1997 that his trial was scheduled at the Old Bailey. By this time, he was in failing health and the jury decided that he was unfit to plead. According to Jon Silverman, a former BBC correspondent and legal expert who followed the issue closely, Serafinowicz, a collaborationist police chief responsible for hundreds if not thousands of deaths, would have been convicted. However, even though Scotland Yard's war crimes unit first became aware of the name Serafinowicz at the end of 1991, it took three-and-a-half years to charge him. Silverman said, 'The police explanation is that they had the wrong spelling. It took eighteen months to track him down in the UK – even though he was in the telephone book and had lived in the same house in Banstead in Surrey since 1956.'[6]

The other individual prosecuted under the Act – and the only one convicted – was Anthony Sawoniuk, whose name was first given to the UK authorities as a war crimes suspect in 1988 but he was not arrested and charged for another nine years. He was jailed for life and died in Norwich prison in 2004 aged 84. Perhaps it was worth bringing in the law to deny Sawoniuk peace in his dotage: he was found guilty of murdering Jewish families when he worked for the Nazis in Belarus.

However, the issue here was not whether the crimes themselves were heinous; of course they were. The fundamental objection to the legislation was not the hounding of elderly men who may have performed hideous deeds half a century earlier. It was unsatisfactory because it proposed legislation which many considered to be profoundly damaging to the rule of law. It is wrong to alter the law for special cases. However ghastly the crimes, they were committed in a foreign country by people who were not British citizens when they were carried out and were therefore beyond the jurisdiction of the UK courts. The intention of the War Crimes Act was to bring them within that jurisdiction after the event. When the Bill was thrown out by the Lords in 1990 by 207 votes to 74 and Mrs Thatcher fell from power, it was imagined that was the end of it. The new prime minister, John Major, had previously been opposed to the measure. Yet early in 1991 it was revived to consternation in the Lords and some sections of the Conservative Party in the Commons, where MPs were given a free vote.

Kenneth Baker, the home secretary, said there were two reasons behind the government's decision to reintroduce the measure: the first was the decisiveness of the Commons vote, when it came before parliament the previous year and was passed by a majority of more than 200; and the second was the nature of the evidence disclosed by an inquiry which considered whether alleged war criminals had taken refuge in Britain.

Mr Baker said: 'The inquiry's published report tells a chilling story of cold-blooded murder on an horrendous scale – killings not committed in the heat of battle, but of civilian populations in circumstances that had no possible connection with military objectives. The inquiry also showed that there is evidence of some of the perpetrators of these crimes actually living in this country.'[7]

The inquiry was conducted by Sir Thomas Hetherington, a former director of public prosecutions, and William Chalmers, former crown agent for Scotland. It looked at some 300 cases and recommended further investigation of 75. It concluded that there were 3 people against whom evidence already existed on which to mount prosecutions and that another 3 cases merited further detailed investigation. Mr Baker said:

> I well recognize the strength of the arguments that the events which the Bill addresses took place half a lifetime

ago, that the suspects are inevitably of advancing years – as are most of the witnesses – and the mounting of trials will not be easy. Few of us would have wished to have to confront these issues again now, or to be reminded of the horrors which occurred. But the fact is that these allegations are before us, allegations so serious that the passage of time, however long, cannot blot them out. I believe that the criminal justice system of this country is capable of ensuring that justice is done in respect both of the victims and of those who are accused of these crimes.[8]

Opposition came from many of the wartime generation including those who, like Edward Heath, had fought the Nazis. The former prime minister denounced the legislation as retroactive, saying the Conservative Party had always objected to backdating. Sir Geoffrey Howe, a former chancellor and foreign secretary, said the Commons should ask themselves whether it would be right to invite a jury to proceed to convict in cases of this kind when the Commons had not been able to persuade the Lords on the legitimacy of their case. Another Tory grandee, Sir Ian Gilmour, said there was no justification for the Commons to use the Parliament Acts to override the Lords on 'this highly objectionable little Bill'.[9]

Even some of the Labour left, where support for the Bill was strongest, had second thoughts. Clare Short said she had reconsidered her views since she voted for the Bill and now thought it would be a 'grave mistake' for it to be approved. She was concerned that there could be no fair trials under the law. None the less, the Bill received a second reading by 254 votes to 88, and the stage was set for another clash with the Lords which only one side could win.

The Liberal David Lloyd George once called the House of Lords 'Mr Balfour's poodle'. It was, in his view, the mere creature of the Conservative Party, and so when it defied his policies as chancellor, he limited its powers. The Parliament Acts of 1911 and 1949 are the nuclear weapon of the lower house, supposedly deployed only in the most exceptional circumstances to assert the primacy of the elected chamber. The first Act came about when the Lords refused to pass Lloyd George's Budget in 1910 because of the taxes it imposed on the landed aristocracy and gentry. The Liberals won a general election called to reinforce the government's mandate and when the Lords refused again to pass the Budget, Prime Minister Herbert Asquith urged the King to create hundreds of new peers willing to support the will of the people. The Lords gave in and also agreed to the Parliament Act which meant that after a two-year gap, a measure insisted upon by the Commons but rejected by the Lords would become law. This was amended to one year in 1949, though since the 1911 Parliament Act was used to get this change through parliament without the Lords' approval, its constitutional propriety has often been questioned.

Despite Lloyd George's claims, the Lords proved themselves anything but a Tory lapdog regarding the war crimes legislation, and again rejected the Bill, inviting the Conservative government to use the powers that he instituted. Arguably, this in itself was a misuse of the Parliament Acts since the Bill was passed on a free vote in the Commons, it involved no constitutional point and there was no question of the Lords defying an electoral mandate.

Many were appalled. A *Daily Telegraph* leader said of the Bill:

> It ignored the difficulties of giving the men concerned a fair trial and of collecting satisfactory evidence after so long. It begged the question of why the full weight of the British body politic should be deployed to make a special case of this category of half-century-old crimes, when so many other horrors remain unpunished, and certainly do not attract such almost obsessive ministerial attention. Above all, it applied a dangerous retrospective principle, putting the alleged murderers under a jurisdiction which

did not apply when the terrible deeds were done. Even more important at this stage than the rights and wrongs of the Bill itself, is the error of a government – especially a Conservative government – choosing this, of all matters, as the ground to take on the House of Lords.[10]

In April 1991, the Lords rejected the War Crimes Bill for a second time by 131 votes to 109, a majority of 22. The government invoked the Parliament Act, a move described at the time by Lord Jenkins of Hillhead as a 'constitutional monstrosity'. Lord Pym, the former Conservative foreign secretary, said the use of the Parliament Acts was 'highly authoritarian and dictatorial and indeed, I fear, an abuse of power'.

The argument had moved away from the efficacy of the legislation itself into a constitutional struggle between the two Houses. The problems with the legislation remained, however: how would a fair trial be possible once it was enacted and an individual arraigned under its terms?

Even Lord Shawcross – a former attorney general who, as Hartley Shawcross, was a prosecutor at the Nuremberg war trials – had grave misgivings, pointing out the difficulties of mounting a defence to the charges which could be brought under a Bill which he believed failed to satisfy the requirements of fairness and justice.

The War Crimes Act became law in the spring of 1991 without further debate, pushed on to the statute book under the provisions of the Parliament Acts for the first time in more than 40 years and the first time they had been used by a Conservative government to assert the primacy of the Commons over the Lords.

Supporters of the War Crimes Act said it was not too late to find and prosecute individuals who had taken part in the genocide in eastern Europe in the 1940s. It was said that more than 100 people were being investigated by the Metropolitan Police War Crimes Unit, staffed by 9 officers. More than £12 million a year was set aside to fund the unit's inquiries.

However, for some the fault lay not with the law but with the half-hearted efforts of the British state to implement it despite spending so much parliamentary time pushing it through. As Jon Silverman wrote:

> In 259 of the 400 cases investigated, there was either insufficient evidence to prosecute or the subject's health precluded a prosecution. Even if only 20 per cent were guilty, that's more than fifty people who lived out their lives in tranquillity, having taken part in the greatest act of mass murder of the twentieth century. Was Britain a haven for war criminals? The answer is self-evident.[11]

THE FIREARMS ACTS 1997 AND 1998

The Dunblane shootings in Scotland in 1996 led to a ban on all handguns. Was this a bad law? While there were many whose response to the horror was to call for a prohibition on guns, there were many others who considered that the fault lay with the killer, Thomas Hamilton, rather than with people who owned firearms for legitimate sporting reasons and would never dream of using them to harm anyone. The massacre, in which 16 children and their teacher, Gwen Mayor, died, was one of the worst mass-killings in Britain's history. The whole nation was appalled, more so because of the innocence of the victims. But whatever the enormity of the incident, did it follow that all handguns should therefore be banned? If a madman with a grudge against society had deliberately driven his high-powered car into a bus queue, killing a dozen children and himself in the process, would all cars have been banned? Would restrictions have been imposed upon the make of car in which he carried out the atrocity? Would sports associated with the car have been shut down and the shops that sold the vehicle forcibly put out of business, with owners receiving compensation that was less than the value of the stock?

The answer to each of these propositions, one would guess, is no, but that is precisely what happened to thousands of gun-owners and shooting businesses after Dunblane. A ban on high-calibre hand guns was implemented by Michael Howard when he was home secretary in the Conservative government and in 1997 Labour extended its scope to cover low-calibre weapons, making prohibition total. The consequences of the ban were that hundreds of thousands of legally held weapons were outlawed and had to be handed over to the police. Target-shooters lost their sport and those competing in international tournaments were required to practise abroad. Small businesses went to the wall and a lengthy wrangle took place over compensation, with owners complaining to this day that they did not receive the amount due for the executive seizure of their possessions. Now you may say that is a good thing, too, because you consider guns to be inherently bad. And it is true that the gun lobby in Britain, unlike that in the US, has few friends. Only a minority owns guns for sport. To most people, weapons are anathema and there was, undoubtedly, popular support for a ban.

Yet, in a democracy, the liberties of minorities are not to be lightly discarded nor their opinions to be gratuitously traduced. If the intention of banning handguns was to reduce the number of weapons in criminal hands then it patently failed. Since Dunblane, the number of offences involving illegally held hand-guns has more than doubled in England and Wales. The most recent Home Office figures show that in 1996 there were 3,347 crimes in which a handgun was used. The numbers fell in 1997 to 2,636 but rose to 5,871 by March 2002. By 2007, the figure had risen to more than 10,000. When, a few years ago, the Tory MP Patrick Mercer observed, not unreasonably, that the ban had 'no effect on gun crime' and suggested that children in rural communities should be taught, as he had been as a youngster, how to use 'non-lethal' weapons such as air rifles as a prelude to the safe use of shotguns – which remain legal, after all – in later life, the roof caved in on his head. Mr Mercer's comments were denounced as 'offensive, crass and appalling' by a group called Mothers Against Murder and Aggression, as though the hapless MP were advocating either. Others demanded that he be sacked from the Tory frontbench and have the party whip withdrawn. For good measure, he was pilloried for the insensitive timing of his remarks, just ahead of the anniversary of the Dunblane massacre.

However, the reason that guns were banned was political not practical. In fact, it is often forgotten that Lord Cullen's inquiry into the Dunblane massacre did not recommend a ban at all. In his report Lord Cullen recommended a series of procedural changes intended to tighten up the possession of handguns, not their prohibition. They included a new certification scheme to be administered properly and robustly by the police, who would be given greater powers to search and inspect. There would also be tighter controls over gun clubs and private owners. The report said:

> Every holder of a firearm certificate should be required to be a member of at least one approved club; and the firearm certificate should specify the approved club or clubs of which he or she is a member and the firearms which he or she intends to use in each of them. Each approved club should be required to inform the police when a holder of a firearm certificate has ceased to be a member of the club for whatever reason. Each approved club should be required to inform the police of the receipt of an application for membership; and the outcome of the application.[12]

Lord Cullen believed that these and other recommendations would plug the gaps in the certification system that had allowed Hamilton to belong to a club and possess a firearm even though he was an unsuitable person to do so and diligent policing of the system would, and should, have ascertained that this was so. He went one step further:

Consideration should be given to restricting the availability of self-loading pistols and revolvers of any calibre which are held by individuals for use in target shooting preferably, by their disablement, while they are not in use, by either (i) the removal of the slide assembly/cylinder, which is to be kept securely on the premises of an approved club of which the owner is a member or by a club official; or (ii) the fitting of a locked barrel block by a club official.

This was clearly Lord Cullen's preferred option, as he indicated himself, and it would not affect ownership of single-shot guns. If this system were not adopted, however, then 'banning of the possession of such handguns by individual owners' could be an alternative.

It was this that ministers latched on to. So great was the public outcry, especially in Scotland, that Michael Forsyth, the Scottish secretary, pushed hard in cabinet for a ban on many handguns. The government, then with a narrow majority and nearing the end of its time in office, faced defeat in the Commons when Tory MPs Hugh Dykes and Robert Hughes tabled a cross-party motion to bolster Mr Forsyth's position. The motion urged 'immediate legislation to raise handguns to the status of prohibited weapons whose use will be restricted to those who can demonstrate professional need, such as the military and the police'. Mr Dykes, MP for Harrow East, said: 'It is an unrivalled opportunity for us in Britain to get away from the American gun culture which is beginning to take root in this country.'[13] With the opposition parties determined to support a ban and rebellion looking likely on the government benches, ministers had little choice.

On 16 October 1996, Michael Howard announced the policy in parliament:

I propose to go considerably further than Lord Cullen has suggested in two respects. First, we shall ban all handguns from people's homes. I do not agree with Lord Cullen that it would be safe to allow single-shot handguns to remain in the home. I believe that they should be subject to the same controls as those imposed on multi-shot handguns.

Howard continued: 'Secondly, we shall outlaw high-calibre handguns of the kind used by Thomas Hamilton. Low-calibre handguns – .22 rimfire handguns – will have to be used and kept in licensed clubs. We believe that a distinction needs to be made between high-calibre handguns, which are principally made for police and military use, and .22 rimfire handguns, which are largely intended for target shooting.' When Labour took office a year later, the ban was extended to these as well.

Was it right that the sport and livelihoods of many people should be wiped out because of the actions, however dreadful they were, of a single madman? The motivation for the ban was the feeling of revulsion towards the gun rather than any rational approach. Had Hamilton killed his victims with a knife, there could not possibly have been a ban on all knives. The fact that the carnage was greater because he was using a semi-automatic weapon is irrelevant to the principle at stake. It is at least arguable that if guns had been more widely available then someone at the school could have shot Hamilton before he caused so many deaths. Nor does the fact that there has not been a similar massacre since mean that the ban was a good law; such events are exceptionally rare even in countries where the populace is routinely armed.

Can this be considered a good law because it clearly has majority support? There are no campaign groups, no marches or petitions demanding the restoration of the right to own pistols. There have been no more killings like Dunblane. Although gun crime has soared, it is almost exclusively confined to criminal elements like drug gangs. If there is a domestic argument, the protagonists are not going to rush to the gun cabinet to settle it. This must, surely, be a good thing. Yet if many thousands of law-abiding people are prevented from acting in a way that would harm no one because of the egregious behaviour of one single individual, is that a proportionate response, however ghastly the crime? As I said earlier, it would not have happened if the weapon had been a car.

The problem with starting along this road is that governments then imagine that they can take this animus against the gun much further. For instance, a new law was subsequently introduced to ban the unlicensed ownership of a gas-powered airgun known as a Brocock. This was owned perfectly legally for many years by around 75,000 people. Since May 2004, possession without a firearms licence would attract a mandatory five years in jail. The reason for the restriction is that the Brocock can be converted to fire live ammunition, something criminals will no doubt continue to do even when those weapons owned by people who would never dream of using the weapon for any nefarious purpose have been incarcerated. The government has also tightened the law still further on possession of air rifles and shotguns for no apparent reason since they have not been used for mass murder. The Home Office has for years wanted to force 600,000 shotgun-owners to obtain a firearms licence, whose provisions are far more restrictive and require a positive case to be made out for ownership. So far this has been resisted.

And where was parliament while all this was happening? Most MPs were in favour of the ban and would say they were representing the wishes of their constituents in supporting one. There were very few voices raised against. One that was belonged to Nick Budgen, the Tory MP for Wolverhampton South West, who delivered what Simon Hoggart, the *Guardian*'s parliamentary sketch writer, called 'one of the last great parliamentary speeches' in the House of Commons in February 1997. Budgen was asked what he would say to the parents of the dead children who wanted a gun ban:

> I would try to be as sympathetic as I possibly could, and I would explain to them that I understood entirely their wish

to have the use of all guns banned; but I would say that people who engaged in the lawful and honourable activity of target shooting were entitled to continue to do that. I would say at the end of the conversation, as quietly and as carefully as I could, that as a matter of fact I thought that their appalling tragedy probably did not make them better judges of legislation, and that it might indeed make them worse judges. I would say that, fortunately, we have in general a rather good system of considering legislation in a way that is somewhat detached from their raw emotions, and that the most important thing was to consider legislation carefully and not in a mood of deep emotion. I think that, on reflection, they would understand that.[14]

Mr Budgen died in 1998. Maybe at the time he still believed that parliament had a good system of considering legislation. It does so no longer.

TALLY HO! THE HUNTING ACT 2005

For much of his adult life, James Barrington was not merely against hunting but a 'sab' who would follow hunts and seek to disrupt them. He regarded hunting as 'barbaric and blood-thirsty' and aged 19 joined the League Against Cruel Sports in 1972. He was the organization's executive director for seven years. Yet in 2008, he joined the Countryside Alliance, a pro-hunting organization that is campaigning to repeal the Hunting Act 2005 which imposed a ban on the sport. What possibly caused Barrington's transformation? He had, after all, achieved precisely what he and his fellow anti-hunters had always wanted: a law that banned hunting and protected the fox. Except, of course, the Hunting Act did nothing of the sort. Its main aim was to make predominantly urban Labour MPs feel better and assuage the consciences of a predominantly urban electorate. If the Act's principal ambition was to help the fox then it palpably failed.

More foxes have died every year since the Act came into force; more animals are getting 'winged' and having slow deaths because they are now being shot rather than despatched by the hounds; and more pregnant foxes are being culled because they don't give off a scent so were rarely killed in the old hunts. The popularity of hunting has increased: more than 300 registered hunts in England and Wales have carried out 100,000 hunting days since the ban. The number of people who subscribe to hunts is said to have increased by 10 per cent.

Barrington was more concerned about the welfare of the fox and the countryside than making a point about class. When hunters protested outside Labour's conference in Brighton in 2005, Tony Blair took to the platform with a derisive 'Tally-Ho' and John Prescott made clear he considered the legislation to be a campaign in the class war. When the Act became law, pushed onto the statute book by use of the Parliament Acts, most Labour MPs who had supported it simply forgot about the fox whose welfare had apparently spurred them on before. Their job had been done: a bloody nose had been given to the toffs, even if many of the supporters of hunts were working people in the countryside.

James Barrington was more concerned to see if the law actually did what it said on the tin and was appalled to discover that it was as flawed as its opponents had maintained throughout the stormy period it was going through parliament. He found that foxes suffered more through snaring, poisoning and shooting than through hunting with hounds. He now saw his former colleagues in the animal rights movement as akin to 'religious fundamentalists' who ignored the scientific evidence by persisting in supporting a measure that had clearly made things worse for the creature it was meant to protect.

Barrington now says, 'I think hunting is a positive and vitally important part of wildlife management, provided it is done within proper rules. Like a lot of people I was quite horrified by hunting and took the view that stopping it would improve animal welfare. But the Hunting Act has failed on every level, not least of all on animal welfare.'[15]

He has recently been working as an animal welfare consultant with the Countryside Alliance and is campaigning to repeal the Act, which bans hunting with dogs in England and Wales, except for using one or two dogs to flush a fox above ground so it can be shot. He says, 'I'm not ashamed of changing my opinion on the matter and I don't think it's hypocritical because for me it was a very long, slow process. If you genuinely want to improve animal welfare and day after day the facts present themselves in a different light, then you are obliged to reassess where you stand.'[16]

As Mark Hill, Master of the Vale of the White Horse Hunt in the Cotswolds, put it: 'Before the ban on hunting in 2005, it was the old, the sick and the injured foxes that we used to catch. Now that we have to shoot them, we think more foxes are being eliminated. The fox has fared the worst out of this ban.'[17]

No other measure during the past 20 years has so conflicted with J.S. Mill's doctrine for a just law – that it must prevent harm to others – than the Hunting Act. Its supporters argue, of course, that it helped prevent harm to foxes; but if that was its aim it failed. Furthermore, there have been relatively few successful prosecutions for illegal hunting and hardly any against properly constituted hunts, and there are more people hunting than ever. Home Office figures show 62 people were prosecuted in 2007 in England and Wales under the Hunting Act. Of that, 48 people were found guilty and faced fines of up to £5,000. However, only three were members of organized hunts and the remainder of the convictions were for poaching offences.[18]

Here, then, was a law fought over like no other during Labour's time in office yet which failed even in its expressed purpose. Parliament devoted 700 hours to debating hunting and only 7 to Iraq, yet still managed to produce a measure riddled with inconsistencies and loopholes. And in order to force the law through a recalcitrant House of Lords, the Parliament Acts were used to secure an outcome that law was never designed to achieve.

In truth, it had been a long time coming. The first attempt to ban hunting was made in 1949 when two Private Member's Bills to ban, or restrict, hunting were introduced in the House of Commons. One was withdrawn and the other defeated on its second reading. At the time the Labour government appointed a committee of inquiry to investigate all forms of hunting. The committee concluded: 'Foxhunting makes a very important contribution to the control of foxes, and involves less cruelty than most other methods of controlling them. It should therefore be allowed to continue.' It was not until 1976 that a ban was proposed once more when the RSPCA came out in favour; and, in 1979, Labour became the first mainstream political party to enter an election with opposition to hunting contained in its manifesto. Yet it was not until the early 1990s that another attempt was made by a backbencher using the Private Member's Bill procedure.

Every year there is a ballot among MPs not in the government for the right to introduce legislation in the form of a Private Member's Bill on a subject of their choosing. The Bills rarely become law because the parliamentary timetable is controlled by the government and unless ministers are ready to back a particular measure – as with David Steel's Abortion Bill in 1967 – it is easy for opponents to use up the available time with a filibuster (i.e. giving a very long, often irrelevant speech to fill up the allocated time so a vote cannot be reached). More straightforwardly, a controversial Private Member's Bill, which is not subject to a party whip like a government measure, can be defeated right at the outset when it has its first debate in parliament known as the Second Reading. This is what happened to the Wild Mammals (Protection) Bill, proposed by Labour MP Kevin McNamara in 1992. But it marked the beginning of a sustained attempt by opponents of hunting to force the issue into the political arena. In 1993, there was another go, this time by Tony Banks, Labour MP for Newham, with his Fox Hunting (Abolition) Bill. In 1995, John McFall, another Labour MP had a go with his Wild Mammals (Protection) Bill. Unlike its predecessors, it actually succeeded at its Second Reading in the Commons but fell in the Lords.

When Tony Blair's Labour Party won office in 1997, it did so with a promise to reach a decision on the vexed issue of hunting. A committee chaired by Lord Burns was established to consider the matter. Like its predecessor in 1949, it concluded that while hunting 'seriously compromises the welfare of the fox' it should nevertheless continue, though under certain conditions. The government decided that a licensing system was the way forward; but the Commons had other ideas and voted for an outright ban, something that was once again defeated in the Lords.

In 2004, the Bill was reintroduced, this time accompanied by the threat of using the Parliament Acts should the Lords object. With the Tories having established the use of the Parliament Acts in 1991 to force the War Crimes Act on to the statute book, Labour also became quite happy to use them for measures for which they were never intended, simply because they had lost the argument in the Upper House. It was used to force a change in voting procedures at European elections after the Lords objected to the closed list proportional representation system proposed. It was used again for the Sexual Offences (Amendment) Act 2000, which lowered the age of consent for gay men to 16. Whereas the original Parliament Act had been born out of a titanic constitutional battle for supremacy, it was now being used by a government with a massive Commons majority that was unable to impose its will on the bit of parliament that remained unelected, even if it had been stripped of its hereditary element.

The main problem with the Hunting Act was that it allowed the activity of riding to hounds to continue (and how in a free country, could it not?) and also recognized that keeping the fox population under control was an important part of countryside conservation and essential for livestock protection. The first line of the act states: 'A person commits an offence if he hunts a wild mammal with a dog', but there is this crucial rider: 'unless his hunting is exempt'. Schedule One of the Act contains a list of exemptions, including: 'Flushing a wild mammal from cover is exempt hunting if undertaken for the purpose of enabling a bird of prey to hunt the wild mammal.' Many hunts have begun using packs of hounds in combination with eagles and falcons.

The Act, therefore, contained the seeds of its own destruction. The fears of opponents that there would be large-scale closures of hunts and that hounds and horses would have to be put down never materialized. The anger in the countryside at what was seen as an urbanite attack on their way of life merely encouraged more people to join hunts and to ride with them. The hunts were identical to those that had gone before; what was not allowed was for the pack to pursue and kill the prey; but another exemption allowed for the fox to be flushed out by two hounds and shot. To comply with the law, the huntsman must go into a wood or undergrowth with their hounds and try to flush a fox out in the direction of either a bird of prey or a gun. But it is not clear where 'flushing out' ends and 'pursuit' begins.

The way hunts used the exemptions to continue their pastimes was brilliantly captured in an article in the *Guardian* by Stephen Moss, who spent several days with the Heythrop hunt in Oxfordshire to find out how the Act was working:

> The Heythrop prove to be indefatigable hunters. Having set off at 11, they are still hard at it in near-darkness six and a half hours later. Though hard at what is difficult to say. I overhear one rider say that a fox has been killed, and afterwards ask Stephen Lambert – chairman not just of the Heythrop but of the Masters of Foxhounds Association,

too – what had happened. He had been riding all day, so ought to have known. 'I haven't a clue,' he says (diplomatically?). 'It's not impossible [that a fox was killed], but if they had done, they probably wouldn't tell me. I'm told things on a need-to-know basis. If we catch a fox, occasionally we tell the police, but other times not. The one thing that is absolutely vital is that we do not set out to be above the law.' Lambert is willing to admit that the hunts are 'testing' the law. Hence the questionable use of birds of prey. He mentions one hunt in Wales that has a falconer but no bird. If the police pitch up unexpectedly and say 'Where's the bird?', the master points up at some distant speck, and says 'There he is. You must need your eyes tested.' Lambert says: 'If we were 100% saintly we wouldn't keep our staff. The huntsman would lose interest.' There is also a fear that if hunts did just trot around exercising the hounds and hunting trails, all those hunt followers who threatened civil disobedience when the ban was under discussion would go their own way and set out to break the law. 'It's a very difficult balance to strike,' he says, 'but it's crucial that we don't put our fingers up to the law. Instead, what we want is to show that the law is ridiculous and unworkable.'[19]

How could any of this still be within the law if hunting was supposed to be banned? The only way to find out was to test it. A few weeks after the Hunting Act came into force in February 2005, Tony Wright, huntsman of the Exmoor Foxhounds, took two hounds from the kennels near the village of Simonsbath to a meet at Prayway Head. Six months later he was served with a summons to face a private prosecution by the League Against Cruel Sports. A Magistrates Court in Barnstaple found him guilty, despite the fact that he was using just two hounds to flush foxes to a gun, as he thought the law allowed. He appealed and in December 2007 the Crown Court in Exeter threw out his conviction, finding that he had been hunting legally and observing that the Hunting Act 'is far from simple to interpret or to apply'. The matter then went to the High Court in London, where the Crown Prosecution Service (CPS) argued that people like Tony Wright, who was carrying out exempt hunting, should prove that they were hunting legally and that the mere act of searching for a mammal should be included in the offence of 'hunting'.

This line of argument was rejected by the High Court. In its judgment, the court limited the definition of 'hunting' to the pursuit of a mammal with dogs and upheld the presumption of innocence for people involved in legal hunting by putting the burden of proof on the prosecution to provide evidence that any hunting is illegal. It also confirmed that under the terms of the Act, 'hunting' can only be intentional: you cannot hunt by accident.

In March 2009, as a result of the Wright judgment, the CPS also dropped charges against Julian Barnfield, of the Heythrop Hunt. He had been charged with four offences of hunting a fox between November 2008 and February 2009. The Wright case effectively rendered the Hunting Act a colossal waste of parliamentary time and effort. The CPS conceded that the judgment made the Act 'wholly unworkable'.

In July 2009 the law became even more confused when the prosecution of two Yorkshire farmers, Peter Easterby and John Shaw, for allowing illegal hare-coursing on their land ended at Scarborough Magistrates Court after two-and-a-half years of legal argument. They had given permission only for legal activity; so although they were found guilty and have a criminal record they were granted an absolute discharge. A measure intended to enhance animal welfare had achieved the opposite while at the same time alienating rural communities and criminalizing upright and law-abiding citizens

As Simon Hart of the Countryside Alliance put it: 'The Act has failed completely, but a law which promotes so much conflict and causes so much confusion cannot be allowed to remain in force. There are no reasonable arguments left for retaining the Hunting Act so getting rid of it need not be complicated or time consuming. Bad laws should be repealed, and this is a very bad law.'[20]

Table 3 Number of defendants proceeded against at magistrates courts for offences under the Hunting Act 2004, England and Wales 2005 and 2006

Police Force Area	2005	2006
Cheshire	–	2
Durham	–	1
Essex	–	4
Humberside	–	4
Merseyside	1	–
Thames Valley	2	–
Total for England and Wales	3	11

Notes: These data are on the principal offence basis. Every effort is made to ensure that the figures presented are accurate and complete. However, it is important to note that these data have been extracted from large administrative data systems generated by the courts and police forces. As a consequence, care should be taken to ensure data collection processes and their inevitable limitations are taken into account when those data are used. Where a police force area is not listed in the table then no prosecutions have been reported to the Ministry of Justice.

Source: Court proceedings database – Criminal Justice Evidence and Analysis – Office for Criminal Justice Reform.

Table 4 Number of defendants proceeded against at magistrates courts, found guilty and fined at all courts, for offences under the 2004 Hunting Act, England and Wales, broken down by police force area, 2005 to 2007

Force	Proceeded against			Found guilty			Fined		
	2005	2006	2007	2005	2006	2007	2005	2006	2007
Avon and Somerset	–	–	2	–	–	2	–	–	2
Cheshire	–	2	1	–	2	1	–	2	1
Cleveland	–	–	1	–	–	1	–	–	1
Derbyshire	–	–	2	–	–	2	–	–	2
Durham	–	1	–	–	–	–	–	–	–
Essex	–	4	–	–	3	–	–	3	–
Hampshire	–	–	4	–	–	4	–	–	–
Humberside	–	4	8	–	–	8	–	–	7
Lancashire	–	–	2	–	–	2	–	–	2
Lincolnshire	–	–	7	–	–	7	–	–	7
Merseyside	1	–	25	1	–	19	1	–	17
Northumbria	–	–	6	–	–	–	–	–	–
Suffolk	–	–	2	–	–	1	–	–	1
Thames Valley	2	–	–	2	–	–	2	–	–
North Wales	–	–	2	–	–	1	–	–	1
England and Wales totals	3	11	62	3	5	48	3	5	41

Notes: The 2004 Hunting Act came into force on 18 February 2005. The statistics relate to persons for whom these offences were the principal offences for which they were dealt with.

Source: Hansard.

CHAPTER 4

LAWS AND THE CRIMINAL JUSTICE SYSTEM

By definition, the criminal justice system relies upon laws. They are its fuel. Parliament passes them and the criminal justice system enforces them through the police, who make the arrests, to Crown prosecutors, who bring the charges, and the courts that dispense the penalties. But what happens when there are so many laws that the criminal justice system finds it hard to cope with them?

Developing new criminal laws was always a gradual process. Many crimes have been crimes for centuries, like theft, murder or assault. When governments have felt the need, they have overhauled the system with a major Criminal Justice Act. Other than during times when significant and systemic changes were being made, as in the Victorian era, these have tended to be relatively unusual and they are noteworthy as a result.

The Criminal Justice Act of 1877 remained in force until 1948, though there were various proposed reforms in the prewar period, such as the extension of probation and the abolition of corporal punishment that were to have been contained in the abortive Criminal Justice Bill of 1938.

After Labour's victory in 1945, work began on another major piece of legislation which became the Criminal Justice Act of

1948, proposing a graded system of imprisonment depending on the seriousness of the crime and the offender's criminal record. This introduced corrective training, as well as attendance and detention centres for young offenders. The right of the courts to impose corporal punishment was abolished.

The next major piece of criminal justice legislation was the 1967 Act aimed at reforming the prison system, overhauling the sentencing practices of courts, changing the way juvenile offenders were handled and abolishing capital punishment for murder. It introduced the suspended sentence for prison terms of up to three years, while sentences of six months or less were automatically suspended. Magistrates were discouraged to apply imprisonment for relatively minor offences. This was later amended under a Conservative government.

In order to reduce the prison population, a parole system for convicts (who had completed 12 months or one-third of their sentence) was introduced. This reduced sentences in cases where further rehabilitation was thought to be redundant. Recommendations for parole were to be made by an independent review body. Another Criminal Justice Act in 1972 incorporated the idea of community service as a non-custodial rehabilitative measure.

These laws were relatively rare attempts to reform criminal justice policy as society changed and expectations of how prison and other punishments should be used became transformed in the 1960s and 1970s. By and large, governments and parliament considered tinkering around with the criminal justice system to be something that should happen rarely and only when deemed necessary. Today it is done almost routinely and often simply to make a political point.

To put into context what has happened consider these statistics: between 1851 and 1996, there were 122 pieces of criminal justice legislation, 39 of them primary measures, or Acts of Parliament; between 1997 and 2009, there were 212 pieces of legislation, 26 of them primary.[1]

If we take our earlier two tests for what constitutes bad laws, how many of these have been proportionate and necessary and how many have worked, in that they made tackling crime easier? It is difficult to measure their efficacy in any scientific or statistical way, but the practitioners in the criminal justice world seem to be in no doubt that most of these new criminal laws have made matters worse, not better.

The philosophy underpinning this legislative hyperactivity was outlined by Tony Blair in a major speech in February 2002, entitled 'Rebalancing the Criminal Justice System'. This was a departure from the earlier 'tough on crime, tough on causes of crime' approach in that it emphasized the former and was less enthusiastic about the latter. However, the assumption was that to get tough on crime required more law rather than more order. Mr Blair made clear that his beef was not so much with how effectively the criminal justice system worked but with the way it was organized and dispensed its sentencing. He also suggested that today's criminal justice systems, not just in the UK but around the world, were 'under strain' and were 'grappling with new forms of crime'. In fact, they were just grappling with old forms of crime carried out by a different means.[2]

This speech resulted in a blitz of law-making the like of which had never been seen before. It contained this sentence: 'It is perhaps the biggest miscarriage of justice in today's system when the guilty walk away unpunished.' As Helena Kennedy QC said later: 'In a single sentence ... the Prime Minister sought to overturn centuries of legal principle, a complete reversal of the approach to justice that every mature democracy in the world respects, whereby the conviction of an innocent man is deemed the greatest miscarriage of justice.'[3]

Why is it necessary to have more criminal-justice measures when the government keeps telling us that crime is going down (even if it is the only one who thinks it is)? Each time it introduces another law-and-order measure, it confuses the courts, ties up the police and makes it more difficult to achieve its objectives. Was the criminal law such an unholy mess that more legislation was needed in 12 years than in the previous 50? Are we safer as a result? Ministers also cannot understand why 'fear of crime' remains stubbornly high. There are two possible explanations: either crime really is high, or the government is contributing to an atmosphere of anxiety by talking up the need for new legislation all the time. This approach, however, was designed to give the Labour government the justification for another torrent of criminal justice legislation.

Tony Blair stated baldly that 'most accept there is a need for radical reform' of the criminal justice system without any evidence that this was a view held by most people in the country let alone in the system itself. He suggested he wanted to make the law more understandable to the man in the street:

> We have a system with no overall direction; no overall lines of management or accountability. It is a system with rules of evidence and court procedures that suffer from what Lord Justice Auld (in his Royal Commission report) called 'centuries of haphazard statutory and common law accretion' . . . All this must change. Let me emphasise our central principle: that above all, the time has come to rebalance the system so that we restore the faith of victims and witnesses that the court hearing will be fair to all participants.[4]

Within a few years of this speech and countless pieces of legislation later, the verdict was handed down by Lord Phillips of Worth Matravers, the former Lord Chief Justice for England and Wales. He said:

> The work of all who sit in the criminal jurisdiction, whether in the Magistrates' Court, the Crown Court, the Court of Appeal or the House of Lords has been rendered infinitely

more arduous than when I sat as a Recorder by a cease-less torrent of legislation, adding complexity to substantive law and to the sentencing exercise. Some of this legislation is needed to deal with changing circumstances, and this includes some of the new terrorist offences. Ruling on the ambit of these occupied quite a lot of my energy last year and is continuing to do so, sometimes in appeals that challenge my own rulings. Other legislation is less easy to justify, including the subdivision of sexual offending into an astonishing number of different offences, some of which have yet to see the face of an indictment. Changes in the law relating to hearsay and bad character were bound to provide a fruitful source of appeals, and these show no sign of falling off.[5]

Shortly after he took office, Lord Judge, the new Lord Chief Justice, took up his predecessor's cudgels with another swipe at Labour's obsession with passing new laws. In a speech to the annual Lord Mayor's dinner for judges in July 2009, the showpiece event for the judiciary, he cited six major Acts with more than a thousand separate sections and 68 additional schedules that went on to the statute book in 2003 alone.

Lord Judge said: 'I'm getting a little confused.' If he's confused, what about the rest of us? He made a request 'which has been frequently addressed, but so far without success: can we possibly have less legislation, particularly in the field of criminal justice?' He added: 'In a rough and ready calculation, it seems to me that if every line of recent criminal justice legislation had been guaranteed by a payment to the Bank of England of £10,000 a line, the credit crisis would have been funded.'

In his response at the same event, Jack Straw, the justice secretary, used Labour's stock answer to any criticism, which is to accuse their detractors of being wrong: 'People find it easy to complain in general terms about the volume of criminal legislation, but when they are asked which of the new offences should be repealed, they struggle to find an answer.' In other words, Labour introduced more laws than the system can cope with and far more than were necessary and then challenged everyone else to say which ones should be repealed. (It is, incidentally, the same approach Labour adopted with public spending: increase annual public expenditure to eye-watering levels – far in excess of inflation – and then when the country runs out of money invite the rest of us to say what should be cut.)

Mr Straw may have been convinced that Labour had taken the right approach by bringing in so much criminal justice legislation; but he and his cabinet colleagues are almost alone in believing this.

Every year, *Archbold*, the 'bible' of the legal profession, bemoans yet another cascade of criminal justice legislation. *Archbold* is the leading criminal law text used by nearly all advocates and judges in English and Welsh courtrooms. Its preface routinely contains a withering commentary on the way the Labour government has used, even abused, the legislative system to tinker with the criminal law.

The preface to the 2009 edition, written by James Richardson, said:

> The willingness of the Labour government to continue its practice of legislating by trial and error has shown no signs of abating even in its eleventh year in office . . . The state of the criminal statute book is a disgrace. The Criminal Justice and Immigration Act 2008 is the usual hotchpotch of measures, with no theme, with much of the detail tucked away from close scrutiny in the schedules, and consisting in large part of textual amendment to earlier legislation. Much of the amendment is by way of undoing this government's earlier legislation.

Richardson is by no means alone in the criminal justice world in believing that a fetish for legislating to grab headlines is having a devastating effect on the system that the laws are supposed to improve. One of his observations is that much of the amendment to law is by way of undoing the government's own earlier legislation. Many people would be astonished at the number of laws that are brought in and never enacted or whose enactment is delayed for years. Some are repealed before they have even taken effect. Finding out exactly how many is another matter, though information given as part of parliamentary written answers give some idea (see Tables 5 and 6).

CRIMINAL JUSTICE ACT 2003

The Ministry of Justice said the government had proposed 'new laws to Parliament which have considerably strengthened the criminal justice system in this country' and said it was for parliament to decide whether to create an offence and whether it is necessary and proportionate. This may be true; but the trouble is that parliament often does not do this job effectively, if at all. Too much law is not scrutinized properly, which is important with criminal justice law since judges often look to the intent of parliament when they make rulings that then become precedents for others to follow. It is impossible to do this if parliament has not actually debated the matter at hand. A classic example of the confusion that this can cause came with the Criminal Justice Act 2003, the 'great daddy of them all', as Lord Judge called it.

While this measure was going through parliament, the home secretary, who at that time was David Blunkett, lost a key ruling in the European Court of Human Rights which stripped the executive in the UK of the right to set the tariff, or minimum sentence, for murderers. This had been a political decision ever since the abolition of the death penalty in 1965. The European Court said it should henceforth be a judicial one.

Table 5 Criminal Law: Measures enacted in criminal justice legislation since 2003 which were not in force by the end of 2007

Act	Provisions not in force
Crime (International Co-Operation) Act 2003	32 sections (10–12, 20–25, 90, 54–75) and 2 schedules (3 and 4).
Criminal Justice Act 2003	26 sections (33–5, 43, 50–54, 56, 62–6, 137–8, 151, 154–5, 181, 188, 280–3) and 7 schedules (4, 11, 21, 22, 25–7). Partially in force: 26 sections (14, 15, 22, 27, 29–31, 39, 41, 48, 182–7, 196, 204, 213, 216, 244, 266, 279, 300–301, 303) and 8 schedules (2–3, 10, 31–2, 35, 37–8).
Domestic Violence, Crime and Victims Act 2004	13 sections (9, 12–13, 15–16, 46, 48–53, 57) and 2 schedules (8–9). Partially in force: 1 section (54) and 3 schedules (10–12).
Drugs Act 2005	1 section (2).
Offender Management Act 2007	23 sections (1–15, 21–4, 28–31) and 2 schedules (1–2). Partially in force: 3 schedules (3–5).
Police and Justice Act 2006	14 sections (7, 14, 19–21, 34–41, 43) and 4 schedules (5, 8, 11–12). Partially in force: 1 section (46) and 1 schedule (1).
Serious Organised Crime and Police Act 2005	6 sections (117, 120–1, 158, 167, 170). Partially in force: 18 sections (60–70, 79–81, 144, 162, 165, 167) and 7 schedules (4, 5, 9–10, 13–14, 17).
Violent Crime Reduction Act 2006	22 sections (1–20, 59, 61).

Source: Hansard, 3 December 2007, col. 858W.

Table 6 Home Office Legislation: Provisions of Acts passed since
1 May 1997 which were not in force by September 2007

Act	Sections not in force
Anti-Social Behaviour Act 2003	85 (5), Schedule 2 (2).
Anti-Terrorism, Crime and Security Act 2001	78.
Asylum and Immigration Treatment of (Claimants, etc.) Act 2004	16.
Crime (International Co-operation) Act 2003	10–12, 20–5, 54–75, Schedules 3, 4.
Criminal Justice and Police Act 2001	78 (7), 80 (2, 4), Schedules 6 (para 21), 7 (para 6).
Domestic Violence, Crime and Victims Act 2004	19, 12, Schedules 10, 11 and 12 (in part).
Drugs Act 2005	2.
Identity Cards Act	1 (1–4), 1 (5–8), 2–24, 27–35, 39, 41–43, Schedule 1.
Immigration and Asylum Act 1999	16–17, 117 (5).
Immigration Asylum and Nationality Act 2006	4, 15–18, 20–2, 24–6, 31–9, 44, 47, 50 (3–6).
Nationality, Immigration and Asylum Act 2002	10 (5a), 17 and 18 (for certain purposes), 19–34, 35 (1a–g, i, 2, 3), 36, 37, 39, 40 (2) and (3), 41 (2) and (3), 44–7, 51–3, 124.

Act	Sections not in force
Police and Justice Act 2006	7 (1), 14, 7, 19 (1–9, 11), 20, 21, 34–8, 39 (1–3, 5–7), 40 (1–3, 5–7), 41 (in part), 43 (1), 46 (part) and Schedules 3, 8, 9, 11 and 12, and Schedules 1, 2, 5, 13, 14, and 15 (all in part).
Police Reform Act 2002	45.
Private Security Industry Act 2001	17, 21.
Proceeds of Crime Act 2002	Schedule 11 paras 17 and 21, Schedule 12.
Racial and Religious Hatred Act 2006.	No provisions commenced.
Serious Organised Crime and Police Act	120, 114 (9), 117 (part), 162 (3), Schedules 4 (part), 9 (part), 10 (part), 14 (part).
Vehicle (Crimes) Act 2001	8, 34, 35, 36, Schedule paras 1 and 2.
Violent Crime Reduction Act 2006	1–22, 27, 31–4, 36–41, 43–4, 47, 50 (part), 59, 61, 64, Schedules 2 (part), 5 (part).

Source: Hansard, 3 September 2007, col. 1838W.

Blunkett decided at a very late stage in the progress of the Bill through parliament to bring in a new sliding scale of tariffs that would bind the judiciary to a decision of parliament rather than leave them to make such decisions at their own discretion. Indeed, it was so late in the day that the amendment was never even considered by MPs because by the time it was due to be reached for discussion the guillotine had fallen. The government's business managers could have moved an amendment to change the timetable, but they didn't. The consequences of this became apparent a few months later when it transpired that the new law allowed for a reduction in sentence lengths for murderers who entered a guilty plea. There was uproar. Politicians blamed the judges until it was politely pointed out by the Lord Chief Justice, Lord Woolf, that parliament had passed this law but they clearly did not have a clue what they had done. Blunkett was furious.

In a statement issued on 20 September 2004, Blunkett accepted that the 2003 Act provided for a reduction in sentence for all offences, but he argued that, because of the 'unique nature of the offence of murder', the normal reduction should not be automatic in all cases but should reflect 'genuinely exceptional circumstances'. He further stated that 'this was clear from debates in Parliament when the Act was passed'. The Commons home affairs select committee decided to hold an inquiry to find out whether Blunkett was right or wrong on this.

The committee said, 'The fact that the provisions in the Act governing reduction for guilty pleas apply to the Act's new arrangements for murder tariffs does not appear to have been remarked on at all during the parliamentary passage of the Act.' It added: 'There is no mention in the Act (or in parliamentary debate during the passage of the Act) of any restriction of these provisions to, in the Home Secretary's words, "genuinely exceptional circumstances".'[6]

The committee went on in a similar vein:

> It is a classic illustration of the truth of the maxim, 'legislate in haste and repent at leisure'. We hope the lesson will be learnt by the Home Office and the House that it is highly undesirable for major criminal justice provisions to be put before Parliament at a late stage in proceedings on a Bill. The House and the public have the right to expect that in future adequate time will be allowed for effective scrutiny of major legislative proposals.

The committee's conclusion was devastating, both for Blunkett's claim that the matter had been debated in parliament but also for the Commons which had allowed such an important law on to the statute book without it ever being discussed by MPs. Do voters know this is how their laws are passed?

WOULD DANTE HAVE BEEN GUILTY OF HARASSMENT?

Some laws that on the face of it must be good laws turn out to be flawed or unjust, tackling a crime that could be dealt with in another way. Take, for example, the crime of harassment. This did not exist until it was introduced as one of the last measures of the John Major government, with Labour support. Obviously, harassment existed but not as a crime. There have been great harassers in history and in literature. Conceivably, it is harassment for a man to bombard the object of his affections with flowers, love letters and poems. At what point does unrequited passion become alarming or distressing? Would Dante have received six months for his 30-year pursuit of Beatrice or Cyrano de Bergerac have been fined for harassing Roxanne? Could Andrew Marvell's coy mistress have obtained an injunction?

Clearly, women – or men for that matter – who are stalked by unhinged admirers or jealous former lovers that make their lives a misery or even threaten them with violence need the protection of the law. The Protection from Harassment Act 1997 brought in a new criminal offence – attracting a maximum of five years in jail – of using words or behaviour 'on more than one occasion' which would put the victim in fear of violence, intentionally or otherwise. It also introduced a new civil tort of molestation. This allows an alleged stalking victim to obtain an injunction forbidding further harassment. A breach of the injunction is a criminal offence, again carrying a sentence of up to five years or an unlimited fine, or both. Neither of these provisions could be considered contentious and have been used in several high profile cases to bring relief to people who have endured years of mental anguish,

However, this law also has a 'low level' criminal offence that covers 'the use of words or behaviour, on more than one occasion, which would cause the victim to be harassed, alarmed or distressed, either intentionally or in circumstances where a reasonable person would have realized that this would be the effect'. On conviction, this offence carries a maximum penalty of six months or a £5,000 fine, or both. Crucially, this is also an arrestable offence. The test of whether a reasonable person would regard the behaviour as harassment would only be made in court, but when a complaint is made, police could make an arrest. To prevent legitimate activities being caught in the legal net, the government included a defence of 'acting reasonably and necessarily in pursuit of a business, trade or profession, or other lawful activity'. But someone who has parted from his wife, husband or lover and seeks to re-establish the relationship might fall foul of the law if the target regards the entreaties as harassment, intended or not.

Increasingly, this law is being misused. In an article in the *Spectator* magazine in November 2006, Tessa Mayes explained how it had enabled the police to issue warnings to people when they have simply had a quarrel. While real harassment involving a threat of violence is a serious matter, Mayes felt that too often the law had been applied 'absurdly' – with the result that harassment cases are often thrown out of court. Among those affected in this way was Michelle Collins, a television actress who was accused of harassment after allegedly being abusive to a woman on the phone and was issued with a warning by police. In another incident, a man was accused of harassment after trying to flirt with a fellow commuter on a train. He was acquitted. A 22-year-old woman was taken to court for harassment by her father after their relationship broke down following the death of her mother. The daughter was found not guilty. A mother and father were charged with the harassment of their daughter following a disagreement about her marriage. They were cleared on appeal.

Mayes found that an increasing number of petty and even dishonest harassment complaints were being made to the police. The most bizarre case involved a Yorkshire man convicted of making rude hand gestures at his neighbours and playing a fart machine over several years. In 2005–6, the police recorded 218,817 incidents of 'harassment', more than double the number recorded 5 years previously. Yet only 680 people were found guilty of actually putting people 'in fear of violence' in 2004.[7]

Even though the Protection from Harassment Act was introduced by a Conservative government, Mayes maintained that it was under Labour that sight was lost of the original purpose of the law. More than that, the 1997 Act has been extended on a number of occasions to apply to groups as well as individuals who harass people. Furthermore, the law was amended so that individuals who commit an act only once (the original legal definition of harassment was to commit an act twice) can also be convicted, if they are part of a group responsible for the behaviour. Mayes said:

> The Act was misconceived from the start. It defines harassment as two or more acts of behaviour causing alarm or distress which a 'reasonable person' would agree is harassment. Behaviour that counts as harassment is also defined on the basis of whether the victim feels alarmed, distressed or fears violence and on whether the perpetrator knows or ought to know that. It is supposed to fill a legal gap, applying to situations where individual acts are not in themselves necessarily that bad and can't always be prosecuted, but where the repetitive nature of the act is unpleasant or threatening to a victim. Yet critics argue that the law is too vague. Any repetitive behaviour could feel like 'psychological assault' to one person yet be acceptable to, or laughed off by, another.

The Protection from Harassment Act is also being used to control protest. A woman who sent two emails to a pharmaceutical company politely asking a member of the staff not to work with a company that did testing on animals was prosecuted for 'repeated conduct'.[8]

The genesis of the Act was the 1996 case of Tracey Morgan, who was stalked for nine years by Anthony Burstow, a former close friend and was driven to distraction by his attentions. There must be protection for people like this. Mayes said: 'Yet basing legislation on extreme cases doesn't necessarily make for a good and just law. There are already plenty of laws dealing with all kinds of harassment – among them the Offences Against the Person Act (1861), the Criminal Justice and Public Order Act (1994) and the Malicious Communications Act (1998).'

On taking office as prime minister, Gordon Brown surpassed even his predecessor's record for law-making, introducing 2,823 new laws during his first year in office. This was 40 per cent higher than the annual average created by Margaret Thatcher. Meanwhile, disputes between neighbours, and often trivial harassment cases, are increasingly likely to come to court. This legalistic approach is disquieting. We are overburdening the law *with social and political problems*, and undermining it in the process.

TEENAGE CANOODLING IS OUTLAWED

> It would be absurd for us to provide coherent
> sanctions to protect children from sexual abuse by
> adults but not by other children.
> Home Office spokesman, April 2004

Who among us does not remember our first teenage sexual fumblings, a lengthy snog, a hand under the jumper or, most daringly, up the dress? It might amaze you to learn that under the Sexual Offences Act 2003 this is now unlawful if both participants are under 16 and it is considered a sexual assault. The Act was introduced after a consultation period, ostensibly to make sense of a disparate amount of sexual offences laws, many dating back centuries. The aim was to bring the law up-to-date, which meant, for instance, removing an existing legal barrier against group homosexual activity. At the same time, though, a clinch behind the bike sheds by a 15-year-old boy and a 15-year-old girl became illegal. The Act states that sexual touching, includes doing it 'with any part of the body', 'with anything else' and 'through anything'. Technically that includes 'snogging' and most other sexual activities indulged in by teenagers since the dawn of time. Guidance notes with the legislation say this could include 'where a person rubs up against someone's private parts through the person's clothes for sexual gratification'.

This law was introduced in 2003 and it will not have escaped your notice that there have not been any high-profile court cases involving a couple of embarrassed teenage lovers. Why? Because it was made clear from the outset that although this was now a crime, there was no intention of enforcing the law. The government told the Crown Prosecution Service that it should not normally prosecute the under-16s for having consensual sex, let alone for 'sexual touching'. It is true, of course, that under previous laws, sexual intercourse below the age of consent was illegal, but the sort of sexual activity outlined in the Act had never been specified as unlawful.

The Home Office said at the time that failing to include definitions in the measure would have run the risk of legalizing consensual sexual activity between children, something the government was not prepared to do. The Home Office said: 'We are putting safeguards in place to ensure that these cases, which are not in the public interest, are not prosecuted – by amending guidance to the police and Crown Prosecution Service.'

However, Terri Dowty, a campaigner for Action on Rights for Children, said: 'It's astonishing that the government could consider legislation with the prior intent of issuing guidance to countermand it. I worry about the message it sends to young people – it seems to say that sometimes the law means what it says and sometimes it doesn't.'[9] Dowty also feared that private prosecutions could be brought by an aggrieved individual, perhaps an angry parent who didn't like their child's boyfriend or girlfriend.

Professor Nicola Lacey of the London School of Economics was also unconvinced:

> What the Home Office would say was that they wanted to use the criminal law for symbolic impact, to say that it's not a good thing for kids to be having sex. My counter-argument is that the criminal law is too dangerous a tool to be used for symbolic purposes. With this on the statute book, it will give police and prosecutors a lot of discretion. It could be used as a way of controlling kids who perhaps the police want to control for other reasons. Kids who perhaps are a nuisance or who belong to a group who attract the attention of the police in some way.[10]

Despite not wanting its new law to be used, the Home Office is, however, concerned that children can behave in a sexually abusive way to each other. 'Adults do not have a monopoly on child abuse and we cannot assume that sexual relationships between young people will be fully consensual just because they are the same age.'[11]

Here is another example of a law whose expressed purpose was to make a social and cultural statement, a sort of legalistic tut-tut. But the Sexual Offences Act was also spectacularly badly drafted. Since it repealed parts of earlier legislation, notably the 1956 Sexual Offences Act, there was supposed to be a transition period to cover the situation where a defendant is charged under the old legislation where some offences had different definitions. Although ministers were given powers to make these transition arrangements, they never did so; if a defendant was accused of committing a sexual offence but the prosecution could not prove it happened before the new measure came into force on 1 May 2004, they had to be acquitted regardless of the evidence against them. In 2005, the Court of Appeal upheld the decision of a judge to acquit a defendant for precisely that reason. Lord Justice Rose observed: 'If a history of criminal legislation ever comes to be written it is unlikely that 2003 will be identified as a year of exemplary skill in the annals of Parliamentary drafting.'[12]

THE RISE OF SUMMARY JUSTICE

Ministers sought to justify this incessant tinkering by claiming that crime had fallen substantially. Yet prison numbers rose inexorably throughout Labour's time in office, from 50,000 in 1997 to more than 80,000, suggesting that tougher sentences and more serious offences were having an impact. However, there were not enough prison places to cope with the numbers likely to be sent there, the courts threatened to be overwhelmed and the police were spending too much time in their stations processing arrests.

So just as activities that were once not considered criminal were turned into crimes, so offences that had always been considered serious crimes, like theft, were turned into mis-demeanours punishable by a fixed-penalty fine, like parking. If you were in a shop and watched the person standing next to you take a £200 suit, or dress, from a clothes rail, stuff it in a bag and walk out of the door, would you regard that as a minor offence? I suspect most of us believe the individual should be taken to the police station and charged with theft, later to appear before magistrates and punished, usually by way of a hefty fine. Theft has always been seen as a serious crime. It carries a maximum jail term of seven years on indictment. Properly, small thefts are treated proportionately; but the crime itself goes to the question of a person's honesty. Yet since 2004, a shoplifter who purloins property worth £200 or less is not normally arrested and tried but given a fixed-penalty notice of £80; in other words, they are treated in the same way as a motorist whose car has remained too long in a parking space. This 'on-the-spot' fine system (a misnomer because the fines are not paid on the spot, if they are paid at all), which was introduced to provide instant punishment for anti-social behaviour such as drunkenness, has also been extended to criminal damage.

Police are told that if the value of the stolen property is under £200 or the cost of the criminal damage less than £500 then a fixed-penalty notice should be issued. The first obvious flaw with such a policy is that it is no deterrent, which is one of the foundations of the punishment system. If anything, it is an incentive. If, by stealing something valued in hundreds of pounds, the worst that is going to happen to you is an £80 fine, then it is worth taking the risk. Exasperated retailers say there is no deterrent to shoplifting because so few are prosecuted anyway. That is not an argument for diminishing the gravity of the offence but rather for pursuing the offenders more robustly.

Both approaches, of course, rely upon the presence of a police officer somewhere in the vicinity to issue the fine or make the arrest. Yet, as Home Office figures show, less than one-fifth an officer's time is spent on so-called 'frontline' patrol so finding a police officer is no easy matter.

The rationale behind the fixed-penalty scheme was to spare the police from having to make arrests, with all the paperwork that goes with it, so that they can spend more time out and about on the streets. While that may make sense when the offence is one of poor behaviour and low-level disorder, did anyone imagine it would apply to theft as well? Shoplifters dealt with by way of an on-the-spot fine avoid any criminal record, which is a bit odd given that the offence exposes a predisposition towards dishonesty.

How will all those groups that are forced to rely on the Criminal Records Bureau for information about a potential employee discover if they are about to give a job to a thief? The Home Office says low-level shoplifting, such as taking sweets, often goes unpunished because of the length of time that it takes the police to process the offender. However, such crimes are usually committed by children who would benefit from a trip to the police station and a good ticking off to stop them doing it again. But by what measure does the government think an adult stealing something worth £200 is a 'minor' theft?

Like so many of our bad laws, the ambit of this scheme was extended by way of a Statutory Instrument, which was debated not on the floor of the Commons but in a committee. Hazel Blears, the Home Office minister, said fixed-penalty notices 'will mean that the offender is properly dealt with'.[13] Yet most thefts from shops are carried out by drug addicts seeking money to feed their habit, so it is unclear how handing a ticket to them will help. At least if an addict is brought before a court, there is always the opportunity for other agencies to intervene. This policy kicks against the whole thrust of another Home Office strategy which is to tackle offending behaviour by getting abusers off drugs.

Persistent shoplifters, says the Home Office, are arrested and tried; but if they carry out a series of thefts in different police-force areas, and each time receive a fixed-penalty notice, how is their pattern of behaviour going to be noticed? A passing policeman does not know that the thief is a serial offender without taking them to the police station, which would defeat the object of the exercise. In any case, the guidance even accepts that two or three or more fixed-penalty notices can be issued to an individual thief. We are witnessing the decriminalization of crime, not least because many offenders do not pay the fines.

This law was meant to free the police to focus on more serious crimes but the force, motivated by targets, has lent heavily on them even when dealing with serious crime. In 2007, the police issued 207,544 fixed-penalty notices, often for serious crimes such as violence, including to repeat offenders, something we were assured would not happen.

This development has alarmed the judiciary. Lord Justice Leveson, the senior presiding judge in England and Wales, said that the use of fixed-penalty notices in some cases had become a farce.[14]

In one case an offender had accumulated fines of £960 for 'no fewer than eight notices for theft, presumably shoplifting, and one for drunk and disorderly'. They were 'all unpaid, with no real prospect of ever being able to pay a single one of them', the judge said. He also expressed concern that another out-of-court penalty, a conditional caution, could undermine 'our system of summary justice' because decisions were being made 'behind closed doors'.

The rise of summary justice at the expense of formal hearings in the courts led to 51 per cent of offences being dealt with in 2007 by a caution, on-the-spot fine or warning for cannabis possession. This was the first time in modern criminal history that more than half of offences were dealt with by out-of-court punishments. Courtroom convictions as a proportion of all offences brought to justice in England and Wales have fallen by almost 20 percentage points since 2002. Convictions in court accounted for 49 per cent of all offences brought to justice in 2006–7, compared with 68 per cent in 2002–3. Cautions increased by 17 per cent to 350,000 in 2007, fixed-penalty notices issued by the police rose by 37 per cent to 210,200 and warnings for cannabis possession rose from 57,700 to 83,000. Only 52 per cent of the fines were paid in full.[15]

Lord Justice Leveson has emphasized that penalty notices for disorder and conditional cautions could still be useful, but:

> There has been some concern that their use is extending far beyond those cases and, far from underlining the importance of complying with the law, risks bringing it into disrepute.

It is not a question of not trusting the police or the Crown Prosecution Service, or challenging the will of Parliament. It goes back to our system of summary justice, carried out in public by members of the public appointed as magistrates, whose decisions can be scrutinised by the public.

Cindy Barnett, chairman of the 30,000-strong Magistrates' Association, said: 'We are concerned that cases that should be decided judicially in open court are being decided outside the courts system – with the potential for miscarriages of justice.[16]

ASBOSTOSIS

No criminal justice law has more association with New Labour than the Asbo. It is not, in reality, a criminal law at all but a civil one. However, it can lead to criminal proceedings, as it did for Caroline Cartwright. When she made love to her husband she made a noise. A lot of noise. Her neighbours did not like it, but it cannot surely have ever crossed anyone's minds that her screams of sexual pleasure should result in Mrs Cartwright going to jail. Yet that is exactly what happened – because she was given an Anti-Social Behaviour Order, commonly known as an Asbo. Mrs Cartwright, from Sunderland, was served with the Asbo by local magistrates after 250 complaints and was fined £515. She was prohibited under the terms of the order from playing loud music or 'making excessive noise, knocking, shouting, screaming or vocalisation that can be heard in neighbouring properties or outside the house'.[17]

Although an Asbo is a civil order, breaching one is a criminal offence. So when Mrs Cartwright and her husband started up again, she was arrested and remanded in custody. It was the first known instance anywhere in the world of a woman being sent to prison for having an orgasm. She said, 'I can't stop making noise during sex. It's unnatural to not make any noises, and

I don't think that I'm particularly loud.' We have a law, in other words, that not merely seeks to change what is considered to be anti-social behaviour but one that results in a punishment which most reasonable people would consider to be out of proportion to the offence committed. It falls, therefore, into the definition of a bad law.

This is not to say there is not a problem with anti-social behaviour. The issue is whether the law should be used to combat something that used to be constrained by social mores, proper policing and community enforcement. And if it should be, is this the right law to achieve that goal?

The Asbo was one of New Labour's first anti-crime initiatives, introduced by Jack Straw when he was home secretary in the Crime and Disorder Act 1998. Asbos allow the police, local authorities and social landlords to obtain an order to prohibit a person aged 10 or above from engaging in behaviours specified by the order. Violation of the order can result in criminal prosecutions and a custodial sentence of up to five years. Asbos make explicit that a type of behaviour is not acceptable and impose a clear condition or punishment for those who breach the order.

Implicitly, the legislation accepted that bad behaviour should not be a criminal offence, however objectionable it might be. As a civil remedy, it means that the burden of proof can be the lesser test of 'a balance of probabilities' that an individual has been up to no good rather than the higher criminal test of 'beyond reasonable doubt'. However, since a breach of an Asbo is an offence punishable by jail, the law means that behaviour many may feel is anti-social or plain bizarre has become criminalized. In addition to the unfortunate Mrs Cartwright, there are numerous stories of people facing jail for behaving in an anti-social way.

What was the genesis of this particular law? It was a Labour manifesto promise before the 1997 general election to bear down on the sort of behaviour that has long afflicted many inner-city areas and housing estates where swaggering bullies and generally selfish people make the lives of others a misery. In his speech on the Second Reading of the Crime and Disorder Bill Jack Straw explained his thinking: 'The Bill has a simple, practical ambition: to build a safer and more responsible society. My wish is that everyone should enjoy that most basic of human rights: the right to live life free from fear and free from crime.'

Straw also set out how the legislation had come about:

> The Bill marks out the new approach to policy making by which my right hon. Friend the Prime Minister [Tony Blair] transformed my party from one of opposition to one of government. The Bill represents a triumph of community politics over detached metropolitan elites. In the early 1980s, my party lost its way, not least by failing to listen to those whom we claimed to represent, and by failing to learn from them. My right hon. Friend broke decisively with all that and ensured that our policy making would be inspired above all by our constituents. Among many other things, that led us to a serious examination of how to reverse the apparently inexorable rise in anti-social behaviour and teenage crime.[18]

There is something immediately amiss here. This legislation was as much about trying to show that Labour was a 'different' sort of party from the one that had previously appeared to be the criminal's friend. It was to bolster the impression that Tony Blair (using a phrase actually coined by Gordon Brown) was tough on both crime and its causes. The logic of this position should have been to put all possible effort and resources into rebuilding the remnants of community authority. The problem was not with the law: there were plenty of those making certain acts illegal and there had been for generations. The real crisis was in the absence of order on the streets caused by a retreat of police to their stations, a decline in police numbers and the dismantling of the informal network of authority figures, from the park warden to the concierge, who once helped maintain order. In addition, adults were less inclined to carry out the sort of self-policing of their own community which was once commonplace. Adults who insisted on youngsters behaving in a proper way were usually backed up by other adults and by the official authorities. There was a feeling this was no longer happening. Adults feared they would end up in prison themselves or would be attacked because of the absence from the streets of any uniformed presence. They began to look the other way.

Alexander Deane, a former adviser to David Cameron, went so far as to blame the middle classes themselves for retreating from their obligation to impose some sort of order on society even though, arguably, the Metropolitan Police were set up by Robert Peel so that the working classes could police themselves and leave the middle classes alone. Deane recounts observing an incident of a child vandalizing a bus in front of adults: 'Individuals would once have been much more likely to have acted to halt such behaviour . . . The ethos was more conducive to intervention in the misbehaviour of the young but now is not, not only because of the removal of the tool of physical chastisement but also because of a culture of fear.' Deane says we fear the repercussions for ourselves of intervention, if it ends in the errant child being physically restrained, 'but also we fear violence from those that once would have been held in check by a culture of respect'.

Deane's thesis is that the middle classes have relinquished their duty to uphold decent standards of behaviour, both among themselves and by insisting upon them when others transgress: 'Moral opprobrium and peer condemnation are the most effective tools in enforcing cultural behaviour patterns. The refusal of the new middle class to wield these tools has undermined all our traditions and standards.'[19]

However, law-abiding adults have not abandoned these

codes; they simply no longer know how to enforce them. When a teacher is assaulted and the lout responsible is allowed back, unpunished, into the school a few days later; when a woman driven to distraction threatens a group of yobs with an airgun and is jailed; when a father remonstrates with vandals for stoning his car and is beaten to within an inch of his life; when the criminal justice system acts swiftly to prosecute an adult who has lost his temper after years of harassment yet leaves the yobs themselves alone; when politicians talk incessantly about the rights of children and set up a commissariat to enforce them; when a government promises to reform a welfare system that actively encourages bad behaviour, yet fails to fulfil its pledge; and when the liberal elites spend decades undermining the one institution – the traditional family – that contains within it the elements of deference, respect, responsibility and duty that are the basic structures of a decent society, then is it any surprise that the middle classes have abandoned the role of moral policeman?

It is a bit late to lament the absence of respect when the progressive Left did so much to erode any notion of deference to those who by dint of their job or age should command it. It was Tony Blair, after all, who was so derisive of the 'forces of conservatism', those old fashioned virtues of law, order, respect and decency that provided the societal glue yet were sneered at by the Left. Most of us still subscribe to them, so Deane was wrong to say they had been abandoned, but correct to say we are frightened to uphold them, not because of the law but because of the absence of order. Rather than seek to rebuild these lost values, however, Labour reached for the statute book. They wanted to see if they could legislate bad behaviour out of existence.

In his 1998 speech to the Commons, Straw said he felt the government was required to deal with the emergence of a new phenomenon when in fact it was merely the continuing manifestation of a very old phenomenon – people behaving badly, though this time there was not the wherewithal to keep it in check. He said:

> As shadow home affairs spokesman, I was struck by the degree to which the problems and experiences of my constituents had changed since I was first elected in 1979. Then, the great bulk of my constituency case work concerned housing complaints and social security, but that changed from the early 1990s. More and more people came to me complaining of intolerable anti-social behaviour, of harassment and of intimidation. Much of the trouble was caused by children and young people who were out of control. The criminal justice system appeared to be incapable of enforcing decent standards of public behaviour on children and adults alike.[20]

Straw continued:

> The Bill is, therefore, born out of the experience of our constituents, and out of their sense of frustration with the current criminal justice system. That frustration is shared by the police and by other dedicated and skilled professionals who are expected to solve the problems, but who have been hampered by a slow, inconsistent and ineffective system. Our manifesto spelt out the need to modify and to modernise the criminal justice system to get it working effectively. The Bill is the first major step in that process. It begins our root-and-branch reform of the youth justice system, and it will establish new ways for agencies and communities to work together to support a safer, more responsible society. It will equip the criminal justice system overall, better to respond to disorder and to protect communities from sex offenders, from drug-misusing offenders and from racist thugs.

It seems a bit harsh, in view of the noble motives for this

legislation to call it a bad law. Straw spoke for all reasonable people in what he said; and he was right to identify the wretched existence that many people had because of whom they lived next door to as something that had to be addressed. The question is whether this was the right way to do it. To begin with, the Asbo which was introduced under the 1998 Act looked like a total flop. For the first few years of its existence it was hardly used at all. Just a few hundred were issued up and down the country. Those that were handed out attracted widespread coverage – and, unusually, the recipients, including children, could be named whereas children in youth courts accused of more serious criminal offences cannot be identified.

These children included Stephen Blowes, 15, from Cambridge. He received an Asbo for persistent 'hedge-hopping' and causing a nuisance to his neighbours. The order imposed by Cambridge magistrates banned the teenager from entering any rear garden in the city without permission from the owner. The order also ruled that he must not create a disturbance or use threatening or abusive behaviour within a designated area of the city's Arbury district, where he lived. In Tower Hamlets, east London, a four-year-old child was threatened with an Asbo for throwing a plastic football at a car, even though the minimum age for an order is ten.

One of the most notorious Asbo cases was Aneeze Williamson, of Shipley, West Yorkshire. He was 11 and described as 'out of control, the ring-leader of a pack of local hooligans' who 'appears to have no regard for other people's property and belongings'.

A local shopkeeper who had been the victim of theft, criminal damage and abuse, said: 'Young kids like to hang around on street corners, it's the way of the world I suppose. But things change when Aneeze Williamson and a couple of his friends join the group. He's only 11, but he's a dangerous kid in my eyes.' The long list of crimes committed by Aneeze includes numerous thefts from homes and shops, assault, including one offence of causing actual bodily harm, as well as many burglaries, arson and cases of criminal damage.

Another was Michael Ashton, 13, from Manchester who had been accused by neighbours of trespassing in gardens, tormenting residents, vandalizing property and shouting abuse. A court heard the complaints – some submitted anonymously – and granted an Asbo banning Michael for two years from areas of the north Manchester estate where he lived. If Michael, who had never been convicted of, or even charged with, a single crime, was caught simply standing in a forbidden street, he would be committing a criminal offence that can carry a sentence of up to five years. 'All that for knocking on doors and running through gardens! Isn't that what kids do?' said his mother.

Well, not all of them do and there are many long-suffering residents on estates terrorized by this sort of yobbish behaviour who welcome any respite. The question arises again, though: is recourse to the law the best way to tackle this sort of behaviour? Once it would have been dealt with by policing and some harshly administered parental discipline.

Furthermore, as soon as a power like this is available it gets used in the most bizarre ways. Some Asbos have included a ban on riding a bicycle in the city centre, on meeting more than three non-family members in public, on wearing a bala-clava in the street and on wearing a single golf glove. One Asbo forbade Zach Tutin from saying 'grass' until 2010. The order also outlaws the words 'slag', 'cripple' and 'Paki', and bans Zach from using the main thoroughfare of Moston, east Manchester, where he lives with his mother. In another case, a magistrate banned a 16-year-old boy from misbehaving in school. If he disrupts a class, he can now be sent to prison. This was something that used to be, and still should be, sorted out by the school. Yet increasingly heads are calling the police to sort out the aftermath of playground scraps or bad behaviour. In County Durham, Dean Bell, 15, was banned from playing football in the street. At one point police confiscated 12 balls from the youngster in the space of a fortnight.

For a party that came to office promising to be tough on the causes of crime as well as on crime itself, the Anti-Social Behaviour Order was a strange invention by Labour. As Decca Aitkenhead wrote in the *Guardian* after investigating the use of orders in Manchester:

> Anti-social behaviour has manoeuvred socialists into positions they remember sounding rightwing 20 years ago, and induced the zealotry some need to steady their nerves. Fighting the behaviour with Asbos has given many on the left their first authentic sense of victory – of wielding power on behalf of the vulnerable – and the fight has the pleasing ring of populism. It communicates the party's transfer of faith from the delicacies of moral idealism to the dogma of what works. It is probably because of this that Asbos tend to be discussed in black-and-white terms. Do they work or not? Are they right or wrong? The political debate has such appealingly sharp edges that it is tempting to hope the same definition can be found in the actual lives of people who behave in an anti-social fashion. My experience of three families with Asbos was that all of these questions were simpler to answer the less time one spent with them. Proximity to their lives blurred the edges so quickly that any hope of answers vanished, and even the questions became almost meaningless, lost in the drama of domestic turmoil.[21]

Ministers are convinced Asbos are a success and will be one of the Labour government's enduring legacies. However, what they have done is to turn a whole lot of activities that were once considered irritating into potentially criminal offences punishable by up to five years in jail, while at the same making crimes that were once considered serious, like theft and vandalism, subject to the legal equivalent of a slap on the wrist.

STOP THE TORRENT

At a press conference in 2004 to launch a 'five-year plan' for crime, David Blunkett, the home secretary, was asked whether it was his intention to call a halt on new laws against anti-social behaviour and low-level crime and let those that he and his predecessor, Jack Straw, introduced take effect. In other words, could he promise a moratorium on criminal justice legislation? Blunkett, flanked by Lord Falconer, the lord chancellor, and Lord Goldsmith, the attorney general, literally laughed at such a preposterous suggestion. 'What would we do with our lives?' he said, only half in jest.

Yet when Blunkett became home secretary in 2001 he appeared to recognize the problem of over-legislating in criminal justice. He told the Commons in his debut speech in the post: 'There are few countries in the world that have the constant debate on these matters and the constant change that we have. There is more legislation than it is possible to spend time reading in this area. No sooner has a Bill been passed than another one is being passed to update it.' He added: 'It is time to get a grip on what we want to do.' Since those fine words were uttered, we have had more criminal justice measures than ever before.

The Labour government has spent years trying to reimpose through the legal system those values of deference and respect for one's elders that the very same progressive elites who supported Blair and Brown spent decades undermining and belittling. Blair once said: 'People like a society that is less deferential. They want a society free from old prejudices. But a loss of deference is very different from a loss of respect for other people. Society without prejudice should not be one without rules.'[22]

If by 'free from old prejudices' he meant no forelock tugging to the landed gentry, most would agree. But if he considered deference towards hierarchy, authority, age and gender to be a 'prejudice' that must be resisted, then his appeal for greater respect was meaningless. Respect is not possible without some deference on the part of young people, especially to parents, teachers, police officers and other adults. There was a time – and this is not the myth of the golden age – when misbehaving youths were brought into line by other adults and, by and large, accepted the rubrics of hierarchy and authority even if they didn't especially like it.

Old social mores have been supplanted by child-safety orders, local child curfews, parenting orders, reparation orders, action plan orders, referral orders, detention and training orders, spot fines, drug treatment and supervision orders. In place of the commonsense society, we have the Asbo society, and more laws than you could shake a stick at.

SOME MORE OFFENCES INTRODUCED SINCE 1997

- To wilfully pretend to be a barrister (a provision of the Legal Services Act 2007 aimed at modernizing the legal profession and increasing competition between barristers).
- To obstruct workers carrying out repairs to the Dockland Light Railway (the offence is created under legislation designed to boost capacity on the DLR in the run-up to the 2012 Olympics in London).
- To attach an ear tag to an animal when it has previously been used to identify another animal (a regulation introduced last year to tighten up identification of cattle).
- To land a catch at a harbour that includes unsorted fish without permission (regulations to control fish taken from seas around Britain).
- To fail to use an approved technique for weighing herring, mackerel and horse mackerel (brought about by the Natural Environment and Rural Communities Act 2006).
- To allow an unlicensed concert in a church hall or community centre (the 2003 Licensing Act introduced a maximum penalty of six months' prison for breaking the law).

Table 7 Criminal Justice Act 2003:
Sections not in force by November 2007

	Number of sections	Percentage of sections
Wholly in force	276	84
Partially in force	26	8
Not in force	26	8
Repealed	1	–

Source: Hansard, 21 November 2007, col. 964W.

CHAPTER 5

SEND IN THE CLOWNS:
THE LICENSING ACT 2003

Clive Fairweather is one of the West Country's leading storytellers, sometimes performing as 'Old Fairweather', a nineteenth-century farm-labourer, or as 'Augustus Hare', a Victorian notable. For more than 40 years, he has regaled village pubs and festivals with his tales of England's history; and, for 39 of them, he did so without needing to apply for a licence. Yet after the Licensing Act came into force in 2005, Old Fairweather discovered that his annual visit to the Totnes Festival in Devon would not be so straightforward any more. He had to fill in six forms, four for the council, one for the police and one to be pinned (next to the No Smoking sign) on the door of the medieval guildhall where he was due to perform so it could be inspected 'by a constable or other authorised person'. Although the cost of the licence was just £21 and the forms were easily completed by a former teacher, the sheer pointlessness of the exercise irritated Mr Fairweather beyond measure:

> I was engaged in two hours of storytelling in a building where free speech has been current for 900 years. There will be no alcohol, no amplification, no subversion of the state, no threat to public order. But for the first time in 40 years of storytelling, I was obliged to buy a licence – at a time when

the Government is urging us to celebrate our Britishness, to rediscover our national stories and to re-establish a sense of community and social commitment.[1]

Mr Fairweather was by no means alone in his bewilderment that a perfectly innocuous and culturally beneficial activity could be turned into a bureaucratic rigmarole, ostensibly to prevent violent activity breaking out. Consider the children of a small Derbyshire village, generations of whom had engaged in the somewhat paganistic ritual of well-dressing for many hundreds of years. In the spring, they put together floral displays and walk around the heads of the local wells and decorate them with the flowers. When the Licensing Act came into force in 2005, this activity required a licence or, instead, something called a temporary event notice (TEN). However, a TEN could only be granted for an event attended by fewer than 500 people. The police judged that more than 500 would be attracted to the well-dressing ceremony and objected to the application. The organizers cancelled the event because they felt they could not put up with the bureaucracy.

When an Oxfam bookshop advertised in a local paper that it was to hold an evening of readings by four poets, accompanied by a didgeridoo player to provide an 'atmospheric background', before a maximum audience of 25 people, the police and the council told the manager that it could not take place without a temporary event notice. Faced with this obvious threat to life and limb, the evening was postponed until the various forms were filled in. In another case, a folk club made up of 'elderly gentlemen' who meet once a year in a small room above a pub in the English countryside to sing, unaccompanied, had to cancel their gathering because the landlady was told she would need a variation to her premises licence to allow entertainment of this sort.

These are among the countless examples of harmless and often ancient activities that have been either abandoned or made more difficult to put on because of the Licensing Act. How did this happen? Few laws introduced by the Labour government excited as much controversy and generated as much comment as the Licensing Act 2003. It is an object lesson in how governments with too much time on their hands simply seek to intrude where they are not wanted, imposing burdens – financial and bureaucratic – on people who were merely minding their own business. It is also a classic example of where politicians failed to do their jobs properly and left the promulgation of this measure almost entirely to the zealous officials who would simply not accept that they were heading off down the wrong track.

Ministers thought the Licensing Act, which would allow extended licensing hours for the sale of alcohol, was a good wheeze because the civil servants told them it would be hugely politically popular: 'Just think, minister, of the votes you will get by allowing round-the-clock boozing.' Indeed, shortly before the 2001 election, the following text message was sent to young voters: 'Don't give a xxxx for last orders? Vote Labour.' But the Licensing Act was not just about drinking.

We need to go back to before the 2001 general election to see the first shoots of what would grow into a mighty thicket of rules, regulations and, inevitably, fees. After it came to power in 1997, Labour had signalled it wanted to liberalize the drinking laws. Ministers had this wonderfully naive idea (either that or they had been too much at the scotch) that a Continental-style cafe-culture could be imported into Britain provided people were allowed to drink around the clock. The implications of flexible drinking hours for law and order are a matter of debate, with some official figures showing declining crime around the period when drinkers used to get thrown out but increasing disorder later in the night. Accident and Emergency (A&E) centres report more late night injuries from drink-related fights or accidents. This cannot be shown to be the direct result of the later drinking hours, as opposed to generally deteriorating behaviour, though circumstantial evidence for blaming longer hours is strong.

The government's intentions were set out in a white paper, *Time for Reform: Proposals for the Modernisation of our Licensing Laws*, published in April 2000. It claimed there were complexities and inconsistencies with the existing laws which dated back many years and provided for over 40 different kinds of licence or permission. The idea was to introduce a single integrated licensing scheme, administered by local authorities.

The main proposals were:

- A single integrated scheme for licensing premises which sell alcohol, provide public entertainment or provide refreshment at night.

- A new system of personal licences which allow holders to sell or serve alcohol for consumption on or off any premises possessing a premises licence. (Places providing public entertainment or refreshment at night, not involving alcohol, would require a premises licence only.)

- The legal age for drinking alcohol on licensed premises and for buying it there, whether as off-sales or on-sales, both to be 18.

- New measures to back-up restrictions on underage drinking including: a new offence of buying alcohol on behalf of a person under 18; a new offence of knowingly permitting a sale to a person under 18 years; test purchasing to be placed on a statutory footing; a new duty on people selling alcohol to satisfy themselves about customers' ages.

- Personal licences to be issued for 10 years to those aged 18 or over without a relevant criminal record following a test of knowledge of licensing law and social responsibilities with provision for endorsement or withdrawal of licences within that period.

- Abolition of the 'fit and proper person' test in respect of licences to sell alcohol.

- Premises licences to incorporate operating conditions (e.g. hours, noise, fire exits, capacity) limited to crime and disorder/public safety/nuisance factors, and set locally on basis of the balance of operator's requirements/resident views/police and fire authority assessments.
- To minimize public disorder resulting from fixed closing times, the introduction of flexible opening hours, with the potential for up to 24-hour opening, 7 days a week, subject to consideration of the impact on local residents.
- Tough new powers for police to deal instantly with violent and disorderly behaviour by closing premises that rogue licence holders have allowed to become the focus of such behaviour.
- Children to be allowed access to any part of licensed premises at the personal licence holder's discretion; but licensing authorities to have the discretion to restrict (e.g. by requiring adult supervision) or deny access for children to unsuitable licensed venues.
- Personal and premises licences to be issued by local authorities.
- An avenue of appeal for parties (including the police and local residents) to the Crown Court.
- Licences to be supported by a flexible range of sanctions (including temporary reduction in opening hours) instead of present single all or nothing sanction of loss of licence.
- New arrangements for non-profit making registered clubs supplying alcohol to their members which preserve their special status.

This was meant to be as much an exercise in deregulation as in the modernization of antiquated laws. Yet it was carried out in such a ham-fisted fashion that hundreds of thousands of people were left fuming with frustration at its complexity and were out of pocket because of its expense. From live musicians to village hall managers and from sports clubs to small wine merchants – who have all had to wade through mountains of paperwork to obtain their alcohol or entertainment licences – there were screams of irritation from the very beginning.

These idiocies were visited upon village halls and community centres, on schools and working men's clubs; on rugby associations and cricket pavilions; on musicians whose only offence was to sing folk songs while wearing an Arran sweater. These licensing requirements seemed to be introduced because of the obvious danger to public order posed by a clown or a rendition of 'Wild Rover'. And yet the one activity that did not have to be licensed was the provision of televised big-screen sport in front of hundreds of drunken fans. This exemption had nothing to do, of course, with the clout of Rupert Murdoch's Sky TV.

The aim of the regime was to make the system 'more flexible for the vast majority of responsible drinkers and licensees while giving more powers to local communities and the police to deal with those few licensees that cause problems'. Not for the first time, such laudable aims ended up causing headaches for pub-owners, local authorities, club entertainers, circus managers, small shopkeepers, late-night kebab stallholders, sports clubs, carnival organizers and thousands of volunteers who manage village halls up and down the land. All of these groups – and there are many others – have been affected in different ways, but the essential cause of their difficulties was that they were required to convert existing alcohol and entertainment licences into the new premises and personal licences required under the Act. This involved filling in a 21-page form, to which 60 pages of explanatory notes are attached, a daunting enough task for a full-time publican whose livelihood depends on getting it right, but an onerous burden for a volunteer running a community hall.

Rodney Tate, chairman of the Swineshead village hall management committee, explained in 2005 when the Act came into force how the new 'flexible' legislation had affected his life:

> It will have taken me about a full week of my (unpaid) time, including attending two seminars, to understand sufficiently

the conversion process and complete the application papers. The Act may have the admirable objectives of the prevention of crime and disorder, public safety, prevention of public nuisance and the protection of children from harm, but we haven't suffered from any of these issues in our small village. So we are being afflicted with an expensive bureaucratic nightmare for no useful purpose.[2]

Why on earth did village halls, where the most violent outburst is likely to involve some tut-tutting over the declining standards of cake-making at the bring-and-buy sale, find themselves subjected to this regime? MPs who sat on the committee that steered the Bill into law were suitably chastened. Malcolm Moss, the Conservative MP for North East Cambridgeshire, said: 'I am embarrassed not to have been able . . . to make any fundamental changes to the Bill. I regret that.'[3] Mark Field, MP for the Cities of London and Westminster, said: 'Many people did not realize the great implications for the range of village hall-related events. The issue has the makings of an absolutely horrendous mess.'[4]

It beggars belief that such legislation can be passed into law without those whose job it is to scrutinize it fully appreciating its implications, but it happens all the time. Another characteristic feature is the government's unwillingness to listen. Peter Luff, the MP for Mid-Worcestershire, warned ministers that they were serving up a legislative dog's breakfast; but he might just as well have banged his head against a wall for all the attention they paid. He set out the charge sheet during a debate in Westminster Hall shortly after the provisions of the new legislation took effect. 'The Licensing Act means villages in every corner of the country will say goodbye to the traditional touring circus, see more village shops go to the wall, watch local sports clubs forgoing much-needed income and lose their village halls, despite no accidents, no anti-social behaviour and nothing worrying having occurred in, outside or even remotely close to them.'[5]

Was it beyond the wit of government to devise a licensing regime that dealt with the problem of alcohol-fuelled violence (which it didn't) without making life more difficult for the decent citizen? The anxiety and costs that this exercise generated were completely out of proportion to the likely benefits. The number of temporary events that can be held without a full licence has been restricted, causing great inconvenience. The regime introduced a personal licence that someone must possess if alcohol is to be sold. The holder of the licence was known as the designated premises supervisor and must go on a training course to obtain an 'accredited personal licence qualification'. This was madness and was finally recognized as such when the government in 2009 amended the law so that a committee rather than an individual could take responsibility.

Characteristically, this change in the law was announced by the government as though it was doing everyone a favour. A press release from the Department for Culture, Media and Sport issued on 29 July 2009, stated:

> A new measure to help village halls and community halls came into force today. Instead of having to have a designated person apply for a personal licence, responsibility for the supervision of alcohol sales can, on application, fall to the management committee.
>
> This measure will reduce the burden on individual volunteers, save hundreds of pounds in training costs and volunteer time and should also give halls greater flexibility to sell alcohol during community and fundraising events.

Gerry Sutcliffe, the licensing minister, said:

> I am pleased that we have managed to help out those who help run village and community halls. Most of these halls are kept going by volunteers who individually cannot devote a large amount of their time to putting on

events or attending training courses. This new measure will mean that people who run the halls can apply to take collective responsibility, making it easier for them to put on community and fundraising events where alcohol is sold.[6]

But who made life difficult for them in the first place? By the time Mr Sutcliffe issued his self-satisfied press statement many volunteers, unwilling to take on the personal responsibility, had already been driven away.

The change took nearly four years to obtain from when the Act came into force. Other failings in the Act have still not been addressed despite mountains of evidence that it simply does not work as was intended. Yet ministers, briefed by officials who do not wish to admit they are wrong, just stonewalled. When he was the licensing minister at the Department for Culture, Media and Sport, James Purnell was asked what assessment had been made of the likely consequences of the Licensing Act on the income of village halls. He replied: 'There is no cost to village halls applying for a premises licence for the provision of public entertainment. Only where they wish to add the supply of alcohol to their licence will the vast majority pay no more than £190 on initial application and £180 as an annual fee. For many halls, the fees would be £100 and £70 respectively.'[7]

However, Gloria Gower, secretary of the Rotherfield village hall in East Sussex, did not want a premises licence for the hall. She wanted to apply for TENs, only to find that the Act restricted the number that can be obtained to 12 a year. In the year before the Act, Rotherfield hall had 29 trouble-free bookings where alcohol was served. Restricting it to 12 meant turning away bookings, thereby putting the future of the hall in jeopardy because of a fall in income. Mrs Gower said: 'The National Village Halls Forum has been campaigning on this issue for some time but the people who drafted this legislation seem unwilling to admit that they got this part wrong and to make the changes necessary to keep the facilities for the majority of the population who elected them.[8]

This did not just affect village halls, Stefan Reynolds, who operated a Surrey wine company that transacted its business by letter, fax and internet, and delivered orders directly to customers from home, was required to apply for a new premises licence for the small room under the garage at his parent's house where he stored the wine. These were not premises ever visited by the public and therefore unlikely to play any part in achieving the ostensible objectives of the Licensing Act – the prevention of crime and disorder, public safety, prevention of public nuisance and protection of children from harm. Mr Reynolds said, 'It is absurd. Equally absurd is the fact that my local council is unable to let me know the cost because the fee structure is based upon the business rateable value of a property, which does not apply in this case.'[9]

TEARS OF A CLOWN

The Licensing Act also had a big impact on circuses. The circus was actually invented in Britain. The first was a riding school established on land owned by St Thomas' Hospital, London, in 1768. It was set up by Philip Astley, a sergeant-major who had served in the 15th Light Dragoons in the Seven Years War. He was a gifted horseman and when he retired from the Army, he became an equestrian trick-rider and performed at pleasure gardens. When Astley opened his riding school, he set up a ring, calling it 'the circus' from the Roman word. In 1772, Astley introduced some variety by hiring jugglers, acrobats, tightrope-walkers and clowns, thereby inventing the modern circus. Circus spread from this small ring adjacent to Westminster to Russia and the court of Catherine the Great, and to the rest of Europe and to America. For centuries, circuses travelled the country entertaining millions without needing too worry much about red tape, local government bureaucrats or form-filling. They could go from place to place largely unmolested. After all, whom did they threaten?

Then came the Licensing Act and for the first time, circus-owners had to apply for an entertainments licence – and to do so at every venue they visited. It cost them money, which was a problem for circuses operating at the margins of profitability. It took ages to fill in the forms – one for each of up to dozens of local authorities that might be visited in a season. It led to lunacies whereby circuses that had needed to uproot themselves because of floods had to travel hundreds of miles because they had to wait 10 days for a licence to come through. They found themselves subject to the complexities of live musical enter-tainment licensing. If music is 'incidental' (though the Act, rather unhelpfully, does not provide any definition for incidental music) it does not need to be licensed; if it is integral, it does. Is the music for a circus act incidental or integral? Why on earth should it matter? But in mad, rule-obsessed modern Britain, it does.

When Zippo's Circus pitched up in Birmingham in 2008, the council's licensing department insisted upon alterations to the clown act. Three Spanish clowns, Nicol, Michael and Pappa, who would normally have introduced themselves with a blast of trumpets, were refused permission to do so. Also cut was the moment when Nicol sounds three notes on a tuba, which then explodes, the bell landing on another clown's head while Nicol blows a puff of smoke from his rear. The licensing officer insisted that if the clowns sounded their trumpets, or blew the exploding horn, it would be a live music performance and the big top would require a licence.

Martin Burton, the long-suffering proprietor of Zippo's Circus, who has battled with the bureaucrats for years over this law, was able to retain the deadpan humour of a professional clown: 'I'm a big fan of silent comedy, but this is ludicrous,' he said.[10] Mr Burton has managed to negotiate an exemption with most of the local councils whose areas he visits. He explained:

Zippo's Circus will write a very detailed letter to the local licensing officer explaining what is in our circus and explaining why we think that is non-licensable and they will write back and agree or disagree with us. Increasingly licensing officers have declared my circus and its content as non-licensable. Clearly there are activities which bring a form of entertainment within the Licensing Act and clearly not all circuses are the same, although most touring ones are quite similar to mine. If we look in the recent past, then 80% of licensing officers that we have asked have declared my circus non-licensable.[11]

However, Mr Burton said that while this had been achieved through negotiation, the problem itself had not disappeared 'because you do not know when somebody is going to turn round and suddenly say, "Yes, this is licensable," which is what happened to me in Birmingham.'

Mr Burton had spent hours negotiating with the city council over an exemption from the Act, without which he would have to pay £1,000 every time his circus arrived at one of the 30 venues visited every year. 'There was some discussion about whether skipping on a tight-rope was dancing. Tight-rope walking is not regarded as regulated entertainment requiring a licence; dance is.'[12] Mr Burton thought he had persuaded the council that the music in their act was purely incidental: 'It's just a quick blast of trumpets at the start. Then three notes from the exploding tuba: pa-pa-pa-bang!'

Malcolm Clay, secretary of the Association of Circus Proprietors of Great Britain, said:

It is this grey area which is so difficult to contend with. If we have a juggler (and juggling is not a licensable activity) and the juggler has a girl assistant who wiggles about and passes him his hoops and clubs, is she dancing? Where on the scale does the juggler's assistant come into the area of dance? At the moment Zippo's Circus has a Spanish boy on a low wire who kicks his legs and dances. Is dancing on the tight wire, although it is a circus skill, included within the definition of dancing? The dancing is only an artistic way of expressing the routine. We have these grey areas. Licensing officers are saying, 'We don't really want to be bothered. We've never had problems with circuses.'[13]

Malcolm Clay also said the difficulty is not merely the sheer pettiness of it all but the cost.

When we started licensing we calculated that the licences were costing £1,000 a time. The public notices column of the local paper is the most expensive column to advertise in. If we could have advertised in the entertainments column it would have been cheaper . . . The cost has been a problem and it is a problem that has diminished slightly and the industry has had to cope with it. The real problem with all of this is the flexibility. You know what your licence is going to cost and the industry, by the nature of the people who run it, is quite resilient, but you cannot cope with arriving in a town and not being able to trade for a week because your expenses remain exactly the same.

This lack of flexibility hit home during the summer of 2008 when heavy rains caused floods at the places where the circus traditionally set up. 'Zippo' Burton gave a graphic account of what happened to his circus.

We were due to open in Sheffield and my circus was in Twickenham. We went to Sheffield the week before and made the necessary inspections with the council officers and the parks officers and everything was fine. On Monday morning the first vehicle pulled onto the park in Sheffield and within ten minutes I had a phone call from the Mayor's office saying our event was cancelled. You will remember that Sheffield had terrible floods last year and this was right in the middle of all of that. Pre licensing what I would have done was I would have phoned up Meadowhall shopping centre and moved my circus from the council park to Meadowhall ... However, because of the Licensing Act 2003 we had to turn round. I literally had lorries coming off the motorway onto the slip road and I told them to go back onto the motorway and back to London. The only place we had a premises licence that we could use was for Barnes in London. So we went all the way back to Barnes and opened in Barnes ... it is one thing to re-advertise the change of location from one part of Sheffield to another, it is another thing to advertise a change in location from Sheffield to Barnes. That caused us real hardship and we lost serious money that week, plus the next venue was Perth in Scotland and the idea of Sheffield was it is halfway to Perth. I then drove from Barnes to Perth without a break, which was another extremely expensive exercise. That was as a direct result of the Licensing Act causing us real hardship.[14]

This concept of incidental music was never in the legislation but was added to statutory guidance in order to prevent the barminess of Morris Dancing becoming a licensable activity, something that was sufficiently potty to make the legislation potentially a laughing stock. Also, as a result of lobbying by the Church of England, religious services were exempted from the need for a music licence. But carol singing, in some circumstances, is licensable, though when the legislation first came in this was by no means clear. The Department for Culture, Media and Sport issued advice to would-be carollers that was more convoluted than a rendition of 'In Dulce Jubilo'. If a performance is 'spontaneous, incidental to other activities or part of a religious service', it is not licensable. However, if a carol concert has an audience, it will be regulated entertainment and will need a licence. So, did that include a group of carol singers performing on a station concourse or in a shopping centre? The department says:

> If a carol service is organized, advertised and provided for an audience there would seem to be little doubt that this would be licensable. However, a group of carol singers (players) outside a shop could be construed as incidental to the activity of people going about shopping and therefore exempt from the requirement for a licence. It would make no difference whether or not they were seeking voluntary contributions to charity from passers-by. This is different from a scenario where a shopping centre or individual business has organized a carol performance for an audience in a shopping mall which would require a licence or temporary event notice.[15]

In other words, organized carol singing in a big shopping centre is licensable; door to door singing isn't, though why that should be so is itself a mystery since singing could hardly be 'incidental'. The reason the guidance was drawn up in this way is because officials suddenly realized that their legislation would be fatally undermined if people could not sing the odd carol at Christmas. If singing is part of a religious service it is incidental and therefore not licensable. This gave one West Country choir a brainwave. It had for years performed at the local harbour to raise some money for charity only to be told by the local authority that they would require a licence under the new Act. To get around this they now invite the local vicar with them to bless the harbour, transforming it into a place of religious worship, and therefore exempt from the legislation.

You know a law is a bad law when a choir is reduced to jiggery-pokery simply to sing by a harbour wall to collect money for charity.

PLAYING MY PIANO – OR NOT, AS THE CASE MAY BE

Other groups have not been able to avail themselves of a religious exemption, particularly pubs wanting to put on live music. Licensing entertainment was nothing new but this used to be done on a more informal basis. There were discrepancies and exemptions, one of them being the two-in-a-bar rule, which the new system abolished. As its name suggests, it meant two singers or musicians could perform together without having to get a licence. Once the Act came into force, this was no longer possible. It was to have a significant impact on live music, the complete opposite of what the government had claimed would happen.

This was apparent almost from the outset. After the Act became law, the first set of research published by the Department for Culture suggested that more than 60 per cent of smaller venues had a licence to put on live music. While this sounded good, it was roughly the same proportion that existed before the Act. In other words, a lot of people had gone through costly and time-consuming form-filling just to stand still. Actually, these 'encouraging' figures, as the department called them, hid anecdotal evidence of a big impact on the smallest venues – those that used to operate under the two-in-a-bar rule. The department figures showed that 30 per cent of these venues simply did not bother to get a licence because it was too expensive and too much hassle. According to the British Pub and Beer Association a licence costs in the order of £1,500 to £1,600, which for a small business whose main interest is not the provision of live music is not a viable proposition. So many pubs simply gave up providing music.

One of the affected landlords was Ged O'Sullivan, who owned Ryan's Bar in Stoke Newington, London. Before the Licensing Act, this was a lively music venue using the exemption for performances in an intimately fuggy basement. Under the new law, Mr O'Sullivan needed an entertainment licence for the first time, triggering a nightmare of bureaucracy and expense. The local authority demanded new gas-fittings, new electrical wiring, acoustic-limiters (even though he has only ever had one complaint about noise), a new alarm system and CCTV cameras. Planning problems arose and a neighbour objected to drinkers and diners in the garden in the summer. So he installed a fence with acoustic matting around the 80ft perimeter and needed to pay legal bills. It cost him tens of thousands of pounds to get a licence that he previously did not need.

Hamish Birchall, a jazz musician and indefatigable campaigner for live performances, said: 'Under the old regime, all premises with an alcohol licence could have one or two live musicians whenever they were open. The justices' on-licence was, in effect, a licence for one or two musicians – without it you could not even have one performer.'[16] A simple law was made complicated and expensive for people trying to get by. The Act meant that a public concert by pupils in a school is illegal unless licensed, but exempt if performed in a church; a private concert in someone's home to raise funds for charity is illegal unless licensed; unamplified music is exempt if performed with Morris dancers, but illegal unless licensed if there are no dancers; a piano provided by a pub for the regular use of customers is illegal unless licensed, but jukeboxes are exempt; and televised sport – or anything broadcast – on big screens with powerful amplification is exempt, anywhere, anytime. It is no surprise that many bar-owners have simply given up.

Licensing the performance of live music was introduced in 1753 to curb rowdy alehouses in the City of Westminster but is it still necessary to do so? When the Bill was going through parliament, the minister, Lord McIntosh, made a statement in the House of Lords and quoted from Chris Fox, president of the Association of Chief Police Officers (ACPO), saying: 'Live music always acts as a magnet in whatever community it is being played. It brings people from outside that community and others who come and having no connection locally behave in a way that is inappropriate, criminal and disorderly.'[17] Few people in the live music world recognized that description but the government maintained there was potential for trouble at music gigs, which may be true if hundreds attend. But if alcohol is being served, it is already licensed; so why is it necessary to license the music?

This point was made to a Commons committee hearing by Dr Martin Rawlings from the pressure group Pub is the Hub:

> In essence, live music cannot possibly be said to be some-thing that is bad and evil. We have accepted that we need to sell alcohol under licence – it has some bad effects, does it not? The only reason for regulating live music at all is in terms of the crowd control that you might have to have; but if you already have a licence that will cover that – and most pubs do one way and the other – then why do you need specific permission to run a couple of guys playing a guitar?[18]

More to the point, why should you need a licence simply to provide a piano? This is now a potential criminal offence under the Licensing Act 2003. Pianos must be licensed as 'enter-tainment facilities' because, as the Act stipulates, their provision might be detrimental to the safety of the public. The maximum penalty for the unlicensed provision of a piano, where a licence is required, is a £20,000 fine and six months in prison.

This requirement was enforced vigorously by London coun-cils when 30 pianos were set up in London streets in the summer of 2009 under the 'Play me I'm yours' scheme. As Robert Hardman reported in the *Daily Mail*:

> Every piano has required both planning permission and a temporary events licence, not to mention meetings with the police and a constellation of local government functionaries. There would actually be more pianos

scattered across London were it not for the red tape and local jobsworths. Notting Hill, for example, likes to bang on about its wonderful carnival and its million-plus multicultural punters. Yet a few local residents have objected to a solitary, unamplified piano there. Without the time or resources for a planning battle (she has a shoestring budget of £14,000), Colette [one of the piano event organizers] has just taken that particular piano elsewhere. Some pianos have only been given council permits as long as they are padlocked all night. That would make sense if they were all in residential areas. But why, say, at Liverpool Street station? How is Knees Up, Mother Brown going to make more noise than the Stansted Express? When a trial piano went into action next to the Millennium Bridge the other day, a police community support officer was on the scene in an instant to check its credentials. You can burgle to your heart's content, but if you try to play Greensleeves on an unlicensed piano, matey, you're nicked.[19]

In a letter to the *Guardian*, Tim Clement-Jones, a Liberal Democrat peer, wrote:

Back in 2003, ministers called the new Licensing Act 'a licensing regime for the 21st century', yet where live music is concerned, they actually turned the licensing clock back more than 100 years. A case in 1899 (Brearley v Morley) established that a pub landlord could let customers use a piano on his premises without an entertainment licence. Today, such a landlord could face criminal prosecution where the maximum penalty is a £20,000 fine and six months in prison.[20]

Lord Clement-Jones sought to bring forward a live music Bill to 'clear up the bureaucratic minefield of the Licensing Act and breathe new life into the live music scene' but as with all private member's legislation it would only become law with government backing and that was not forthcoming. But why on earth was it withheld since the legislation has been shown to be a dog's breakfast?

This measure could also have profound implications for schools, which need to obtain a licence for their pianos if they are putting on concerts.

It is, as always, the small venues that have been hit hardest by this law. Big-screen musical entertainment is exempt and large-scale venues can afford the time and people to jump through bureaucratic hoops. Feargal Sharkey, the former lead singer of the Undertones, who chaired the Live Music Forum established to examine the impact of the Act, told the Commons committee inquiry that while big venue music was growing as a business, 'we have some issues surrounding smaller venues where we do not think that level of growth is continuing'. He said: 'There has been extraordinary growth in large outdoor, large-scale festivals particularly over the last four or five years . . . We are quite clearly of the opinion that it has become increasingly burdensome and increasingly difficult for small-scale premises, particularly those whose main activity is not providing live music, i.e. bars, restaurants, that kind of thing.'[21]

It is at these small venues where, as Sharkey acknowledged, tomorrow's star performers cut their teeth. If they go, then the next wannabe Feargal Sharkey may not get his chance. The government's own research showed that there had been a decrease of 5 per cent in live music taking place on smaller premises. Sharkey added:

> We would have the concern at this moment that that descent is accelerating and the impact of that is increasing. We are very focused on the idea of good regulation and we are very content and happy with intervention when it is reasonable, necessary and appropriate. There are specific issues we have relating particularly to smaller premises where we do

not feel this legislation is fit for purpose. Long term we feel that ultimately the only real solution will be to repeal live music from the Licensing Act and to have a standalone bit of legislation more suitable, more sympathetic, more reasonable and more proportionate to the impact that we believe live music has on local communities.[22]

Why did the police give the government the support they needed to justify a licensing regime on music? Chris Fox's letter was quoted time and again to defend the measure yet other senior police officers did not recognize the world he was describing. Feargal Sharkey said:

I did discuss that particular letter and that particular issue at length with ACPO and . . . they did eventually retract it in that they eventually acknowledged that they had no evidence on which to substantiate the allegation that people who attend live music concerts behave in a way that is 'criminal'. Music should not automatically be treated as a disruptive activity, which will inevitably lead to nuisance and disorder.[23]

The Commons committee called on the government to exempt all venues with 200 people or less from needing a licence. It also said the two-in-a-bar rule – where it is legal for any venue to have two musicians playing as long as it wasn't amplified – should be reinstated.

WILL ANYONE DRINK A TOAST TO THE LICENSING ACT?

Surely someone must think the new law was an improvement on what went before, which was, after all, presumably the only point for introducing it? Or was it deliberately intended to cause the problems that it did?

How about local councils, who became the licensing authorities, taking over from magistrates who did the job perfectly well for centuries? They were pleased, weren't they? Actually, no; and the new regime has cost them £100 million or more to implement, passed on to the council taxpayer, of course. In a submission to the Commons select committee inquiry into the way the Act was introduced, the Local Government Association said: 'The legislation restricts councils to such a degree that the transition period has been more bureaucratic, more painful and certainly much more costly than it needed to be.' The new system, which is meant to be self-financing, has proved hugely expensive. Councils have received, or expect to receive, some £53 million in fees against an outlay of £130 million, causing significant deficits for many. Westminster Council, which probably has more licensed premises than any in the country, said: 'We were given an impossible job to do . . . It was not properly planned. Regulations governing the application process were published far too late, were unnecessarily prescriptive, too complicated for licensees and badly thought out. Guidance . . . was confused, contradictory and unhelpful.' And here is a familiar refrain: 'Obvious measures to simplify the process were resisted by government. Licensing authorities were not sufficiently involved in decision-making, or their views were ignored.'[24]

It took a long while for this madness to get reported much beyond specialist music magazines, though I wrote several of my columns in the *Daily Telegraph* on this subject dating back to 2004. In 2009, the sheer insanity of it all was summed up well in an article by Terence Blacker in the *Independent* newspaper:

Six years ago, the Blair Government decided, for reasons which were and remain mysterious, that live music – that is, any music, acoustic or amplified, played by one musician or more in a public place – causes a threat to public order. It passed the Licensing Act, which required pubs or clubs to fill out a complicated form and pay for a permit from the local council.

There would be no exceptions. A person playing a ukulele accompanied by someone else on a triangle would be breaking the law if the act appeared in a pub without the required licence. There was no control, on the other hand, over noise blaring from a large TV screen or from recorded music.

Blacker went on in a similarly baffled vein:

> Could someone in government, in the ministry, in the police, explain the thinking behind this idiocy? Surely even the most blinkered, legislation-addicted minister can see that it is not music which causes trouble when people are gathered together, but alcohol. It is asinine to blame musicians for what is a general social problem.
>
> Is the reason why politicians fear the kind of music which is not controlled by sponsors or huge marketing interests that it represents freedom? A government which likes to boast of the country's 'creative industries' is one which deals with life as if it were part of a big business. Everything must be licensed, controlled.[25]

Well, at least the pubs must be happy. They were getting longer opening hours, so what did they have to complain about? Quite a lot, actually. The British Beer and Pub Association, representing some 60,000 outlets, told another Commons committee investigating the implementation of the Act in 2005:

> The form is complicated and the process is complicated. Applications had to be delivered separately to eight different 'responsible authorities', five of which are housed within the council itself. The association estimates that the cost of obtaining a licence during the six-month transitional phase

that began in February has been £1,830 per pub – £95
million across the sector – with a further £33 million to be
spent on hearings and appeals.[26]

There was also a disproportionate impact on the ordinary
citizen, whether they are a small trader or a single musician or
a charity volunteer or a community hall manager – all of whom
either operate on small profit margins or give their time free, and
yet were expected to grapple with an intolerably complicated
process. The Federation of Small Businesses, whose members
represent one-fifth of the total number required to obtain new
licences, said filling in the 21-page application form was only
part of the problem:

> In addition to the length of the forms and the difficulties
> that small businesses have had completing them, is the
> issue of floor plans, sound-proofing and other measures
> that some businesses have been required to introduce if
> they wished to vary their licences . . . The costs for small
> businesses requiring a licence to sell alcohol has increased
> sharply and architects' plans and the cost of sound-proofing
> premises further compound this. One member stated that
> the whole process would cost him 'in excess of £4,000'.
> This is a clear demonstration of a system that has not been
> properly thought through and has not taken account of
> small business needs.[27]

One online wine merchant, working from home, who does
not sell directly to the public or store any significant amount of
alcohol at his house, said:

> I have to perform seemingly absurd actions, such as
> submitting a scale plan of my house. Why? I'm not changing
> anything, merely working from my bedroom. I will have to
> pay a surveyor to do this. Why do I have to post a 'pale

blue' notice outside my house, telling people what I'm doing? This will only attract the attention of undesirables, who will think I have lots of whisky in my house.[28]

Even hairdressers became entangled in the Act. Norwich City Council wrote to all salons in the city ordering them to get a licence if they want to serve complimentary alcoholic drinks at Christmas or face a maximum of six months in jail, a maximum fine of £20,000, or both. Jason Taylor, owner and director of Kinki which has two branches in the city, said: 'If we were having parties and getting everyone drunk then I could understand but it is a token tipple, a stubby bottle of three per cent beer or a small glass of wine.'[29]

Sports clubs have also been adversely affected. Their inclusion in the regime is especially bizarre given the objectives of preventing disorder public nuisance and protecting children from harm since sports clubs do not contribute to any of those. The only justification for imposing new regulations on any sector is either to make their lives easier or protect others who are being placed at risk by their activities, yet this simply does not apply where sports clubs are concerned. As Kevin Smyth, secretary to the Committee of Registered Club Associations, said: 'You cannot argue with the basic idea of why it was wanted but the actual benefit as far as clubs go has been minute and the costs have been horrendous.'[30]

Small clubs, once they have obtained their ten-year licence still have to pay an annual fee of £295 a year. What for? The only possible ongoing cost is that of the bureaucracy itself.

Not for the first time, those most adversely affected by new regulation are required to pay for it. They also have to place advertisements in newspapers as well to inform the public of events, which is expensive. The government has recently proposed even more onerous requirements on clubs under its 'Safe, Sensible, Social' consultation from the Department of Health. It proposed mandatory training for staff, 'sensible drinking messages' in entrances to bars and all premises, and information at each point of sale saying that it is illegal to sell alcohol or buy alcohol for those under the age of 18.

There are many more examples of such absurdities but the government still avers that it got the law right and teething problems are to be expected with such a major reform.

When, after an exhaustive and well-informed inquiry, the select committee reported in 2009, there was a widespread welcome for its conclusions, both on the need to reduce the bureaucracy and to give live music a break. These were matters that could have been addressed many years ago but never were.

The committee's main findings were these:

- That although the Licensing Act has simplified and improved the licensing process there is still concern that the system is too bureaucratic, complicated and time-consuming, especially where a premises is run by volunteers. We conclude that the Government should, together with local authorities, licence applicants and other stakeholders, evaluate the licensing forms with the aim of making them more user friendly.

- We are concerned that sporting and not-for-profit clubs should face the same licensing costs as the commercial sector. We believe that it is highly unsatisfactory that such clubs, with modest turnover and laudable aims, should be treated in exactly the same way as commercial operations. This is particularly the case with sporting clubs, which play an important role in ensuring community access to affordable opportunities to participate in physical activity. We conclude that in the case of not-for-profit clubs only the bar area should be taken into account when assessing the rateable value of the premises for the purpose of determining the appropriate licensing fee. In the case of sports clubs we recommend that they should be placed in a fee band based on 20% of their rateable value.

- We conclude that the time is right for a modest increase in the number of TENs which can be applied for to 15 and a relaxation of the rule on the number which can be applied for by any individual. We recommend that the Government should consider implementing a reduction in the cost of applying for a TEN in order to lessen the burden on voluntary, community and not-for-profit groups.

- To encourage the performance of live music we recommend that the Government should exempt venues with a capacity of 200 persons or fewer from the need to obtain a licence for the performance of live music. We further recommend the reintroduction of the two-in-a-bar exemption, enabling venues of any size to put on a performance of non-amplified music by one or two musicians.

- We note the huge difficulty and expense experienced by circuses in complying with the new regime. We conclude that it is right for circuses to be subject to the Licensing Act but that they should be issued with a portable licence by their home authority. We further recommend that the Government should consult on exempting certain low risk, small-scale travelling entertainments such as Punch and Judy, and activities which add to communities' cultural life, such as travelling plays by mummers.[31]

And what did the government do with these recommendations? It rejected them. True it did accept many other, mainly administrative, suggestions. It did change the law to give some relief to village-hall volunteers who did not want to be solely responsible for alcohol licensing; but that happened too late for many of them. On the proposal that there should be more

TENs, the Government said: 'We have considered increasing the number of notices per year to 15 following the Independent Fees Review Panel's recommendations. However we believe that the current limits are a good balance between maintaining necessary public protection and keeping the temporary event notice system as a light touch regime.[32]

OK, but how about cutting the cost of applying for them? The government said it had already made changes to 'lessen the burden for committees running community premises, encouraging more to apply for a licence to supply alcohol'. It added:

> We estimate that the overall potential savings under this proposal could be around £200,000 per year. It is not a huge sum of money, but it is the removal of red tape that will make a difference to volunteers on hard working village hall committees. It will also make it easier for such groups to obtain a premises licence to supply alcohol, removing the need for them to rely on temporary event notices. The Government believes that this is a more effective method.[33]

And the government, of course, knows best.

But what about the musicians who wanted a bit of sanity to prevail? The government rejected the committee's call to exempt venues with a capacity of 200 persons or fewer from the need to obtain a licence for the performance of live music; and it also refused to reinstate the two-in-a-bar rule. However, they did promise another review. As Feargal Sharkey said:

> After six years of legislation, eight consultations, two government research projects, two national review processes and a Parliamentary Select Committee report, all of which have highlighted the harmful impact these regulations are having on the British music industry, Government's only reaction is yet another review. At a time when the British music industry is facing significant recessionary pressure

and Government's own research indicates a 5% decrease in the number of venues available to aspiring young musicians and performers, we had hoped, wrongly, that this Government would endeavour to provide the most supportive framework possible for our industry.[34]

Reading the government's response you would not have thought there had been any problems at all with the Licensing Act 2003. Yet it has managed to infuriate, inconvenience and impose extra costs on almost all of those who have been affected by it. The new licensing regime was supposed to rationalize a system that had become cumbersome, boost live music, be a fillip to pubs at a time when many were facing closure by extending opening hours and afford councils and the police greater opportunity to shut down rowdy premises. Arguably, it failed on every count. It was, and remains, a bad law.

CHAPTER 6

IT'S A FREE COUNTRY, INNIT?

There has been no period in recent peacetime history when so many laws have been passed in the UK to curtail so many freedoms. Some commentators on the Left have defended the use by Labour of powers that they would have denounced had they been wielded by the Right. Their argument appears to be that even if they look like the sort of powers that should not normally be available to democratic governments, these are difficult times (terrorism) and they are in the hands of decent social democrats (New Labour) so it does not matter. This is a dangerous doctrine. To begin with, if the powers are themselves wrong then the political stripe of those who use them should not matter. To remove or restrict the right of free speech is not a benign move in the hands of progressive thinkers and a malign one in the hands of conservatives. Yet this view is offered by the progressive Left as a justification for some of the illiberal policies of the Labour government. The second problem, of course, is that decent social democrats, liberals or conservatives are not always going to be in office in Britain even if, by and large, they have been for the past two centuries. Relatively recent European history has demonstrated how democratic procedures can be hijacked to dictatorial ends.

The changes we have seen since 1997 have been considerable whatever Labour's cheerleaders on the Left would have us believe. Each individual incremental reform on its own might have a rationale; but taken together they amount to a greater diminution of freedoms, checks and balances in 13 years than had been seen in the previous 100. Many of these changes were carried through in the name of fighting terrorism or curbing organized crime and so anyone who questioned their purpose was deemed in favour of terrorism or serious crime. Consider what we have seen since 1997. Jury trials have been abolished where there is a risk of intimidation or in complex serious fraud cases; the ancient rule of double jeopardy has been dispensed with; legislation has been passed for ID cards backed by a national identity database; there has been a huge extension in CCTV camera coverage; the Regulation of Investigatory Powers Act (RIPA) or 'snooper's charter' allows a wide range of government bodies and quangos to watch over people, check on what they are doing and monitor their communications by collecting personal details about the use of phones and emails; an assets-recovery agency has been established to allow the civil courts to take away the wealth of people suspected of making their money from crime, even if they have not been convicted of anything; a new law has made incitement to religious hatred a criminal offence; the European arrest warrant allows for fast-track extradition for such non-existent crimes as 'xenophobia' to jurisdictions with no habeas corpus protection; so-called Henry VIII provisions were included in the Anti-terrorism, Crime and Security Act to let the home secretary amend any provision without further recourse to parliament; and various attempts have been made to lock away people with psychopathic personality disorders who may attack someone, but have not done so as far as we know.

Then there is the aforementioned Civil Contingencies Act, the sort of measure that used to be triggered only in wartime, which vests in the home secretary extraordinary powers for use in an emergency as determined by the government of the day. This could involve the requisition, confiscation or destruction of property without compensation and restrictions on the free movement of people, without the prior approval of parliament.

Any single measure on this impressive list may well be justified either to 'tilt the criminal justice system back towards the victim' or 'to further the war on terrorism'. However, taken collectively, they amount to the most sustained attack in recent memory on liberties and legal certainties (such as the presumption of innocence) that were once taken for granted and which were fundamental to the concept of a 'free country'.

AN ENGLISHMAN'S HOME

. . . is his castle, isn't it? Apparently not. The powers of bailiffs to enter homes and seize property are wider today than they have ever been, which is just as well given the large numbers of house repossessions and council-tax defaulters. Bailiffs prey upon the misery of others, but someone has to do it. However, former protections for homeowners have been taken away. Even the most rapacious Dickensian bailiff did not have the power of his modern counterpart: Neckett in *Bleak House* had to be invited in to serve his warrant for debt on Skimpole. This is because, for centuries, bailiffs were unable forcibly to enter a home under a common law right of citizens established in around 1300 and reaffirmed on many occasions by the courts, as in the judgment of the Peter Semayne case in 1604 from which the 'Englishman's castle' concept derives, and by successive governments throughout history.[1]

In 1760, William Pitt (the Elder) made a famous declaration of this right. 'The poorest man may in his cottage bid defiance to all the force of the Crown. It may be frail, its roof may shake, the wind may blow through it. The rain may enter. The storms may enter. But the king of England may not enter. All his forces dare not cross the threshold of the ruined tenement.'[2] This right to refuse forced entry held for centuries until the current Labour government, with its puritanical pretensions but cavalier disregard for personal privacy, came along.

In 2004, it introduced the Domestic Violence, Crime and Victims Bill, which contained a power to force entry in connection with unpaid fines imposed for criminal offences. This was such a significant departure from the common law that it merited a wide debate; yet it was included in a measure that, on the face of it, had nothing to do with bailiffs. The government maintains that it was fully considered by parliament, but it depends what you mean by fully. The Bill was already in its final day in committee when ministers tabled 'urgent' new proposals to show they were 'getting tough' with fine dodgers. The minister, Chris Leslie, explained: 'These amendments give enforcement officers the power to enter premises to execute a warrant of arrest, commitment, detention or distress where the officer has a reasonable suspicion that the offender who is a subject of warrant is present.'[3]

The MPs on the committee seemed to have little idea that they were being asked to set aside an ancient liberty and Mr Leslie certainly did not spell it out. Dominic Grieve, the Tory spokesman and now shadow justice secretary, smelled a rat but did not want to sound soft on fine dodgers.

> We are about to give considerable powers to non-uniformed individuals ... We are allowing them to enter private premises, which will not necessarily be the premises of the person whom they are seeking, to carry out searches ... I am a little surprised that we are apparently introducing such potentially draconian legislation without paying real regard to the consequences on the ground on a day-to-day basis.[4]

Despite these doubts the Bill went through. Her Majesty's Courts Service issued helpful guidance to bailiffs about how their powers should be used: 'If a person locks himself in their home, it might be reasonable to break open the door, but probably not to smash a hole in the wall.'[5]

In 2007, the government sought to extend these powers in the Tribunals, Courts and Enforcement Act 2007, allowing bailiffs to use physical force against householders to restrain or pin down them down. Jack Straw, the justice secretary, thought better of pursuing this proposal at a time when thousands of people were losing their homes. The headlines would not have looked good, after all. Even without the additional power to sit on a little old lady while her TV is being loaded on to the back of a lorry, the liberties of 'the poor man in his cottage' were simply tossed aside, with the barest of parliamentary scrutiny.

BUT AT LEAST WE STILL HAVE FREE SPEECH, DON'T WE?

Free speech, after all, is what Britain is renowned for. It is one reason why we have so many terrorists, since militants whose own countries did not want them ended up here, churning out their jihad literature and denouncing their home country's leadership. But how free are we to express ourselves? Arguably, since the *fatwa* was issued on Salman Rushdie over the publication *The Satanic Verses* in 1989 there are some things that we cannot say or write any longer: usually they are things about Islam.

In retrospect, *The Satanic Verses* affair was a turning point in the country's history of free speech, an event that appeared to demonstrate indomitability, yet turned out to be a defeat. An unambiguous stand was taken on Rushdie's behalf by the government of the day, which denounced the threat to his life and broke off diplomatic relations with Iran. Sir Geoffrey Howe, then foreign secretary, told the Commons: 'This action is taken in plain defence of the right within the law of freedom of speech and the right within the law of freedom of protest.'[6] Despite mass book-burnings, protests around the world, including in Bolton and Bradford, and threats of violence, the work continued to be published and sold. How could it be otherwise? This was Britain, after all, the citadel of free speech. We would not be browbeaten into denying the rights of one of our citizens, or anyone else for that matter, from having their say, however controversial or offensive their opinion might be.

Sadly, the past two decades have seen a pusillanimous flight into cowering capitulation. We seem to have forgotten what free speech entails, how hard it was fought for and how important it is to defend. It is the value with which this country is most associated throughout the world. It is why Britain has been home, over the centuries, to so many political dissidents who would have been persecuted elsewhere, and why those who live in autocracies that brook no criticism tune into the BBC World Service. They see this as a place able to accommodate opinions that are obviously crazy, offensive or even seditious, a country where a view can be held and expressed, provided – and this has always been true – that it does not foment violence.

Geert Wilders, the Dutch MP, was refused entry to Britain in February 2009 because of his anti-Islamist stance. It was his opinion that the Koran was inherently inflammatory as a text and he made a 17-minute film, *Fitna* (an Arabic word meaning test of faith) setting out this thesis. He wanted to show it to peers in the House of Lords but the Home Office would not let him enter the UK on the grounds that his presence would not be conducive to public safety. The film, therefore, must have been appallingly racist or obscenely violent. It was neither. It contained some unpleasant images of bomb explosions, of captured hostages facing death and of chanting mobs interlaced with passages from the Koran. Wilders, whose Party for Freedom would later win several Dutch Euro seats, claimed that these verses from the holy book of Islam are being used today to incite modern Muslims to behave violently and anti-democratically. You may think he is wrong to say this; you may agree with him; you might, like the Lords who invited him to Britain, think it is something worthy of discussion, given the obvious problems caused around the world by radical Islamism and the violence perpetrated in the name of the religion. It is hard, in a free country, to understand why it is a view that must be suppressed.

What, then, possessed the Home Office to ban Wilders – an unprecedented action against a democratically elected politician from a European state, who is entitled to free movement within the EU? By any measure, it was an extraordinary decision; yet it was not even raised in parliament, the supposed guardian of our freedoms, though some MPs have commented on the ban, largely to support it. If Wilders was a terrorist preaching violence against particular groups, it could be understood on public order grounds. The order issued by Jacqui Smith, the home secretary, read:

> The Secretary of State is of the view that your presence in the UK would pose a genuine, present and sufficiently serious threat to one of the fundamental interests of society. The Secretary of State is satisfied that your statements about Muslims and their beliefs, as expressed in your film Fitna and elsewhere would threaten community harmony and therefore public security in the UK.[7]

Yet what possible threat to public security is posed by a Dutch MP showing a film, in private, to a smattering of peers on a Thursday afternoon in February? Of itself, the film does not call for violence against Muslims; indeed, it suggests that Islam is a cause of violence, a view with which you are entitled to agree or feel strongly about, but not to prohibit. The reason for the ban appears to have been the possibility of protests by some Muslim organizations against Wilders' visit. In other words, his freedom to express a view and the liberty of peers to hear it in an institution supposedly devoted to free speech were set aside in the face of intimidation – the opposite of what happened in the Rushdie case, even if that author was forced into hiding.

Had a foreign parliamentarian who disliked Christians and

considered the Bible to be inflammatory planned a visit to Britain, does anyone imagine he would have been prevented from doing so? No, and neither should he have been. This must work for everyone. Free speech is about understanding that some people hold a different view from you, whether you like it or not. It is not about the denunciation of opinions expressed in private, as when Rowan Laxton, a Foreign Office diplomat, was reported to his superiors for railing at the Israeli invasion of Gaza from his exercise bike in the gym or Carol Thatcher was sacked from her BBC show for describing a French tennis player as looking like her childhood 'golliwog' as she chatted with colleagues and guests in the 'green room'. When we start to alert the authorities to 'thoughtcrimes' we really are one step away from the dystopian world that Orwell invented as a warning, not a prophecy.

People have always been free under the criminal law to speak their minds, provided they did not, in doing so, incite others to commit violence or infringe public order. Rabble-rousers trying to whip up the mob have never been the beneficiaries of this latitude: there is, in other words, a difference between licence and liberty. However, it is necessary to demonstrate that the words complained of are likely to stir up hatred and public disorder, not merely to complain that they are unpleasant or objectionable to some. Imams have been allowed to continue preaching in mosques when it could be argued that they have overstepped this mark, as when they have called for the death of homosexuals or Jews.

Wilders was no advertisement for free speech – after all, he wanted the Koran to be banned – but that is not the point. It is what this affair says about us, not him, that matters. Is Britain now adopting a position where people who support suicide bombers and jihad are able to make known their opinions without legal challenge, whereas those who oppose them cannot?

But what happened to Geert Wilders (who was eventually allowed into the UK) was not an isolated incident. Parliament, in its infinite wisdom, agreed to a clause in the Serious and Organised Crime Act which specifically forbade protest of any sort within a 1km radius of the Houses of Parliament without express permission from the Metropolitan Police. The first anyone heard of this ludicrous law was when a young woman Maya Evans was arrested near the Cenotaph where she was caught in the dastardly act of reciting the names of British troops killed in Iraq. A police officer decided that ringing a bell and reciting a list of names constituted a protest for which an arrest could be made because prior authority had not been sought. How could Parliament pass such a law, when it is so patently inimical to the freedom of speech that this country once considered fundamental? Why did MPs, who are meant to be the custodians of our values, let it happen? The government decided to use this legislation to create a security cordon around Westminster and framed the law in such a way that it would apply to individuals and not just gatherings of people.

This was done to gag Brian Haw, the man whose long-standing vigil in Parliament Square so irritated MPs. It soon transpired, however, that Mr Haw was the only person in the land immune from its impact, since the courts ruled it could not be made retrospective and, therefore, his protest continued, albeit scaled down. However, because of the way the clause was drafted, anyone else taking part in an unauthorized demonstration within 1km of the Palace of Westminster could be prosecuted, even if they were simply standing on their own, neither posing a threat nor inconveniencing anybody else.

The justification given for this extraordinary measure was to protect MPs from possible threats to their security and to ensure they are able to go, unhindered, about their daily business of passing increasingly outlandish legislation. Yet the area covered by these restrictions was so extensive that a nurse protesting against pay and conditions outside St Thomas' Hospital on the other bank of the Thames would be breaking the law unless authority had been obtained in advance from the police.

Although the general principle behind the new law was contained in the Serious and Organised Crime and Police Act, the actual order that put it into effect was passed using delegated powers by a special standing committee, which is stacked in the government's favour so that it can get its legislation through. When the committee debated the measure, serious concerns were voiced on all sides; but Paul Goggins, the Home Office minister, saw nothing wrong. He said: 'We value the importance of demonstrations. In a democracy, we have a right to be able to demonstrate our opinions and our views . . . I therefore make it absolutely plain that that is my belief and that is the view of the Government, and nothing in the order changes any of that.'

But it quite clearly did; and it is absurd that the police, not parliament, were left to define what is meant by a demonstration. The Act deliberately did not define what is meant by a demonstration – so a judgement of whether one was taking place was left entirely to a constable. Mr Goggins said constables would exercise their good sense and only those acts that a 'reasonable person' would regard as a demonstration would fall foul of the law. So, what definition could Mr Goggins offer? 'The whole point of a demonstration is to convey a point of view. Someone demonstrates their point of view; that is a demonstration. It can be an individual person who so arranges their demonstration that they make their point.'[8]

By this measure, any expression of an opinion close to the Houses of Parliament – including, presumably, even one that is laudatory of the government – is to be considered a demonstration and, therefore, an arrestable offence if prior authority has not been obtained from the police.

ALL RIGHT, THEN, WE WERE WRONG

Despite Mr Goggins' insistence that this law was reasonable, a view apparently accepted by the parliament which passed it, this measure attracted so much derision that Jack Straw, the justice secretary, eventually agreed that it should be repealed. The relevant clauses 132 to 138 of the Serious Organised Crime and Police Act 2005 are to be repealed by the Constitutional Reform and Governance Bill which was before MPs at the time of writing. As a result (and should the repeal take effect) it:

> will no longer be a requirement to give notice of demonstrations in the designated area and there will no longer be an offence for such demonstrations to be held without the authorisation of the Metropolitan Police Commissioner. There will no longer be an offence under the 2005 Act for a person to use a loudspeaker in the designated area; the use of loudspeakers will continue to be governed by section 62 of the Control of Pollution Act 1974 and section 8 of the Noise and Statutory Nuisance Act 1993. Repeal of sections 132 to 138 of the 2005 Act also means that there will no longer be a designated area around Parliament as set out in the Serious Organised Crime and Police Act 2005 (Designated Area) Order 2005 (S.I. 2005/1537). Additionally, repeal will restore the applicability of section 14 of the Public Order Act 1986 (imposition of conditions on public assemblies) to a public assembly in the vicinity of Parliament.[9]

So why do it the first place?

SMILE: YOU ARE ON CCTV (UNLESS YOU ARE A CRIMINAL)

The most gratuitous invasion of privacy is to be filmed whatever you are doing. A London council even placed cameras in baked bean cans to spy on householders leaving their rubbish out on the wrong day. But if you are to be the most snooped upon nation this side of Pyongyang, it is important that the surveillance works. Since it is our contention that a bad law is one that patently fails to deliver what it says on the front of the Act, then the various bits of legislation setting up a forest of CCTV cameras in Britain ranks among the worst.

One of the most common statements made when anyone questions the amount of surveillance in this country is that if it stops crime it is worth it. The problem is that it doesn't. We have more CCTV cameras than anywhere else in the world yet we also have one of the highest crime rates. More than that, there is no evidence that CCTV is especially effective either in preventing crime or, in many cases, of leading to the apprehension of a criminal. Consider some of the iconic CCTV images of recent times. There are the pictures of Jill Dando on her way to her London home on the day she died, shopping and walking. It did not stop her being killed nor did it identify her killer. CCTV proved to be nothing more than a video diary of her impending doom. The children leading Jamie Bulger away were not easily identified by the CCTV, either. Nor did the cameras stop the four July 7 suicide bombers caught on CCTV entering Luton station on their way to London to kill 52 people on the transport network. On the other hand, David Copeland, the Brixton nail bomber, was captured largely as a result of CCTV. There is a voyeuristic quality to many of these images but whether they are worth the money, the upkeep (though this is often overlooked) or the political capital invested in them is another matter.

We have more CCTV cameras in Britain than anywhere else in the world. Indeed, we have more than the rest of Europe combined. In the course of a typical day, the average city-dweller can expect to be filmed at least 8 times. Foreign visitors can be seen in London gawping with astonishment at the number of cameras.

We are told that this is necessary to keep us safe and secure, but CCTV cameras they do not fulfil even that basic function. Don't take my word for it. Detective Chief Inspector Mick

Neville of New Scotland Yard says so. He was in charge of the Metropolitan Police's Visual Images, Identifications and Detections Office (Viido) when he called the huge investment in closed-circuit TV technology an 'utter fiasco' that had failed to cut UK crime. Only 3 per cent of London's street robberies are being solved using security cameras. He said 'no thought' had gone into how to use them: 'Billions of pounds has been spent on kit, but no thought has gone into how the police are going to use the images and how they will be used in court. It's been an utter fiasco. There's no fear of CCTV. Why don't people fear it? [They think] the cameras are not working.'[10]

It is often said that there are 4.2 million CCTV cameras in Britain, one for every 14 people. The figure, regularly bandied about, was an extrapolation based on research of CCTV density in a few streets in Putney, south London. It was contained in a working paper published in 2002, by academics Michael McCahill and Clive Norris. The researchers sampled 211 'premises' – banks, estate agents, pubs, shops and office blocks – and found that 41 per cent had CCTV systems, with an average of 4.1 cameras per system. By assuming this was 'broadly representative' of CCTV coverage across the whole of London, the authors estimate that 41 per cent, or 102,910, of the 251,000 VAT-registered businesses registered in London would have a CCTV system. Multiply this by 4.1 and there would be 421,931 cameras.

They then added the cameras operating in other public institutions – such as open-street systems, transport, hospitals, schools etc. – and reckoned that it is 'not unreasonable to "guesstimate" that Londoners are monitored by at least 500,000 CCTV cameras'. The report then estimates that, as London has 7.2 million residents and the UK has a population of around 60 million, the country has at least 4,285,000 cameras, approximately one for every 14 people.

It is impossible to say how reliable this figure is. If it were true at the time, there must be many more now; if it was too high then it may well be true now. There are few other official or unofficial estimates though in 2008, Peter Fry, director of the CCTV User Group, reckoned there were around 1 million, and probably no more than 1.25 million, 'public' cameras. However, he cautioned that, although based on his pretty extensive databases, this isn't 'much more than a guesstimate'.[11]

Fry's figure included official systems such as those run by the police or local authorities, plus 'quasi-public' systems such as those in hospitals, universities, shopping malls, supermarkets, airports, buses and amusement arcades. However, it does not include a private camera in, say, a tiny shop.

It is clear to anyone who travels abroad that the UK has far and away more cameras than any other country, whether democratic or despotic. For a country that prides itself on defending individual privacy and freedom this is odd to say the least. It is only justifiable as part of a trade-off for better security. Yet if DCI Neville is to be believed, there is none, though he is not against CCTV in principle, only when it does not work: 'The CCTV network in the UK has been built up in a piecemeal way, driven by local authorities and the private sector more than by the police. Better training and more intelligent use of the technology are important to the future development of how we use CCTV.'[12]

Ken Pease, from the Jill Dando Institute of Crime Science, at University College London, said looking through hours of footage could be 'tedious' for officers. 'If you look at the data, and I have done some of the research myself, they do have an effect. The thing is the effect wears off, and it wears off for the reasons that are pretty clear – which is the non-use of the very tedious job of sifting through footage for less than very serious crimes.'[13]

You might be forgiven for thinking that the lesson to be drawn from this fiasco would be to remove CCTV and concentrate on more effective crime deterrence measures, like more police officers on the street. The problem with being a nation more snooped upon than North Korea is that people actually think the cameras make a difference and believe they are safer than they are. Yet the cameras are not really a deterrent at all. Their main function is to catch people after a crime has been committed and they are pretty useless at that, though sometimes in high profile cases they do succeed.

Instead of accepting that the camera may not be the best form of crime control, more money has been invested in digitizing CCTV. It is not clear how much has been spent on CCTV down the years but it runs into hundreds of millions pounds. Some of this cost must be offset against the savings made by the police not patrolling because they think the cameras are doing the job for them, though whether that really is a saving is another matter.

New laws have been introduced to require camera operators to ensure that their equipment produces images good enough for police investigations. This is a case of the emperor's new clothes. Nobody has the nerve simply to say that most cameras do not serve the purpose for which they were intended and if they do say it they are pretty soon slapped down.

According to the Home Office Policing and Reducing Crime Unit, CCTV systems seem to reduce and deter property crime in public areas, such as car parks or shopping malls, but are not effective at stopping or preventing violent crimes: 'Overall, the best current evidence suggests that CCTV reduces crime to a small degree. CCTV is most effective in reducing vehicle crime in car parks, but it had little or no effect on crime in public transport and city centre settings.'[14]

Although the CCTV systems do help at deploying police officers quickly to violent crimes sites, the offenders may avoid the security cameras, since they are mounted in public zones. A Home Office study suggested that better street-lighting may be more effective at preventing crime than CCTV (you may be surprised to learn that this has been the conclusion of several Home Office studies dating back to 1991):

There are two main theories of why improved street lighting may cause a reduction in crime. The first suggests that improved lighting leads to increased surveillance of potential offenders (both by improving visibility and by increasing the number of people on the street) and hence to increased deterrence of potential offenders. The second suggests that improved lighting signals community investment in the area and that the area is improving, leading to increased community pride, community cohesiveness, and informal social control.[15]

The crime charity Nacro also questioned whether the Home Office should have spent such a disproportionate amount of its crime prevention budget on CCTV rather than other measures. It said good street lighting was up to four times more effective at deterring offenders yet three-quarters of Home Office money allocated to crime prevention – more than £200 million by 2002 – went on CCTV. Nacro questioned the need for so many cameras as a crime-prevention tool when there was little evidence that they worked:

> While CCTV schemes in car parks can be effective in reducing car crime, cameras in town centres have little impact on serious or violent crime. Without the constant oxygen of publicity CCTV schemes can quickly lose their effectiveness. Ironically, evidence shows that the biggest falls in crime linked to CCTV installation occur before cameras are operational, coinciding with the period when publicity is at its greatest.[16]

Nacro's study used the Home Office's own evaluation of 24 CCTV schemes in town centres, housing estates, public transport and car parks. In 4 the crime rate had actually gone up significantly; in 13 there had been a significant reduction in crime; while in 7 CCTV had no effect. The studies showed that while cameras made people feel safer and helped in the capture of criminals, their deterrent effect waned.

Critics of CCTV fear that they have been installed at the expense of more police on the beat. Rachel Armitage, of Nacro's crime and social policy unit, said: 'Areas need to be appropriately policed, not remotely policed. Given the choice between walking down a dark alley monitored by CCTV or having that alley adequately lit, which would you prefer?[17]

However, Lord Falconer, Home Office minister, maintained that cameras had a 'significant' impact on crime levels where they were properly used and maintained: 'People really like to have CCTV cameras because police and the people who live in the areas believe it brings greater security. What the research indicates is that in every area there is a statistical reduction in crime. More research needs to be done to see how more effectively it can be used.' He added: 'In terms of providing people both with security and a sense of security, this is a good investment.'[18]

Mark Littlewood, of the civil rights campaign group Liberty, said:

> It is time for a reassessment of the worth of CCTV in terms of its cost, both financial and in terms of privacy. The report confirms that the effectiveness of CCTV as a tool to fight crime is greatly overstated. Each day we are tracked by cameras and there are inadequate laws to ensure that the footage is not misused and inadequate enforcement of those laws.[19]

That was back in 2002. What has happened since to change anything? The Home Office can always come up with another study that reverses the findings of the earlier one, like this:

> On a positive note, CCTV systems do reduce the public's fear of crime and they do ensure the quick deployment of officers to the incident scene which gives less time for

the offenders to act more violently. To verify if CCTV is effective, the law enforcement body needs to conduct video surveillance evaluations over a long period of time to weed out any inconsistencies in the crime data. Also, if the CCTV operators are well-trained and know the fastest way to deploy the police officers, then the CCTV system will be more effective. CCTV systems are the future for preventing crime, and as the CCTV security cameras become more sophisticated, more offenders will be caught and more crimes will be prevented.[20]

CCTV in Britain has been around since 1956 when the police in London started to use cameras in order to catch drivers running red traffic lights. By 1969, 14 police forces around the country were using CCTV, but there were still only 67 cameras in total. Even as late as 1991, still only 10 cities had open-street CCTV systems. Now, the average Londoner going about their business may be monitored by 300 CCTV cameras a day. Roughly 1,800 cameras watch over London's railway stations and another 6,000 permanently peer at commuters on the Underground and London buses. In other major city centres, including Manchester and Edinburgh, residents can expect to be sighted on between roughly 50 and 100 cameras a day.

We are, then, already a 'surveillance society' but for the time being we are fortunate that the full potential for its abuse is constrained by the pluralist democracy in which we live. However, we only have to look once again at George Orwell's 1984 to imagine the use to which such snooping could be put. In the novel, the state tells its people that the cameras are there for their benefit and to prevent crime, but the crime they are preventing is insurrection. Everyone is watched to ensure they conform. Winston Smith can never get away from the surveillance. At one point, he realizes how dangerous it is even to allow his thoughts to wander in public or when facing the telescreen. Facial expressions were watched closely and could have dire consequences. Giving a disbelieving look when a state policy or a military victory was announced was considered a 'facecrime'.

MIND HOW YOU WALK

OK, so we have not gone that far. But the point is that we could. In the wrong hands, technology that appears benign can be used to shackle. Within the lifetimes of millions alive today, there were totalitarian regimes that would have made the most appalling use of such opportunities. I have no doubt that our political masters believe the rapid expansion of CCTV cameras, for instance, is good for us. Indeed, that would be the view of most people, who seem happy with the cameras. It stands to reason that if you have a camera trained on a shopping centre, a car park, a hotel lobby or a bus stop, we must be safer.

Well, actually, as we have seen, it does not follow at all. But maybe it is the technology that is at fault. A review carried out by Home Office experts and police chiefs has found that too many images are hard to access. The new generation of CCTV is far more sophisticated than the analogue video cameras we have had in the past. They are smart digital technologies able to 'decide' if a crime is about to happen and focus in on suspicious activity, making it easier to go back over the images. These intelligent cameras can tell if someone is spraying graffiti on a wall because they have 'learnt' what normal behaviour should be within their field of vision. Similarly, a camera trained on a car park will be activated only if it detects someone going from car to car. An airport camera can be programmed to know what a departure hall should look like, with thousands of separate movements. A single suitcase left for any length of time would trigger an alarm.

This technology was developed for use in hotels to alert staff to a breakfast tray left outside a room. Soon, it will be coming to a street near you. Why not go the whole hog and have microphones attached to cameras or embedded in street-lights? The Dutch have pioneered a system that recognizes aggressive sounds, without actually eavesdropping on conversations (perish the thought), while Intelligence Pedestrian Surveillance analyses clusters and movements of pixels in CCTV footage in search of 'behavioural oddities'. Surely, though, the prize must go to automatic gait recognition. This identifies people by the way they walk and the government has asked Ministry of Defence scientists to develop it for widespread use. Cameras are programmed to pick up on a particular gait, thereby making it impossible for a suspect to escape by covering his face. Even Orwell did not come up with 'gaitcrime'.

REAR WINDOW

Why has this happened? Henry Porter, a doughty champion of liberty writing in the *Observer*, said:

> We are suffering a collective failure of nerve, which is relentlessly encouraged by the government. Though non-violent crime has declined and levels of violent crime are lower than three years ago, we have got ourselves into a panic. In this climate of fear, Britain is changing faster than most of us understand. What is compelling and worrying is the barely scrutinised extension of police power that is being allowed.[21]

The writer Brendan O'Neill suggests:

> Perhaps part of the reason the British seem to have welcomed surveillance, or at least have treated the rise and rise of CCTV with nonchalance, is that Britain was already becoming an intensely voyeuristic society. Not only are

we being watched, we also watch each other. On reality television, for example, we watch members of the public eating, sleeping and even having sex. Voyeurism is OK.[22]

Like Winston Smith, we have come to love Big Brother.

SURVEILLANCE BY NUMBERS

1: The UK's position in the global league table for ratio of CCTV cameras to people.

12: The number of people per CCTV camera in Britain.

20: The percentage of all the world's CCTV cameras that are in the UK.

300: The number of times a day the average Londoner is caught on CCTV.

0: The percentage improvement in police detection rates of violent offences with CCTV.

NOTHING TO HIDE? THEN BE VERY AFRAID

How did a country that has such a long tradition of cocking a snook at the powers-that-be end up with identity cards, or at least the legislation to bring them in? (We await to see if the Conservatives will be in a position to fulfil their promise to abolish them.)

Ever since ID papers were abolished in 1952, after being retained following the end of the Second World War, the Home Office has been trying to bring them back. We know that the arguments in favour of an ID card are phoney because we have had the debate before, only last time the justification was different. When Michael Howard proposed an ID scheme when he was at the Home Office in 1994, among the reasons advanced were that it would bear down on benefit fraud and could be used to help cut underage smoking, drinking and betting on the National Lottery. There was hardly a peep about international terrorism or illegal immigration because these were not the problems then that they are today. The specious nature of this debate was beautifully exposed in the Commons by Peter Lilley, the former minister who led the cabinet revolt that resulted in the abandonment of the last ID scheme: 'There is no policy that has been hawked, unsold, around Whitehall for longer than identity cards. It was always brought to us as a solution looking for problems.'[23]

How many newly installed home secretaries have had, buried in their in-tray, a fully worked-up proposal for a replacement? Most will have dropped it straight into the bin. A few will have mulled it over and thought, no. Mr Howard bought into it, though only halfway: his scheme would have been voluntary and was junked in any case.

Then along came David Blunkett and 9/11. This toxic combination of a populist home secretary and the worst terrorist atrocity of modern times was just what the Home Office had been looking for. Even before 11 September 2001, officials were pushing ID cards again, using concerns over asylum seekers and economic migration as an excuse. You can hear them saying: 'Minister, think of the political gains. The polls are 80 per cent in favour. It makes you look tough on crime, terrorism and illegal immigration, and is popular to boot.'

What they didn't say, of course, is that none of the arguments advanced in ID cards' favour holds any more water than it did on the previous occasions when they were not proceeded with. To begin with, there are civil liberties objections: many people (your author included) are opposed in principle to being forced to register as a numbered citizen on a national identity database. Labour averred that it won this argument, though on what evidence it bases that assertion is unclear. Leaving aside the civil liberties disagreements, the merits of this law, as with any other, must lie in the practicalities of the measure. If the ID card fails to do what the government said it would do, and costs a fortune as well, then it falls into the category of a bad law.

First, the cost. The Home Office originally estimated this to be around £3.1 billion, most of which would be spent in any case introducing biometric identifiers into passports. The government now expects the total cost to be around £5 billion, but this is the bill to the Home Office only. It does not take into account the hundreds of thousands of biometric readers that the public sector will need to check fingerprints online when it becomes necessary to prove your identity to gain access to public services. In 2004, a Home Office assessment said these could cost between £250 and £750 each. This will be much higher now. The £5 billion figure also does not take into account the cost of the upkeep of the register. The London School of Economics puts the total cost over ten years to be in the range of £10.6 billion to £19.2 billion.

To begin with, the greatest expense was to have been be incurred in setting up the database from scratch. Blunkett said a clean database was essential to ensure any mistakes in existing government-held information was not replicated. However, in order to cuts costs, the Home Office dropped this plan (which, do not forget, was a promise made to parliament when the ID Bill was going through) and instead decided to 'piggy back' on existing Whitehall databases. So the security from error that was to have been built into the system has gone before it is even off the ground.

Second, illegal immigration. The only people who will not have to register on the ID database are foreign nationals in the country for three months or less. How will we know whether they are overstaying if it is not mandatory to carry the card, something the Bill specifically rules out? The government is also reinstating embarkation controls at the ports to check whether someone who entered left when they were meant to, which is a far more sensible thing to do.

Third, social security fraud. Only a tiny proportion of fraud relies on false identity; most is to do with people claiming false eligibility for payments, for instance while working in the black economy.

Fourth, terrorism. The existence of ID cards in Spain did not stop the Madrid bombs in 2005. Determined terrorists, especially if they do not need to have an ID card when they are in the country and do not have to show one in any case, will not be prevented from carrying out their activities. The worst terrorist attack in the country was carried out by British citizens who made no attempt to hide their identity. Why would they as they were going to kill themselves in any case? How would ID cards stop such people? Of the 25 countries worst hit by terrorism over the past 20 years, 80 per cent had national ID cards; almost two-thirds of terrorists operated under their real identities.

And what about crime? The police will have no greater powers than now to demand that an individual identify himself and, since no one will have to carry and produce a card when asked to, this seems to be of limited usefulness. Any coherent argument for an ID card must rely on it being mandatory to carry one; but this is not what ministers proposed, because they know that a large number of law-abiding people will object strongly to being required to produce it. In other words, the civil liberties argument that they declared won is the main obstacle to making it effective. People are going to be pretty miffed in any case when they are fined £1,000 because they forgot to inform the 'authorities' when they moved home, the first time this has been a requirement on the citizen since 1066. Criminals on licence have to tell the police when they move; so do paedophiles on the Sex Offender Register. If you own a car, it is necessary to tell the DVLA when you move so your records can be kept up-to-date. However, it has never been a legal obligation to tell the state that you have moved for no reason other than that you have moved. But it has been since July 2009.

The Government has been careful not to make this a criminal penalty but a civil one, but it is a penalty all the same:

> The Civil Penalty regime establishes a mechanism to deliver a proportionate means of ensuring those who have successfully applied to be on the National Identity Register update any changes affecting the accuracy of their records and surrender their identity card when required to do so. A failure to comply with these requirements may lead to the issue of a civil penalty. A penalty will only be issued after a warning letter has been sent to the individual, and will initially be levied at £125, rising to a maximum of £1000, although the actual amount imposed may be lowered in light of extenuating circumstances. Compliance with the requirement at any stage in the proceedings will normally result in the penalty cancelled.[24]

And if you wondered how much information is to be contained on the ID register, that is also set out in the relevant SI as follows:

Information recorded on an ID card

2. (1) This regulation is subject to regulation 5.
   (2) The following information is prescribed for the purposes of section 6(3)(a) of the 2006 Act (issue etc. of ID cards) –
   (a) the title of the card;
   (b) the number of the card;
   (c) the holder's name;
   (d) the holder's gender;
   (e) the holder's nationality;

(f) the holder's date of birth;

(g) the holder's place of birth;

(h) the date of issue of the card;

(i) the expiry date of the card;

(j) the holder's signature, unless the holder is unable to provide a signature;

(k) the holder's facial image;

(l) subject to paragraphs (3) and (4), fingerprints of any two of the holder's fingers;

(m) information specified in regulation 3 and regulation 4(1) to the extent that such information is available or is applicable in relation to the holder;

(n) references to the United Kingdom being the issuing country and the Home Office being the issuing organization;

(o) a machine readable code;

(p) the symbol of the International Civil Aviation Organization denoting a machine readable document which contains a contactless chip;

(q) the digital signature;

(r) the document signing certificate;

(s) cryptographic key pairs;

(t) information contained in additional security features;

(u) an address in the United Kingdom to which an ID card can be returned, if found and;

(v) contact details that can be used to make general enquiries about ID cards

(3) If the holder is unable to provide two fingerprints, but is able to provide one fingerprint, paragraph (2) (l) is to be modified so as to refer to any one of the holder's fingers.

(4) If the holder is unable to provide any fingerprints, paragraph (2)(l) is to be modified so as to refer to the fact that no fingerprints have been provided.

Additional information that may be recorded on an ID card

3. The information specified for the purposes of regulation 2(2)(m) is –

   (a) any title of nobility held by the holder;

   (b) any other name specified by the holder as a name by which the holder is known except where there is insufficient space on the ID card or where the Secretary of State believes that the inclusion of such names is unnecessary or contrary to public policy;

   (c) that the holder is a member of the Privy Council;

   (d) any clarification required to show that a forename of the holder is not a title of nobility;

   (e) the inability of the holder to provide a signature;

   (f) in the case of a British Subject, within the meaning of Part 4 of the British Nationality Act 1981, the fact that the holder has the right of abode in the United Kingdom;

   (g) the fact that the holder is not entitled to benefit from European Community provisions relating to employment or establishment;

   (h) the fact that the holder is a family member of an EEA national with a right to reside under the Immigration (European Economic Area) Regulations 2006.[25]

The ID scheme was also intended at the outset to have a full set of biometric protections, though no technology is foolproof and always runs a high risk of false-positive and false-negative identifications. Again, the original promise when the legislation was going through parliament was for several biometrics: a digital photograph, iris prints and fingerprints. A report by the National Physical Laboratory said that, in order to avoid false matches in a population of 50 million people, a fingerprint system should use at least four fingers per person, preferably eight; an iris system should use both eyes; and facial recognition could not, on its own, provide a sufficient accuracy of identification.

Even then, 'the practicalities of deploying either iris or fingerprint recognition in such a scheme are far from straight-forward'. It added: 'Such a system would be a ground-breaking deployment for this kind of biometric application. Not only would it be one of the largest deployments to date, but aspects of its performance would be far more demanding than those of similarly sized systems.'[26]

The study pointed out that however sophisticated the system, there will be false matches and false non-matches, which increase the larger the database, and will mean that innocent people will face accusations of fraud. One person in 10,000 does not have an iris that can be used for identity purposes because of a range of inherited conditions; others have missing fingers or scarring that makes fingerprinting impossible. Many people are housebound, so would not be able to attend the enrolment.

The most secure biometric is the iris. A trial for iris recognition conducted among 60,000 returning refugees to Afghanistan showed a high rate, probably one in 100, of false non-matches where the system simply failed to pick up a person's record. We have 50 million people over 16. But, in any case, since the iris print is expensive to capture the government has opted instead to use fingerprints alone – again a decision taken after the legis-lation had already been through parliament. Fingerprints can be taken by a machine in the equivalent of a railway station photobooth or in Tescos.

But why does anyone think these will make the system secure? A report by Privacy International said that all biometrics have been successfully spoofed or attacked and the temptation to do so is greater if people are led to believe that the system is virtually foolproof when it is not.[27] The campaigning group Justice said: 'It is clear that current fingerprint technology is not only susceptible to attack but there are also numerous accuracy and long-term implementation issues that need to be thoroughly investigated before a large-scale fingerprint identification system could be successfully introduced.'[28]

Let's face it. It doesn't matter how well an ID card works when used by millions of honest people: it matters how the system might fail when used by someone intent on subverting the system. In the end, an identity register is not established for the benefit of the individual, but of the state.

AND ANOTHER THING: HOW THE STATE CAN TAKE YOUR HOUSE AND THE MONEY IN YOUR BANK ACCOUNT

Here are a few things you would never have imagined that a British government would do 20 years ago. Under the Housing Act 2004, local authorities have the power to take over an empty property; and under the Dormant Bank and Building Society Accounts Act 2008, it can take money that has been unused for up to 15 years and spend it 'in the community'.

When I was a student a few decades ago, above my bed I had a quotation from the nineteenth-century French anarchist, Pierre-Joseph Proudhon, who in answer to his own question 'What is property?', responded: 'Property is theft'. Labour ministers clearly still subscribe to this doctrine.

Local authorities now have the power to take over properties left vacant for six months or more if the owners, without good reason, refuse grant offers to repair and rent them. The intention is to tackle the under-supply of homes in both the owner-occupied and rented sectors. Councils would carry out repairs if required and the property would revert to the owner once the cost of any renovation had been recovered.

The procedure is called an Empty Dwellings Management Order (EDMO), to be attached only to private-sector residential property held under a freehold. The orders are not issued against commercial or public property, even though the state, especially the Ministry of Defence, owns thousands of houses and other buildings that are often left unoccupied for years on end. There are an estimated 700,000 empty homes in England, or around 3 per cent of the housing stock, about half of which have been vacant for more than six months. In London and the Southeast, where demand for social housing is greatest, there are about 70,000 dwellings that have been empty for six months or more. The government's principal targets are houses left unoccupied because they are dilapidated or abandoned.

No doubt some people manage their property in a way that Labour MPs or housing charities consider to be an unacceptably slipshod manner. But is that any of their business? What about houses that are left empty for investment purposes? These might be in a suitable condition for immediate occupation, but the owner is waiting for the market to improve before selling. Should they be requisitioned? Or what about a home left empty because the owner has gone to live with a partner but does not want to sell in case the relationship does not work out? Should that be subject to compulsory leasing? Or what about a property that has been bought as a retirement home well in advance of any move into it, to take advantage of market conditions? Why should the local council take over the management, however temporarily? Or what of the home left vacant for a few years while the owner works abroad but chooses not to let it out because they do not like the idea of anyone else living there?

As of February 2009, 17 interim orders had been approved by the Residential Property Tribunal Service since the legislation came into effect in April 2006. The government minister Iain Wright said:

> We are confident that the legislation is beginning to work well. We always intended that the legislation should be used only as a last resort where other measures have proved unsuccessful. We want to encourage voluntary re-occupation

of empty homes but this can only work well where there is realistic compulsion to back them up. EDMOs provide this compulsion and should therefore be a key component of a comprehensive empty property strategy.[29]

Did you ever imagine there would be a law like this? Or like this one? Somewhere, there is a bank account in my name that is not used anymore but which contains about £20. Somehow, I have also managed to find myself £11.49 in credit with a card company that continues to send statements every month to inform me of this fact, even though the account was cancelled several years ago. Of course, I should do something about this money – but if I don't, does that give the government the right to say what should happen to it? If everyone in the country had £31.49 sitting around doing nothing, multiplying that by 60 million produces a sizeable sum.

It is not the government's money to dispose of, even if it is given to charity, which is no bad thing. There is probably just as much cash sitting around in loose change on sideboards, in the pockets of little-worn jackets and down the backs of sofas in homes up and down the land, yet Gordon Brown is not telling us – or not yet anyway – to use it in a manner that he sees fit. As far as ownership of the cash is concerned, a bank is merely an extension of the back of the sofa, even if it is more tightly regulated (or at least we thought they were).

When he was chancellor, Brown had a bee in his bonnet about all this money, perhaps because he is so wanton with the taxes he took from us. He sought to cajole the banks and building societies into making greater efforts to reunite it with its rightful owners. The issue even featured in the Labour Party's 2005 election manifesto, which said:

There are many bank accounts that are lying dormant and unclaimed, often because people have forgotten about them or because the owner has died. We will work with the financial services industry to establish a common definition and a comprehensive record of unclaimed assets. We will then expect banks, over the course of the Parliament, to either reunite those assets with their owners or to channel them back into the community.[30]

No doubt there are many who welcome this raid on unclaimed assets because they think financial institutions have too much money anyway. But while the banks might have been wrong to use the cash to make their financial position look rosier than it would otherwise have been, it is not actually their money. It is ours; and it might have lain dormant over many years for a perfectly good reason. Initially, Brown wanted to force the release of money in accounts left dormant for more than three years, but was beaten back, presumably after being advised that such a move would amount to state larceny. There must be hundreds of thousands of accounts containing money put away by grandparents or other relatives for children to be handed over when they reach 18 or 21 and which are never touched again once the initial deposit has been made.

Brown revised his plans to seek the release of dormant funds after 15 years. Of course, there are some accounts that are dormant because the owners have died and they have been forgotten about. In such circumstances, every effort should be made to reunite the money with its rightful owners; but if this is not possible, then, after a period of years, it may well be right that it should go to charity, though parliament should spell out the legal basis for doing so. But if I choose, either through indolence or design, to leave my £31.49 untouched for 10, 15 or even 100 years, why is that any of Mr Brown's business?

There is something unsettling about this. If you do not use the cash you have left in a bank account, the government believes it should decide what happens to it. And if you have a house that you want to leave vacant for two or three years, it could be taken from you because the state says so.

CHAPTER 7

THE THEFT OF CHILDHOOD

Parents of children at a primary school have been banned from taking pictures of their own children at the annual sports day. Mrs Ethelston's Church of England Primary School, in Uplyme, Devon, prohibited photos and video filming, claiming it was due to changes in child protection and images legislation. Parents criticised the move and said they felt there was no legal reason why they cannot take photos for personal use.

Jane Souter, who has a son at the school and is chair of the Parents Teachers and Friends Association, said: 'It is a shame but that is the way it is all going now, you are not allowed to do a lot of things because of rules and regulations.

'A lot of the parents think it is a great shame. There are people who have been there for many, many years and they are upset about it, although they do not blame the school.

'It is sad that you are not allowed to take pictures of your own children. It is all to do with the pictures getting into the wrong hands and the school has to follow its own code of conduct.

'I am sure the school do not like it just as much as we do.'

Another parent, who did not want to be named, said: 'Parents want to record achievements through their child's life and not to be made to feel that they are all criminals and are going to upload dodgy photos to some porn site.'

They added that many parents were upset that they could no longer take photos and fear photography will be banned at every school event. They said: 'Speaking to many parents, they were extremely annoyed and exasperated and no one really knew why they couldn't take photos of their children as they done so in the past. Many seemed just resigned that it was a sign of the times.' They added: 'Please, please, clear this ridiculous nanny state affair up.'

Daily Telegraph, 18 June 2009

Has any group in society endured more legal tinkering than our children? The pressure organization, Action for Children, says successive British governments have made more than 400 major announcements relating to children and young people over the past 21 years, leading to 98 Acts of Parliament, 82 strategies and 77 initiatives, many of which are no longer working. Three-quarters of these policy changes and statements were made in the past decade under Labour.[1] The government department responsible for education within England has changed five times since 1987, with 11 different secretaries of state. It has been called the Department for Education, the Department for Education and Science, the Department for Education and Employment and the Department for Education and Skills. At the time of writing it is called the Department for Children, Schools and Families; I cannot guarantee that this remains its name.

Each year since 1987, Tory and Labour administrations have drawn up four separate Acts affecting children together with

40 Green and White papers. Fewer than half of the pilot projects set up over the past 21 years have been taken up across the country, the charity claims. A total of 51 funding streams affecting young people have been set up by the government since 1987 but Action for Children claims 69 per cent no longer exist and just one in five has been checked to see if it is working. Action for Children says that what children need most is stability; but this is being ignored for the short-term political gain that ministers and officials imagine accrues from making announcements ostensibly showing that they care about children.

Clare Tickell, chief executive of Action for Children, said:

> The last 21 years have seen a massive volume of policy. Not only that, the average life-span of each initiative is a little over two years. Many developments have been laudable and Action for Children has supported them. Yet few would suggest that an environment of such uncertainty is a healthy way of maintaining support for some of the most vulnerable and marginalised children and families in our society. A generation of children and young people has suffered from endless policy-making that reacts to headlines and short-term political pressures, ignoring their basic needs.[2]

The government, needless to say, will have none of this despite the overwhelming evidence that its constant interference is counter-productive. Beverley Hughes, who was the children's minister until June 2009 when she resigned from the government, said:

> Since 1997 this Government has made a real commitment to putting children, young people and families right at the heart of policy – for the long term. We are 100 per cent committed to improving children's wellbeing. This

Government has lifted more than 600,000 children out of poverty, built almost 3,000 children's centres and increased school funding by 87 per cent.[3]

For Labour, spending money on children and passing laws affecting them became an activity that justified the party's existence. Many of its ministers were the parents of young children, including Tony Blair for much of his premiership. Who could possibly question a frenzy of activity intended to improve the lot of our children? They are our future, after all. This self-evidently altruistic motivation meant the government felt able increasingly to intrude into areas that would once have been considered off limits to a state, or certainly a democratic one. The template for all policies in this area was a strategy approach called 'Every Child Matters' set out in a Green Paper in 2003. It was published alongside the formal response to a report from Lord Laming's inquiry into the death in 2000 of Victoria Climbié, an eight-year-old girl who was abused, tortured and killed by her great aunt and the man with whom she lived. Police, doctors and social workers had contact with Victoria as she suffered 128 injuries, but failed to discuss the case with one another.

For as long as anyone can remember, one of the wisest adages of public policy-making is that hard cases make bad law. Labour either forgot this or simply chose to ignore it. The death of Victoria Climbié was an appalling event, but it was to have an impact on the laws affecting children and their parents that was grotesquely disproportionate. A massive edifice of new regulation, law, surveillance, data-collection, target-setting and inspection was constructed upon this single tragedy and anyone who objected risked being denounced by the political establishment for their heartless indifference to the plight of vulnerable children. Just to ensure we got the point, many of the documents subsequently published to back up the new system carried a photograph of little Victoria.

OK. WE GET IT. EVERY CHILD MATTERS

The stated aim of the 2003 Green Paper was to:

*   Increase the focus on supporting families and carers – the most critical influence on children's lives.
*   Ensure necessary intervention takes place before children reach crisis point and protecting children from falling through the net.
*   Address the underlying problems identified in the report into the death of Victoria Climbié – weak accountability and poor integration.
*   Ensure that the people working with children are valued, rewarded and trained.

After a consultation exercise that predominantly involved people working within the children 'industry' talking to one another, the government published a White Paper *Every Child Matters: The Next Steps*, which formed the basis of the Children Act 2004. This established:

> a national framework for local change programmes to build services around the needs of children and young people so that we maximise opportunity and minimise risk ... The services that reach every child and young person have a crucial role to play in shifting the focus from dealing with the consequences of difficulties in children's lives to preventing things from going wrong in the first place. The transformation that we need can only be delivered through local leaders working together in strong partnership with local communities on a programme of change.[4]

From this, much has followed. The government wanted nothing less than what it called 'whole system change', something that was illustrated with an onion diagram (Figure 1) which should be pinned up everywhere and used for target practice.

Source: *Every Child Matters.*

Across the country, 150 local change programmes were instituted to drive priorities and secure 'more integrated front-line delivery, processes, strategy and governance'. A gigantic self-perpetuating and self-justifying bureaucracy has been constructed on these foundations that amounts to the gradual nationalization of childhood. At every level from birth to adulthood, the tentacles of the state are now felt in bringing up children in a way they never used to be. Details of every child in England until their 24th birthday are now to be carried on a computer database called ContactPoint. The information that can be held on ContactPoint is limited by law, as provided by section 12 of the Children Act 2004. The entries for each child consist of:

- Their name, address, gender and date of birth.
- A number identifying them.
- The name and contact details of any person with parental responsibility for them or who has care of them at any time.
- Details of any education being received by them (including the name and contact details of any educational institution attended by them).
- The name and contact details of any person providing primary medical services in relation to them.
- The name and contact details of any person providing to them services of such description as the Secretary of State may by regulations specify.
- Information as to the existence of any cause for concern in relation to them.
- Information of such other description, not including medical records or other personal records, as the Secretary of State may by regulations specify.[5]

The database should not hold case or assessment material or any subjective observations. It can include information of a 'sensitive' nature, defined as issues relating to sexual health, mental health and substance abuse although consent from the child or the child's guardians is needed, and it does not appear as such on the database. However, refusal of consent can be overridden if this can be justified on child protection grounds.

The scope of the database has alarmed civil liberties groups and was considered by the joint parliamentary committee on human rights.[6] Its concern was whether the government could make a case for what was a prima facie breach of Article 8 of the European Convention on Human Rights, the right to a private family life, as the database was to be universal rather than, as previously, a register focused only on children considered to be at risk.

The report stated:

> The Government argues that universal coverage is necessary in order to achieve the aim of ensuring the welfare of all children, and that the interference with children's Article 8 rights is proportionate because there are limits on the type of information recorded and control over access to that information. The question that must be addressed is whether such a general aim as improving the well-being and promoting the welfare of all children is capable of justifying such a serious interference with Article 8 rights. The death of Victoria Climbié, and the inadequacies of communication between state agencies exposed by the Laming inquiry, have generated a sense of outrage and a determination to prevent the same avoidable errors being repeated. Maintaining a child protection register, or even a register of children 'in need' and therefore in receipt of Children Act assistance from the local authority, is a much more targeted measure aimed at protecting vulnerable children. But a universal database seems to us to be rather more difficult to justify in Article 8 terms. Adults are also the beneficiaries of universal services such as health care and other services, such as community care, for which they may be eligible in certain circumstances. It appears to us that the strict logic of the Government's position is that it would be a justifiable interference with adults' Article 8 rights to maintain a similar universal database of all adults in the UK in order to ensure that those amongst them who are or may be entitled to receive certain services from the state actually receive them. We are concerned that, if the justification for information-sharing about children is that it is always proportionate where the purpose is to identify children who need child welfare services, there is no meaningful content left to a child's Article 8 right to privacy and confidentiality in their personal information.[7]

The committee was not only sceptical about the justification for the database; it also questioned the information it can hold:

> The Government accepts that no 'case information' should be recorded on the databases. We welcome the Government's amendment of the Bill to make clear that regulations cannot provide for medical records or other personal records to be included on the database ... However, the information which may be included on the database about a child goes beyond purely objective facts about a child, such as their name, address and date of birth. It includes information, such as contact details of persons providing services including health services, which may reveal very sensitive information about a child, such as the fact that a seventeen year old girl has been referred to family planning services. It also includes 'the existence of any cause for concern' about a child, which is an extremely subjective and open-ended phrase which is almost bound to include very sensitive information about a child.[8]

It has been suggested that other information recorded may include 'family routines', evidence of a 'disorganized/chaotic lifestyle', 'ways in which the family's income is used', signs of mental illness or alcohol misuse by relatives, and 'any serious difficulties in the parents' relationship'.[9] Concern has also been voiced about the security of the information on the database. Ministers have insisted it will be safe and have introduced legal controls over who can see it and how it should be shared. In that case, why was it necessary to introduce so-called 'shielding' arrangements to protect the children of celebrities and MPs from intrusion? Lord Adonis, education minister, told the House of Lords in September 2006: 'Between 300,000 and 400,000 users will access the index. Children who have a reason for not being traced, for example where there is a threat of domestic violence or where the child has a celebrity status, will be able to have their details concealed.'[10] Why, if the system is secure, is this necessary?

As Robert Whelan of Civitas said:

> The Government is showing it has no confidence in this database. There have been all these assurances it is secure, but how can we believe them now? This is just politicians protecting their own. And how is the Government going to define celebrity? It is a very fluid term — an assembly of high-profile clergy, disgraced politicians, topless models, pop singers and reality TV contestants.[11]

Professor Ross Anderson, an expert on database security, said: 'There will always be bent insiders. If you connect all these systems up and if you've got over a million professionals needing to access this every day it will all get out. Paedophiles for example can use the database to find out which children in their neighbourhood are vulnerable and where they live.'[12]

This, then, is the system on which all our children's details are to be entered. Because of what happened in one tragic case, which should have been prevented by the social workers, doctors and police (as in the Baby Peter case in 2007 in the same London borough of Haringey) all children are to be considered potentially 'at risk'. The government says safeguards exist to protect identities but is not sufficiently convinced that they work to allow their own children's details to be included. In addition, as is always the case with these laws, there are powers for the secretary of state to vary the circumstances whereby information can be gathered and what it can be.

THE NAPPY CURRICULUM

In the autumn of 2008, another element of the Children Act came into being: the Early Year Foundation Stage (EYFS). All 25,000 state and private nursery schools, child-minders and playgroups are required to follow a new statutory framework dubbed the 'nappy curriculum'. It involves assessing the progress of children from the age of 2 against 69 'early learning goals' designed to test different writing, problem-solving and numeracy skills. Most of us would, presumably, see nothing wrong with introducing children under 5 to numbers and letters. Quite the contrary: the more who can read before they go to primary school, the better. It is right, too, that people looking after very young children should monitor their progress, as good nurseries do already. But it is the way it is being done that is depressingly familiar: a centralized, Whitehall-driven, top-down, tick-box bureaucracy replete with instruction manuals big enough to act as doorstops.

Thousands of diligent and underpaid nursery teachers and child-minders are being made to jump through another set of hoops that will distract them from the job they are meant to be doing; it is already driving some out of the profession. This is yet another example of good intentions being hijacked by a centralizing fetish that has gripped governments ever since the big ideological issues that previously consumed their time were largely resolved and they looked around for other ways to involve themselves in our lives. Ministers identified a problem: some nurseries and child-minding 'settings', as they call them, are not very good. This means disparities of achievement because, inevitably, the middle classes not only get the better schooling but are more likely to give their children that extra bit of help at home. They get a head start, in other words. In order to try to bring the under-achieving nurseries up to the level of the best, the government has insisted that all – including those doing a perfectly good job – must conform to a rigorous and statutorily enforced regime.

When each child reaches 5, the nursery, child-minder or primary school is required to produce something called an EYFS profile to sum up their development and achievements. These must be recorded against 13 assessment scales, each containing 9 points – 117 criteria – made from observations and previous records. Where are teachers going to find the time for all of this? And will high-achieving nurseries, where these tasks are already carried out, be allowed to continue to do things their way, or will they have to fit into the Ofsted straitjacket? The National Union of Teachers said the 'nappy curriculum' would lead to a narrow focus on academic standards at the expense of giving young children more time to play and that the additional demands would mean that staff paid less attention to individual children. Steve Biddulph, the psychologist and parenting author, said it was 'like ripping open a rose bud to get it to bloom'.[13]

How can this be good for the children? When we were young, if we scrawled a letter or a number we received a gold star in a small assessment book. Now, there is a full report, made available to Ofsted. How long, even though the law currently precludes it, before the results are entered on the ContactPoint database, along with any other information considered of note?

Nurseries are being subjected to a compulsory curriculum for children who are actually under the age of compulsory education. For this reason, it is possible for parents, collectively, to opt out of some of these requirements, though this necessitates filling in a 34-page exemption form, which one campaign group said was 'expertly camouflaged, labyrinthine and bureaucratically complex, appearing to have been intentionally designed to deter anyone from applying'.[14]

Anyway, which nursery in receipt of funding and under the scrutiny of Ofsted would be brave enough to break free of the EYFS? A petition on the Downing Street website urged a rethink of this system because campaigners feared the EYFS curriculum 'may harm children's development, restrict parents' freedom of choice in child care and education, and place an unnecessary bureaucratic burden on those who care for young children'.[15] The fact is that, whatever ministers say, most of the changes in education seen in recent years have been largely ineffective in driving up standards, as opposed to grades. An

Ofsted report called *Early Years: Leading To Excellence Aug 2008* said standards in 40 per cent of nurseries were not good enough. So ministers have a point, but that is an argument to improve them, not circumscribe the rest. Ofsted found that many child-minders were ill-equipped for the new EYFS regime. Yet, at the same time, good teachers and child-minders were being driven away by the form-filling, the constant assessments, the targets, the need to 'observe' rather than teach – in other words, by the sheer madness of it all.

When I was young, few children went to nursery, mainly because most mothers stayed at home to look after us. The world has changed. Now, most children go to nursery or are left with child-minders. This has given the state a captive clientele of children under the age of five that it never had before. It does not, however, give it any more right to dictate how those children should be raised than it had a generation or two ago.

Perhaps this whole trend reached its apogee in June 2009 with a report that proposed giving local councils the power for the first time to enter family homes to inspect children being educated away from school. The ostensible reason for this was, with a reference once again to Victoria Climbié, to ensure home education was not being used as a cover for child abuse, even though Victoria went to school and was subject to social services scrutiny. A review of home education carried out by Graham Badman, former director of education at Kent County Council, recommended forcing all parents to register their children with local authorities every year. The recommendations were accepted in full by the government. This means that officials from local authorities would have the right to access a home with just two weeks' notice and speak to children to ensure they were 'safe and well'. They can then revoke the right to home-schooling if they have serious concerns over their welfare. Parents would also be required to submit a statement outlining what children will be taught over the following 12 months and councils can impose a 'school attendance order' if they believe the education received is not up to scratch, with parents facing legal action if they refuse.

The state would in effect be nationalizing home education even though there is no evidence that home-educated children do worse than those in schools. There is also no evidence that home-educated children are more likely to be abused, though it is self-evidently the case that if they are never seen outside the home it is more difficult to be sure. None the less, 99 per cent of abused children attend school. Parents tend to teach their children at home because they do not trust the standards of the state schools in their areas. The government estimates that as many as 80,000 children could be educated at home. Previous estimates put the figure between 20,000 and 50,000. Yet this government-knows-best approach is now so entrenched that those who question its veracity are regarded as virtually being on the side of child abusers. So much so, indeed, that anyone who wants to work with children in any capacity (and the elderly as well) must consider themselves potential assailants and submit themselves to a check through the Criminal Records Bureau.

ON THE RACK

Even if they have been vetted, people who work with children can be treated in the most appalling way. Take the case of Olive Rack. She lived for more than a year with the threat of seeing her business ruined – even of losing her liberty – because she diligently carried out her job as a nursery teacher. She was a teacher in Kettering, Northants, who in the summer of 2005 was accused of maltreating a child by two nursery advisers from the county council's Children and Young People's Service. They said the teacher had 'dragged' a two-year-old girl across the classroom before 'roughly' placing her in a chair and tapping her twice on the forehead with her finger.[16] One official said the child's 'feet virtually didn't touch the floor', something Mrs Rack denied. The circumstances were important: the toddler had just smashed a baby on the head with a toy brick and was having a tantrum. Mrs Rack, with almost 40 years' experience behind her, dealt with the matter firmly and professionally. Not even the girl's mother complained and continued, indeed, to send her children to the nursery, so confident was she in their safety.

Even though this was an everyday occurrence to which normal people would not have given a second thought, it may well be the case that one, or both, of the inspectors felt the treatment was a bit rough. They were entitled to have said so at the time, even though Mrs Rack had far more experience than they in dealing with such circumstances. One of the inspectors cuddled the girl in what can only have been a gratuitously deliberate attempt to undermine the teacher's position. In a sane world, that is where the matter would have rested. However, sanity went out the window long ago, along with commonsense, judgment and decency.

A month later, Mrs Rack was contacted by Ofsted, the inspectors who have blighted the lives of nursery-owners up and down the land with their nitpicking requirements and pointless form-filling. They told her that a complaint had been made, not by the girl's mother, but by the inspectors. Enter the next link in the chain, the police. Mrs Rack was arrested, her biometrics were taken to be stored on the national criminal DNA database and she questioned about the alleged 'assault'. You might have thought that, at this stage, a senior police officer would have stepped in and apologized to Mrs Rack for wasting her time. But, probably egged on by social services, the police put up prima facie evidence of a crime to the local branch of the Crown Prosecution Service (CPS). Here, surely, the chain would break and a sharp-eyed lawyer would inject the basic gumption that had been sorely missing so far. Let's face it, there are enough serious crimes that go unpunished because the CPS believes there is no case to answer or they do not consider there is a 50 per cent or greater chance of a conviction, the benchmark for launching a prosecution. Yet, in the case of Mrs Rack – where it is questionable that a crime had even been committed – they ploughed on and charged her with an offence that carried a six-month jail sentence. Why? In September 2006 Mrs Rack was cleared by magistrates who ruled that she had behaved perfectly reasonably and used appropriate force. What was driving all these elements – council jobsworths, social workers, police, prosecutors – to pursue a case that they must have known was threadbare at best?

To begin with, there is an animus in government, both local and national, against independent nurseries. They want them all to be state-controlled, as is clear from the way in which ministers are making their lives increasingly difficult by the continual interference that is driving them out of business in their thousands. But there is another reason. It is because Mrs Rack and the many others like her who have been dragged into court are easy prey. They do not go on the run, they aren't hard to find, they won't put up violent resistance or claim the protection of human rights laws. They will get angry and frustrated and bemused at the unfair treatment being meted out. But who cares about them? They are the law-abiding majority, the suckers who pay the salaries of the unholy army of public-sector nonentities who have nothing better to do than make the life of a decent woman a misery. Even Cherie Blair experienced this madness when she was questioned by the police for allegedly assaulting a boy who made a rabbit-ears gesture above her head as they posed for a photograph. If she had not been the Prime Minister's wife, who is to say she would not have ended up in the dock?

In Mrs Rack's case, the council defended its action by saying the inspectors 'had a duty to raise any concerns that may arise through their visits', even though the mother thought it had been blown out of all proportion. Leaving aside whether the incident even merited a report, it was not then incumbent on every other element in the criminal justice chain to hound her all the way to court. Each did so because it feared getting it in the neck from someone elsewhere in the chain if it didn't. Nobody had the courage to put a stop to the nonsense. If they were all following guidelines, then these should be changed. As Mrs Rack said, the prosecution seemed to imply that children could not be touched at all; in which case, how could a nursery worker change a nappy? Mrs Rack said, 'Since I opened in 1987 the red tape and regulations have grown. There are more and more rules, to the point where they are actually strangling the nurseries. It's certainly detrimental to the children, it's spread to their lives as well.[17]

Why was no one in Ofsted, or in the police or prosecutor's office held to account for the ordeal endured by Mrs Rack and others. Until someone is, there will be no end to this lunacy. As one writer and mother put it:

> What do you want from your child's nursery? A secure, affectionate environment run by people who know and like children, or a bureaucratic hell-hole where you are kept neatly updated with your toddler's educational progress, by a coterie of highly-qualified staff who keep the kids at arm's length and react to a high temperature or a display of bad behaviour by picking up the phone and telling you to come and get them? Childcare is under increasing pressure to change its priorities, so that box-ticking and back-covering count for more than confidence and commonsense. Vetted to within an inch of their lives, subjected to all manner of formal inspections, and expected to play the combined role of schoolteacher, social worker, child psychologist and hyper-efficient bureaucrat, those young women who used to be called 'nursery nurses', who worked with children just because they liked them and were good at the job, are burdened under a whole load of contradictory

expectations. Isn't it time someone put a stop to this nonsense?[18]

Indeed it is. But who?

ARE WE ALL SUSPECT CHILD MOLESTERS?

The inevitable corollary of a country that has lost commonsense about how to deal with children is to establish a bureaucracy to keep tabs on adults who might maltreat them. In the past, police records, testimonials and references sufficed to alert potential employers to a possibly dodgy would-be employee. However, a few years ago, the government decided this was not enough; so it set up the Criminal Records Bureau (CRB) under powers set out in Part V of the Police Act 1997 introduced by the last Conservative government to almost universal approval. Who, after all, could gainsay a system intended to provide our children with greater protection from those who would abuse them? Who could possibly dispute the need for a centrally run agency to sift through criminal records to ensure a paedophile does not end up running a Scout troop? Would you not want to be sure that the care-worker looking after your ageing granny does not have a record for assaulting old ladies? Of course you would; which is why few people questioned the need for the CRB in the first place.

Much of the criticism which followed the shambolic failure of the agency to give clearance to thousands of teachers and care-workers when it started work in 2002 has tended to focus on the workings of the system, not its *raison d'être*.

Since its formation, the Criminal Records Bureau has issued 15 million disclosures; but do we need the CRB at all and has it made our lives better? The answers to these questions are almost certainly no. Before the CRB, there was already a perfectly good system for checking on people who wanted to work with children or other vulnerable people. Schools, hospitals and care employers had access to centrally held lists that contained the names of unsuitable people convicted of offences. They also routinely required potential employees to obtain a criminal record check from their local police force, which may have been inconvenient for the police but it worked. What many people failed to appreciate was that the CRB was not set up simply to run checks on public-sector employees working with children or the elderly. It is there to conduct background checks on every one of us, though for financial reasons it has yet to move to the phase where all employers can ask potential staff to produce a basic criminal record check. The two levels of check currently available are called 'standard disclosure' and 'enhanced disclosure'.

The standard disclosure is primarily applied to anyone involved in working with children or vulnerable adults and shows current and spent convictions, cautions, reprimands and warnings held on the Police National Computer (PNC). If the post involves working with children or vulnerable adults, several other lists can be searched: the Protection of Children Act (POCA) List; the Protection of Vulnerable Adults (POVA) List; and information held under Section 142 of the Education Act 2002 (formerly known as List 99). An enhanced disclosure is the highest level of check on anyone involved in regularly caring for, training, supervising or being in sole charge of children or vulnerable adults. It contains the same information as the standard but with the addition of any relevant and proportionate information held by the local police forces, including hearsay intelligence,

The first problem with the CRB is one that applies to all databases: what if the information it holds is wrong? It relies upon the notoriously unreliable Police National Computer for the details, which has already resulted in some people facing the Kafkaesque nightmare of being accused of something they have not done. A few years ago, a distinguished retired RAF officer, living in Dorset, contacted me to describe his experience.

He did not wish to be named. His contact with the CRB took place when he applied to be a volunteer driver for a charity and, as the work involved dealing with disabled and vulnerable people, he applied for a check. A few weeks later, he received from the CRB an enhanced disclosure showing he was someone else with a conviction dating to 1990. At the time of the alleged conviction, the retired officer was living in Switzerland, so he asked the CRB to correct its mistake. They sent a pro forma letter and asked him to provide his fingerprints to prove he was not the man with the criminal record. He refused: 'I do not believe the onus is on me to prove that I am not someone they allege, but for them, if they wish, to prove I am not who I say I am.'[19]

In 2003, the government conceded that records drawn from the PNC are 'seriously inadequate'. The Police Research Group found differing working practices across the police service and variable levels of compliance which adversely affected data quality. Its report identified the main weaknesses in the police use of the PNC and suggested that there was an increasing backlog of case results awaiting entry on to the system.[20]

Her Majesty's Inspectorate of Constabulary (HMIC) produced three reports, the last of which showed that, while there had been significant improvements in clearing the backlog of case results, few forces were consistently achieving the required performance criteria. Inspectors blamed badly designed business processes 'exacerbated by inadequate computerised systems, often implemented piecemeal without strategic vision'.[21]

Although guidelines and codes have been produced in order to tighten up the collation and recording of this information, there has not been a study since to see whether this has happened. Data are also kept indefinitely including of convictions 'spent' under the 1974 Rehabilitation of the Offenders Act. This means old convictions and cautions are retained and can be used in an enhanced disclosure for those who wish to work with children, the elderly or sick people. But are our children any safer? The CRB check can only be as good as the information available and if any is inaccurate it would have been far better to encourage schools and other organizations to make proper use of references and testimonials, instead of constructing yet another state body to peer into our lives. Once an agency like the CRB is set up, its very existence is used to justify all sorts of nonsense. Even foreign exchange trips are at risk because families are being required to undergo checks before taking in children from overseas. Mothers and fathers are now vetted to make sure they are suitable to look after foreign pupils under new rules. Host families are also given basic training in child protection laws, even if they have children of their own.

INDEPENDENT SAFEGUARDING AUTHORITY

Now, anyone working in education, health, leisure and other sectors must register with the Independent Safeguarding Authority (ISA), which started in October 2009, if they come into contact with under-16s. Most have to pay £64 towards the cost of setting up a database, a sum that will certainly rise, and if they work unchecked with children they face a fine of up to £5,000. Just for being an unvetted Brown Owl.

As with the bureaucracy established because of the death of Victoria Climbié, the Independent Safeguarding Agency, established by the Safeguarding Vulnerable Groups Act 2006, is another response to a terrible tragedy: the murders of Holly Wells and Jessica Chapman. The killings carried out by Ian Huntley in Soham in 2002 are often cited as an appalling example of how the system of criminal records checks broke down. Huntley had never been convicted of a crime; however, it transpired after his conviction that he had been the subject of numerous allegations of sexual assault and rape, several of which had been investigated by the police but which were not disclosed by a criminal record check. The official inquiry, chaired by Sir Michael Bichard, reported in 2004 with a recommendation that a registration scheme should be established for those who wish to work with children. In response, the government set up the Independent Safeguarding Authority to determine whether people are fit and proper to work with children or vulnerable adults. This is an awesomely intrusive bureaucracy and effectively has the power of deciding who is fit and proper to work with children from among millions of adults, even after minor reforms belatedly announced by the government after a public outcry.

Staff have been recruited by local authorities to investigate any claim that an adult who works with children – whether self-employed, business staff, volunteers or public-sector employees – may have harmed a child or committed a crime against them, as long as they do not believe it to be totally fabricated. Designated officers have to tell the employee's manager about the allegation, as well as the complainant's parents, and decide if police or social services should get involved. They then track the progress of the claim to ensure it is resolved and must record whether it has led to disciplinary action or dismissal or a criminal prosecution. The officers are allowed to 'canvass views' from the police about whether the accused should be suspended. However, the definitions make it difficult for an employee to remove any suspicion surrounding them.

It is one thing to have had a series of allegations made to the police which, as in Huntley's case, result in an arrest; it is quite another for council officials to retain tittle-tattle about people, whose falsehood they will be required to prove – a reversal of the normal requirements of justice. It is often forgotten that the Soham inquiry reserved much of its criticism for a failure to follow up Huntley's references when he was applying for a job as a school caretaker. Had they done so, they would have been found to be false. Howard Gilbert, principal of the school where Huntley was employed, told the inquiry that he had made a mistake in not checking the murderer's references: 'At the end of the day they should have been called in'. A letter should have been sent to confirm that the references were genuine and authentic.' Some of the references Huntley provided were undated, but Mr Gilbert said that no weight was given to these.[22]

There is a great danger that when these tasks, once routine, are put out to state agencies, these are considered infallible, when invariably they are not. A return to some old-fashioned checking of personal testimonials would be far preferable to the ghastly world of snooping and denunciation into which we are blundering. This was brilliantly set out in a pamphlet, *Licensed to Hug*. Written by Frank Furedi and Jennie Bristow for the Civitas think-tank, it said the dramatic escalation of child protection measures has succeeded in poisoning the relationship between the generations and creating an atmosphere of suspicion that actually increases the risks to children. The paper argued that children need to have contact with a range of adult members of the community for their education and socialization, but 'this form of collaboration, which has traditionally underpinned inter-generational relationships, is now threatened by a regime that insists that adult/child encounters must be mediated through a security check'.[23]

The scope of child protection has become an immense, self-perpetuating industry whose very existence depends upon maintaining the fiction and fear that all adults are potentially harmful to children. Whereas adults would once routinely have rebuked children who were misbehaving, or helped children in distress, they now think twice about the consequences of inter-acting with other people's children.

One of the contributors to *Licensed to Hug* described the culture of fear that pervades what should be ordinary relationships:

My daughter is allowed to play out in the street with kids from the neighbourhood. She said she was going to Semih's house and I said OK. Ten minutes later Semih's mom knocked at my door and said, 'I must introduce myself as we haven't met.' I thought she was going to tell me her name, have a chat, but she said she was CRB checked and her husband was CRB checked and then went away. I still don't know her name!

As Furedi and Bristow commented: 'When parents feel in need of official reassurance that other parents have passed the paedophile test before they even start on the pleasantries, this indicates that something has gone badly wrong in our communities.'[24]

In an atmosphere of mistrust, in which adults suspect other adults and children are taught to suspect anyone other than their parents, there is a feeling that it is best not to become involved. At the inquest of a two-year-old girl who had wandered into a pond and drowned, a man who had driven past and saw her obviously lost said that he did not go to help 'because I thought someone would see me and think I was trying to abduct her'.[25]

This situation has been getting worse over the years and will become even more problematic once the ISA gets fully into its stride. As *Licensed to Hug* observed: 'From Girl Guiders to football coaches, from Christmas-time Santas to parents helping out in schools, volunteers – once regarded as pillars of the community – have been transformed in the regulatory and public imagination into potential child abusers, barred from any contact with children until the database gives them the green light.'[26]

The effect of this treatment is to put some people off volunteering altogether. The Volunteer Survey 2007 found that 13 per cent of men would not volunteer because they were worried people would think they were child abusers and 28 per cent of those who responded to an online survey carried out for *Licensed to Hug* said they knew someone who had been put off volunteering by the CRB process. The former Children's Commissioner, Sir

Al Aynsley-Green, said that nearly 50,000 girls are waiting to join the Guides because of a shortage of adult volunteers, partly caused by the red tape of the CRB process.[27] *Licensed to Hug* suggested that instead of creating an atmosphere of fear and suspicion, we need to 'halt the juggernaut of regulation' and instead behave as if the majority of adults have no predatory attitudes towards children but, on the contrary, can be relied on to help them. If we could encourage greater openness and more frequent contact between the generations, we would all benefit.

We should not forget that volunteers are the bedrock of any healthy society; every year millions of people give willingly of their time to help out in schools, run Scout groups, organize football teams or deliver meals to the elderly. Yet activities that were once commonplace, if praiseworthy, requiring merely the unselfish use of a few spare hours, are becoming increasingly onerous because of this approach. An obsession with health and safety, an unwillingness to accept that there is an element of risk in all we do and a consequent requirement for virtually everyone dealing with children to be subjected to a criminal record check have turned volunteering into something unwarrantedly expensive, bureaucratic and intrusive. David Shrubbs from Sutton Coldfield wrote a letter to the *Daily Telegraph* to point out that he had five CRB checks: one for being a teacher at a secondary school, another for teaching voluntarily at a primary school, a third so that he can run a Cub Scout pack, yet another because he sings in a church choir and a fifth because he is the voluntary licensee of the church club.[28]

Since the Criminal Records Bureau started work in 2002, the number of checks being issued has doubled. They are no longer confined to those employed to work with children, such as teachers, but have spread to cover arrangements that people once made on an ad-hoc basis. Nor are they transferable. The number of errors by the CRB has also continued to rise with many of those wrongly accused of crimes subsequently refused jobs as teachers, nurses and child-minders, or rejected from being youth volunteers.

Of course checks must be made to ensure molesters do not work with children, but they do not all have to be carried out by a state agency. In any case, a CRB disclosure highlights a conviction, not a predilection. It offers no certainty yet gives unrealistic expectations that risk can be eradicated. A far better way to discover if an individual is trustworthy is to follow up testimonials or references with people who know them.

As the Civitas report observed, the informal and unregulated collaboration between grown-ups has throughout history provided the foundation for the socialization of young people. We are now creating a society in which adults start to mistrust others who are not properly 'licensed'. They end up requiring the legitimacy of a security check before being able to exercise any authority. Some adults who upbraid youngsters find themselves charged with assault. Adults whose experience and advice would be invaluable to any young person are giving up volunteering because it is no longer worth the candle. The system as it has developed is just as likely to deter the best as it is to weed out the worst.

Furthermore, there is no evidence that licensing adults protects children from harm. All that a CRB check does is find out what an individual has done in the past. It cannot predict what someone with a licence to work with children may do in the future. The best way to protect children is through encouraging adults to behave responsibly and take a close interest in the wellbeing of young people in their community. Yet this is being destroyed by a culture of vetting and mutual suspicion.

CHAPTER 8

PUT THAT FAG OUT!

On 26 March 2006, it became illegal in Scotland to smoke in an enclosed or semi-enclosed public place. The following year, the law was extended to the rest of the United Kingdom: on 2 April to Wales, on 30 April to Northern Ireland and, finally, on 1 July to England. This followed a trail already blazed (or extinguished) in, of all places, Ireland. The idea that the Irish would quietly stub out their cigarettes and retreat to the garden or the street rather than smoke in the pub had always seemed fanciful. Yet in March 2004, Ireland became the first country in the EU to make smoking at the workplace illegal. Dr Peter Maguire, deputy chairman of the science committee of the British Medical Association (BMA), told the BBC: 'As an Irishman, who in the name of God would have thought the Irish would be the first in Europe to ban smoking in public places? It's a national hobby in Ireland.'[1]

Yet initial suggestions that the Irish would simply ignore the new law and carry on regardless proved wide of the mark and encouraged the governments in Edinburgh and London to follow suit. The ban was also scrupulously followed in Britain. It led to the development of a cottage industry in the production of covered outdoor smoking cabins for pub gardens. Many people who wanted to give up smoking but found the lure of a pint and a cigarette impossible to resist welcomed the ban as an added incentive to quit. Proponents of the ban derided claims that it would seriously damage the pub trade and, indeed, believed it would attract a new clientele of non-smokers and families to enjoy a drink and food in a smoke-free atmosphere. Furthermore, it would be good for the health of pub employees who were at risk of passively acquiring smoking-related diseases like cancer or heart problems.

But hang on. What about the rights of smokers? Why was the law not framed in a way that would reflect the interests both of those who favoured a ban and those who would like to carry on puffing? In the early stages of discussions in Whitehall there was talk of greater flexibility than eventually transpired. There could, for instance, have been exemptions for private clubs or the provision of smoking rooms in pubs and their continuation in workplaces that had already banned smoking in most of their office space. A simpler route would have allowed landlords to have designated their pubs as either smoking or non-smoking establishments, giving people – including staff – the choice of where to drink and work.

By the time the smoking ban had reached its second anniversary in July 2009, the worm had started to turn. A group headed by Antony Worrall Thompson, the celebrity chef, started a campaign for greater flexibility in the law. In a letter to the *Daily Telegraph* on behalf of the organization Save Our Pubs and Clubs, he and a number of publicans wrote:

> Traditional English pubs and clubs are suffering as never before. Around 40 are closing every week and many others are laying off staff in a desperate attempt to survive. Tens of thousands of jobs have already been lost, and many more are likely to follow over the coming months. There are many factors causing difficulties for licensees, from the serious downturn in the economy, to continuing punitive duties on the sale of alcohol. But one factor that could be dealt with – at no expense to the taxpayer – is an amendment to the blanket ban on smoking in public places . . . we urge

politicians of all parties to help save our pubs and clubs by introducing an amendment to the ban. If they don't, the traditional English pub will continue to wither on the vine.[2]

Worrall Thompson was writing against the backdrop of a serious decline for the pub and leisure trade, with an estimated 20,000 public houses at risk of closure, which has serious implications for the communities they serve. Contrary to most predictions, the smoking ban has had a devastating effect on pub trade. When the ban fully came into effect on 1 July 2007 polls suggested that up to 80 per cent of all adults were more likely to visit a pub, but little of that anticipated new custom actually materialized – while regulars have vanished. Research by the *Publican* magazine showed that only one in three licensees have attracted new customers since the ban.[3] At least 78,000 bar staff have been sacked because of a drop in business caused directly by the ban, according to the trade magazine *Morning Advertiser*. Not long after the ban came into force, the British Beer and Pub Association (BBPA) reported an increase in pub closures to 30 a week – nearly 4 every day. It blamed a number of factors, including the smoking ban, the economic credit crunch, increased beer prices and temperamental weather conditions. According to a survey carried out by the association, 1,409 pubs closed during 2007, a sharp increase on previous years. Pub numbers were only down 216 in 2006 after a fall of 102 in 2005.[4] A survey of 1,500 licensees revealed that more than half have seen trade drop since the smoking ban was introduced, with the credit crunch seen as the principal cause followed by the smoking ban.[5]

One perverse outcome of the ban, which was, after all, supposed to protect vulnerable people from the alleged effect of passive smoking, is that many adults stayed at home to smoke, thereby afflicting their children with fumes they might otherwise have avoided. According to the *Morning Advertiser*, two out of three consumers decided to drink at home rather than in pubs.

Pubs across the country closed, especially in urban areas where pubs often do not have gardens. In the Potteries town of Hanley, the Hawkesmore Inn found its takings falling. Landlady Lisa Gascoigne said: 'On the average Saturday night, we would take about £1,000 to £1,200 and regularly have about 60 to 80 people in. After the smoking ban our takings have dropped to virtually nothing, and we can make just £100 on a Saturday night. All our regulars were smokers. Since the ban they have left and not come back.'[6]

Peter Marsden, landlord of the Tandem at Waterloo in Huddersfield, West Yorkshire, was another forced to shut down. 'Last July everything crashed. The smoking ban and the bad weather really hit us,' he said through tears. Marsden and wife Sue remortgaged their home and invested tens of thousands of pounds into refurbishing the pub and putting up a smoking shelter. After months of poor trading, he appealed to Enterprise Inns, which owns the pub, for help but it was not enough to keep the place afloat.[7]

In Lincoln, the Portland Arms shut its doors as takings fell by half. Landlord Phil Seed said: 'When we leave we will have nowhere to live.'[8] In Wales, within a year of the ban, John Price, Welsh secretary of the Federation of Licensed Victuallers Associations (FLVA), said 17 pubs and 3 clubs in the south Wales valleys had closed since the smoking ban. Mr Price, who runs the Bush Hotel in Clydach Vale, said, 'My trade has gone down by 40%. I've lost my elderly regulars. They buy in their drink from the supermarket and stay in front of the television. You can't expect the elderly to go outside in the cold to smoke.'[9] And in Scotland two years after the ban a total of 350 pubs had closed, double the number predicted by the Scottish Licensed Trade Association (SLTA) at the outset. The Scottish Beer and Pub Association admits recent closures have been caused by effects of the smoking ban.[10] Paul Waterson, chief executive of the SLTA, even went as far as advising would-be publicans to stay away from the industry.

Bingo halls and working men's clubs also started to feel the pinch, with operators Gala closing many of its bingo operations, including the only hall – and cinema – on Anglesey, the Empire, where the owner Gareth Jones said: 'Our profit went down 30% after the smoking ban came in, so that contributed towards it. It is a great shame as there are very few entertainment venues on the island.'[11] Cinema-goers were left with a 40-mile journey to see a film because the cinema relied upon the revenue from bingo to survive.

In view of this, can the smoking ban be construed a good law? It will evidently have benefits for the health of people who have been helped to give up smoking or will never take it up, but it is also an unwarranted and unnecessarily inflexible restriction on the freedoms of millions of people. Simon Clark, director of the pro-smoking lobby group Forest, said: 'The smoking ban has been a disaster for many pubs and clubs which are currently closing at a rate of 40 per week. The ban is excessive and although it is welcomed in some quarters, it has had a hugely detrimental effect on many people's lives, socially and economically.' Older people feel 'humiliated' when they are forced to stand outside, especially in winter. He said, 'Give landlords the option of separate smoking rooms in pubs and clubs and people will be able to smoke and drink in a controlled environment. Instead, more people are smoking and drinking at home. This is leading to the loss of hundreds of pubs and clubs with the result that the heart is being ripped out of many local communities.'[12]

For many people, the problem with the legislation was that it was complete anathema to a country with a tradition of individual liberty and for whom the nanny state is already too solicitous. It fed into the Tory attack on Labour intrusiveness; while there was no possibility of the Conservatives reversing the ban, reformers hoped to bring about changes. Shane Frith, director of Progressive Vision, one of the four coalition partners supporting the Save Our Pubs and Clubs campaign, put it this way:

Labour has infantilised the people of Britain with an enormous growth of the nanny state. The smoking ban, affecting private property, is one of the more egregious examples of this attitude. I, as a non-smoker, have never been forced to walk into a smoke-filled bar, yet Labour's nanny state believes I am a victim and need to be protected. If given a choice, I will prefer to stay in non-smoking sections of pubs or visit non-smoking pubs, but as an adult I deserve that choice. The attack on smokers is just part of Labour's 'government knows best' attitude. It is this attitude that brought in the hunting ban, is leading to greater restrictions on alcohol and has produced the hysteria about fatty foods. Even if you are a non-smoker, you likely have something to fear from Labour's nanny state.[13]

With his letter to the *Daily Telegraph*, Worrall Thompson tapped into a deep-rooted disquiet about the ban that few had been prepared to voice openly. Here are some of the replies:

Dear Sir,

I fully agree with the idea of relaxing the laws on smoking in pubs and clubs. An overall ban is draconian and also has completely destroyed some Arabic Hookah bars. If there were just one or two places that could be licensed for smokers, like in Spain for instance, everyone would be happy. I really can't understand why the health lobby has so much power with this issue. I mean drinking is hardly a sport, pubs are not health clubs and people who party til 10 am in some London clubs are not being fuelled by Lucozade!

Dear Sir,

Thank you for publishing the letter from Antony Worrall Thompson about amending the smoking ban to allow choice for all. It has been without doubt the most spiteful and socially unacceptable piece of legislation ever to have been served on the British people. How many publicans have seen their once profitable business wither and die and how many law abiding people, especially the older generation have been left wondering exactly why they are no longer able to be included in any sort of social activity by law. This initiative needs publicity and I thank you for highlighting it in your paper.[14]

How did we get to a point which just a few years ago nobody would have thought possible – a ban on all smoking in public places? As often is the case, it began in the US, where in some parts it is even forbidden to light up in your own home if it is part of an apartment block. In Belmont, California, smoking is forbidden anywhere in the town of 25,000 people except in detached homes and yards, streets and some sidewalks, and designated smoking areas outside.

The law is not quite as draconian in the UK but it is still comprehensive. The legislation was first proposed in the Public Health White Paper in 2004. At the time it was proposed that private members' clubs and pubs that did not serve food would be exempt. In the summer of 2005 the government conducted a three-month public consultation, which concluded in September and was followed by weeks of internal Whitehall discussions in which Patricia Hewitt, then the health secretary, pressed strongly for a complete ban. Other cabinet ministers – mindful of Labour's vote in areas with working men's clubs, wanted a partial ban along the lines promised in Labour's 2005 election manifesto. With many Labour MPs favouring a total ban, a free vote was offered. On 14 February 2006 MPs in the House of Commons voted by a margin of 200 votes for a total ban on smoking in public places. Smoking was to be outlawed in any building if more than one person used it as a place of work. Smoking rooms were no longer allowed in offices even if they were properly ventilated and sealed off from the rest of the building. Lighting up was prohibited in airports, covered bus and railway stations, taxis and minicabs. However, the ban did not cover places of residence like prisons, hospices, care homes and mental-health units where patients are held in secure conditions for more than six months. While public areas in hotels were included in the ban, guests were allowed to continue to smoke in designated rooms.

Under the Act, smoking is banned in any area that is enclosed or 'substantially enclosed', defined as having a roof and more than 50 per cent of the perimeter enclosed by walls. This should have meant that smoking could continue on open-air train platforms. However, train companies took it upon themselves to use by-laws to extend the ban to the entire network. Even if you were standing alone on a station platform in the middle of North Yorkshire you would be breaking the law to light up.

It is even forbidden to smoke in your own car if the vehicle is a place of work, like a taxi, or could be used by another worker, e.g. the cab of a lorry. Smokers driving company cars, vans, lorries and enclosed tractors in England could be fined £50 for lighting up at the wheel if the vehicle might be handed over to a colleague later in the day. This has caused a number of ridiculous anomalies. Employees who have a company car for their sole use are allowed to smoke while giving a non-smoking colleague a lift to work, because the journey counts as private use. But employees sharing a pool car will not be allowed to light up, even if they are all heavy smokers. Enforcement is mainly through fines of £50 rising to £200 for repeat offences. Businesses ignoring the ban can be fined £2,500.

Unlike in Scotland, actors in England can continue to smoke on stage if the play requires it. The totality of the ban north of the border forced actor and comedian Mel Smith, playing Winston Churchill in an Edinburgh fringe show, to abandon the wartime leader's trademark cigar. When environmental officers visited the city's Assembly Rooms an hour before the show opened and threatened to close down the venue, Smith decided to portray Britain's wartime leader without the play's 'integral' smoking scene. William Burdett-Coutts, the artistic director of the Assembly Rooms, was told that he would be held liable if a performer smoked and would face a fine of £200 and the loss of his licence:

> We had a visit from the chief environmental officer this morning who said he would shut down the venue. During the scene, Mel got out the cigar and a lighter but then he put them down to the side. I think it's absurd. In the context of an international festival like this, it's crazy. It's integral to the part of Churchill and it doesn't affect other people.'[15]

One by-product of the ban was the requirement to put 'No Smoking' signs on the door of every business, even places of worship, under the Smoke-free (Signs) Regulations 2007 (S.I. 2007, No. 923). The sensible way of proceeding would have been to put up a sign where smoking is allowed, since there are very few of those. But the government decided to do it the other way around.

An attempt was made to stop this when the regulation came before the Statutory Instrument committee. Dr Andrew Murrison, the Conservative MP for Westbury, moved a motion to reverse the measure after representations from many groups such as schools and churches:

> The last time I saw someone light up in a church was a very long time ago. The whole idea of someone puffing away in the pews is, frankly, ridiculous. A number of clergy have made that point, and they are unhappy that they will have to put up no-smoking signs on their premises. We are concerned about excessive signage in many contexts – for example, countryside clutter – and we should be particularly sensitive about important structures, such as churches, and

how they might be defaced by excessive signage. It may seem a small point, but to many people it is a matter of great concern. The Dean of Southwark said that it would be ridiculous to place no-smoking signs on his church's magnificent doorway, which has been locked for 500 years. However, as the door is theoretically a means by which people might gain access to the church, he will have to put a no-smoking sign over it or around it. The Bishop of Fulham said that the new rules are 'stark, staring mad'.[16]

However, John Pugh, the Liberal Democrat MP for Southport, observed during the same debate:

> There is a significant minority – I can cite individuals – of tobacco-addicted churchgoers. I must say – they are priests. No, they do not light up during services, but that does not mean that they do not light up on church premises. I accept that there are rather fewer in nonconformist Churches, but I have certainly found in the high Anglican tradition a fair number of people with serious tobacco addictions that they satisfy – even, from time to time, on the premises . . . Usually, the only form of passive smoking that occurs in churches is the inhalation of incense.[17]

The government line that all buildings should have 'No Smoking' signs, rather than 'Smoking Allowed' signs, was held by Caroline Flint, then a health minister:

> We have done a bit of mystery shopping in churches and cathedrals for the signage position. Dr Murrison referred to the Bishop of Southwark. At that place of worship, not only are there displayed at the entrances signs dealing with things that cannot be done, such as 'no drinking' or 'no mobile phones', but there is a sign saying, 'We accept Visa.' It is therefore clearly the case that examples of signage

can be found in many heritage buildings and places of worship.[18]

Flint made clear that a 'No Smoking' sign would have to be attached to temporary structures such as a marquee at a fete or a Scout tent since they were enclosed public spaces. The signs have to be at least A5 size. They have to display the no-smoking symbol and use characters that can be easily read by persons using the entrance, stating: 'No smoking: it is against the law to smoke in these premises'. Those three features are required, but the signs can be in whatever colour and font people want and made of any material. There is no power in the Health Act for the government to exempt certain premises that must be smoke-free from the legal requirement to display 'No Smoking' signs. Why wasn't one included?

So, is this a good law because it helps people give up smoking and protects non-smokers from tobacco fumes; or is it a bad law because it is so inflexible that publicans, their staff and their clientele who would like to smoke are forbidden to do so; and places that would never have a problem with smoking have to festoon their buildings with 'No Smoking' signs? It has interfered both with personal freedom and with commercial enterprise. It could have been devised so that those who wanted to smoke could have been allowed to continue doing so, without those who do not like smoking being exposed to tobacco. There could have been a presumption that smoking was not allowed in public places; and where it was allowed, signs to that effect would say so. There would be fewer of them than there are 'No Smoking' signs which have now been placed on every public building in the land.

Just because smoking has been banned in other countries or because some smokers have adapted to the prohibition does not make this a good law. Many still feel enormous anger, resentment and frustration at the extent of the legislation, which is unnecessarily widely drawn. Like many other laws passed in recent years, it has lacked that central element of commonsense that once marked out this country's way of doing things. And if anyone thinks this is a universally accepted law, here are just a few observations from those who beg to differ.

> I am 40 years old and run a transport business employing 60+ people. I used to enjoy going to pubs and was a regular bi-weekly visitor. I don't bother any more. It just isn't relaxing any more. In fact, it is quite the opposite. What a sad country we now live in thanks to the policies of the past few years. Me? I'm just marking time till I can sell my company and retire to somewhere sane like Spain. If all goes well, I'll be out of here in the next five years and this will all just be a very bad dream.

> Martin Cullip, Taking Liberties blog, 24 June 2008

> I'm 43 and perform in a semi-pro pub-duo, singing and playing Irish standards etc. As such, I am someone who is 'protected' by the smoking ban. Well, it's certainly protecting me against earning a living from music and it has utterly RUINED the pub-going experience, not just in the winter but, for landlocked city pubs, at any time. No smoking inside, no drinking outside. Result: near-empty, atmosphere-free pubs. Personally, I feel pretty unwelcome in any public space, so I go out much less. I don't travel by train any more. Booking hotel rooms has also become fraught, as I refuse to stay anywhere that won't accommodate my preference.

> Adrian Brown, Taking Liberties blog, 24 June 2008

> As a mental health sufferer this ban has been devastating. One of the most important things for people like me is getting out and not stagnating at home, however, with this vicious ban there is nowhere for us to go out to and relax.

Ergo, we don't go! By not going out we are not meeting new people, who possibly have the same or similar problems and with whom discussion can be very beneficial to both sides. Effectively we feel isolated, have an increased feeling of unworthiness, and an even blacker outlook on the future. Cigarettes have been my lifeline for nearly 40 years and, if anything, I smoke more now than I did prior to the ban. However, I am determined not to line this government's pockets so I buy my cigarettes abroad where there is a more tolerant attitude to smokers and we are still treated as human beings.

Lyn Ladds, Taking Liberties blog, 23 June 2008

Is it really right that old people should be forced out into the rain and inclement wintry weather or mentally-ill patients denied the one thing that acts as a coping strategy? If passive smoking is really that bad (and any intelligent person knows that the claims of ill-health are a fairytale), they should have the courage to ban all tobacco products – period.

Bill C, Taking Liberties blog, 21 June 2008

I am 41 and a manager in a leading insolvency practice. I have seen at first hand the devastation caused by this ban due to the massive increase in clients who have earned their living in the hospitality business. It is not just pub owners. Singers, DJs, comedians, karaoke acts etc are all struggling, and their income is dropping dramatically. Many have said that they originally thought the ban would be a good idea, but now that they stand to lose everything, would be more than happy to perform in premises where smoking was allowed.

Michael Peoples, Taking Liberties blog, 20 June 2008

I hate having to run the gauntlet of workers, strewn across the pavement outside pubs, restaurants and offices, spewing clouds of smoke over you, and think that it was a whole lot better, and tidier, when there were designated areas for smokers.

> Steve Court, Bournemouth Echo, 17 June 2008

One of the most common British social interactions was traditionally a pint and a cigarette and friendly chat/banter with the locals and your mates. The total smoking ban has all but destroyed all that typically British social interaction. We are reduced to oscillating in and out of our local between the front and back doors like some sort of misfit, socially inferior, low-level, potential criminals.

> Malcolm Andrew McLeod,
> *Lancashire Telegraph*, 8 June 2008

The smoking ban has caused enormous social upheaval. My wife and I used to enjoy going to the local for a couple of beers to catch up with each other and friends with a cosy chat, and smoking was part of that. Our local is now mostly empty; it's like a ghost town. I wouldn't mind if that now smoking is banned all the non-smokers who have been campaigning, and others, were now filling the bars, but no. All this has done is remove yet another part of local community life.

> Russ from Poole, BBC News forum, 9 January 2008

CHAPTER 9

DNA DATABASE

There have been few advances in criminal technology more beneficial than DNA testing. It has brought killers and rapists to book years after the crimes they thought they had got away with committing. It has led to the release of people convicted of murders they never committed. Sean Hodgson was freed from prison after serving 27 years of a prison term for the murder of barmaid Teresa De Simone, 22. He was near the murder scene in Southampton in 1979 and his blood group matched the killer. He confessed to the killing while in prison in 1982 for another offence. However, Hodgson was also a compulsive liar who could not have carried out the murder, as DNA tests on genetic material left at the murder scene subsequently proved. He was released in 2009 aged 58.

DNA testing has also brought to book the most appalling killers who might otherwise have escaped justice. Forklift-truck driver Steve Wright, 49, one of Britain's worst serial killers, is serving life for the murder of five prostitutes in Suffolk in 2006. His DNA details were entered into the national criminal database after he was convicted of stealing £80 while working as a barman. A pair of gardening gloves that were marked with his DNA and that of his fourth victim, Paula Clennell, proved the key to his conviction, though it was diligent police work that led to his capture.

Mark Dixie, 37, a chef, is serving at least 34 years in jail for murdering 18-year-old would-be model Sally Anne Bowman in a frenzied attack in front of her Croydon home. His DNA was entered into the criminal database when he was arrested by police for his part in a pub brawl during a World Cup football match nine months after attacking her. When Dixie was in custody police discovered a history of sex crimes. Other killers in jail because of DNA evidence include Ian Callaghan, serving a life sentence for killing 66-year-old Shirley Leach in a toilet at Bury bus station in 1994 and Colin Pitchfork, found guilty in 1988 of the separate murders of two schoolgirls, Lynda Mann and Dawn Ashworth, both 15, in Leicestershire. DNA evidence that has been matched with family members has also resulted in convictions, including that of Craig Harman, jailed for six years after admitting the manslaughter of lorry driver Michael Little, 53, in March 2003. He threw a brick from a bridge onto the M3 in Surrey, which hit Little. He was caught after DNA on the brick was checked against the national database and was similar to the DNA of one of his relatives.

DNA profiling is the most powerful forensic tool available to police and its discovery can significantly enhance a prosecutor's chances of obtaining a conviction compared with crimes where no DNA is found. The technology exploits the fact that small sections of our DNA repeat themselves over and over, and that different people have different numbers of repeats. These genetic 'stutters' can be counted, producing a digital read-out. Current tests produce a sequence of 20 numbers. Such a read-out is highly specific to an individual. The chances of a stranger's DNA exactly matching each of the 20 numbers that make up your profile are about one billion to one. These numbers that pinpoint a person from their genes can be stored and accessed through a computer network.

Gary Pugh, director of forensic services at Scotland Yard, said the technology should be considered a profound asset in fighting crime:

The technology exists to locate, scan and search marks from

the crime scene with a suspect potentially being identified in less than 30 minutes and the arresting officer to be waiting outside the perpetrator's last known address when he returns. The use of forensic biometrics is arguably one of the most effective safeguards for society against being wrongly accused or falsely convicted. As some recent high-profile cases have shown, investigators can be convinced they have the right suspect and juries that defendants are guilty, but one fingerprint comparison or DNA test can exonerate the innocent.[1]

So the law governing the criminal DNA database cannot be a bad law, can it? Surely it must be an unmitigated boon to society and one emulated around the world. But this is not the case. Britain has by far the biggest DNA criminal database in the world, for the simple reason that more than a million profiles that it contains are not of criminals at all. This is the problem with which those who defend the database must grapple: why should it be allowed to develop in such an ad-hoc way that is clearly unfair to the innocent people whose profiles it contains? Why should they be treated differently from other innocent people? The tired old argument that if you have nothing to hide you have nothing to fear won't wash; nor will insulting and ignorant attacks on the 'paranoia' of those concerned about this issue, usually from people who have themselves been political extremists and who seem to have no compunction about the state ownership of people.

The legislation governing the taking of DNA in Britain has been deliberately allowed to develop into a mess of unfairness and injustice. Bizarrely, some of its greatest cheerleaders are those who would also champion the human rights court that has decreed that it is wrong and a breach of privacy to take a sample from an innocent person. And why would they do that? Do those commentators and criminal justice practitioners who argue that there is nothing untoward about the DNA profile of an innocent person appearing on a criminal database volunteer their own DNA for inclusion? And if not, why not? The way the DNA database has developed is a classic piece of British legislative fudging.

DNA profiling began in the mid-1980s when the police were first allowed to ask doctors to obtain a blood sample to help with the investigation of serious crimes, with the consent of volunteers. Over the next ten years, forensic DNA technology gradually developed and in 1993, the Royal Commission on Criminal Justice recommended that a database be established to hold the profiles that had by then been accumulated. Partly, this was motivated by the fall-out from some notorious miscarriages of justice, notably the imprisonment of six men for an IRA bomb attack in Birmingham. This had caused a decline in public confidence in the criminal justice system which the government hoped a routine use of DNA could help rectify. In other words, one of the principle reasons why the database was initially conceived was as a more objective form of forensic identification, with the potential as much to eliminate suspects as to secure convictions. In 1994, the Criminal Justice and Public Order Act amended the rules that already existed governing the invasive collection of tissue samples by reclassifying saliva samples and mouth swabs as 'non-intimate' and changing the circumstances where such a sample could be taken without consent: 'The police could now take samples without assistance from a doctor and could collect mouth scrapes and hair roots by force if necessary.'[2]

The 1994 Act also gave the police power to search the database speculatively for matches between DNA profiles. It also changed the definition of the type of offence eligible for DNA matching. Instead of a 'serious, arrestable' offence it was extended to any 'recordable' offence, which covered everything apart from the most trivial misdemeanours. So began the process of widening the pool of potential suspects, something parliament was not clear was going to happen, though the government was. Michael Howard, then home secretary, said it presaged a 'massive expansion' of DNA testing.

He told the Commons:

> Part IV of the Bill is aimed at the complex area of body samples, in particular those taken for the purpose of DNA analysis. As techniques have improved, DNA has become a powerful tool in the investigation of crime, but the law has lagged behind. The Bill will end the current arbitrary restrictions on the police use of body samples and of DNA analysis ... At the moment, samples can be taken only for the investigation of serious arrestable offences. The Royal Commission recommended that the power to take non-intimate samples without consent should be extended to include offences of assault and burglary. We agree with the thrust of the royal commission's recommendation, but we want to go further. It would be simpler and more logical to treat DNA sampling on precisely the same basis as fingerprinting. As a result, the Bill allows the police to take samples from anyone who is to be charged with a 'recordable' offence, and to use the samples to search against existing records of convicted offenders or unsolved crimes. In time, a national database will be built up. Those powers will be of real practical help in the investigation of crime. For example, in a sample of people convicted of rape, eight out of 10 had previous convictions for other offences. They will be easier to catch and convict when their DNA profile is in the database.[3]

There were no speeches opposing the idea of a database. Most of the contributions made clear that they considered it to be a criminal database containing the profiles of people convicted of an offence. The law stated that if the person from whom the sample was taken was subsequently found guilty, the information could be stored on the database and their sample kept indefinitely; if they were not charged or were acquitted, the data and the sample had to be destroyed. In 2001, this was expanded significantly, however, by the Criminal Justice and Police Act. It amended the Police and Criminal Evidence Act 1984 to allow all samples (and fingerprints) collected in England, Wales and Northern Ireland to be retained indefinitely, irrespective of whether the person had been acquitted. Another amendment also allowed samples to be retained indefinitely from volunteers taking part in mass screenings, on the condition that they had freely given their consent.

In 2003, police powers were extended once again by another Criminal Justice Act which allowed DNA profiles, fingerprints and other information to be taken without consent from anyone simply arrested in England or Wales on suspicion of any record-able offence and to retain this information indefinitely, even if the person arrested is never charged. The Counter-Terrorism Act 2008 further extended police powers to allow DNA and fingerprints to be taken from persons subject to control orders; to be collected during any authorized secret surveillance and retained indefinitely; to be searched against material held by the Security Service or Secret Intelligence Service; and to be used 'in the interests of national security'.

As a consequence of this accretion, the National DNA Database is the largest in the world, yet it was set up without a single piece of primary legislation establishing its parameters and governing its use. It was never envisaged at the outset that people who were not criminals would be on the database; but anyone who suggests this might be wrong is accused of wanting people to get away, literally, with murder. There is another answer to the injustice of including some innocent people on the database, which is to include everybody on it.

Shortly before he ceased being prime minister, Tony Blair visited the Forensic Science Service in London and voiced his opinion that a DNA database containing the profiles of the entire population might be worth considering. Ministers always say they have 'no immediate plans' to extend the DNA capture scheme to the whole population but many are sympathetic to the idea. Tony McNulty, a security minister at the Home Office, said that while there were no plans for a national, universal DNA database he was 'broadly sympathetic' to the idea: 'We would never say never.' Senior police chiefs have gone so far as to suggest that everybody's DNA should be taken at birth and stored on the database. At present, 30,000 profiles are added every month. More than 5 per cent of the population is now covered. For such a scheme to make any sense, though, all foreign visitors would have to provide their DNA as well. There are 30 million visitors every year and the impact on the tourist industry of requiring them all to hand over a mouth swab with their ticket can only be guessed at. However, at least they would know what it is like to arrive in a country where everyone is considered to be a potential suspect in a crime.

A DNA database covering the whole population has powerful proponents including Lord Justice Sedley, one of the country's leading judges. In an interview with the BBC he said a national database was being built up by stealth in an 'indefensible' way, but he did not conclude from this that it should, therefore, be confined only to those who have criminal convictions: he suggested that it was such an important crime-fighting tool that it should cover everyone. He conceded that such a move would be 'authoritarian' but said the current random additions to the database were unfair: 'We have a situation where if you happen to have been in the hands of the police, then your DNA is on permanent record. If you haven't, it isn't. It also means that a great many people who are walking the streets, and whose DNA would show them guilty of crimes, go free.' He was concerned, too, about the disproportionate number of ethnic minorities on the database.[4]

Lord Justice Sedley's acknowledgement that a universal DNA database would be 'authoritarian' would, for most of us, be considered a sign of disapproval, though it is by no means clear whether he regarded this as a good or a bad thing. He is, unusually (perhaps uniquely for an Appeal Court judge), a former member of the Communist Party. But leaving aside his previous political dalliances, he was highlighting something important on which he had been required to pass judgment: whether an innocent person, once on the database, could be removed.

There is, in fact, discretion for chief officers of police to remove profiles if requested to do so if they were taken from an individual who subsequently is never charged. Lord Justice Sedley, who as a radical lawyer in the 1970s and 1980s, was a strong supporter of incorporating the European Convention on Human Rights (ECHR) into British law through the Human Rights Act. Therefore it is surprising that he was among the Appeal Court judges in 2002 who dismissed a case brought on behalf of an 11-year-old boy whose DNA was kept on the database even though he had been declared innocent of any offence. The court said it did not breach human rights laws. Yet in 2008, this was overturned by the European Court of Human Rights.

The case was brought by two people from Sheffield, Michael Marper and 'S'. The former was arrested in 2001 and charged with harassing his partner but the charges were dropped, while the latter was arrested in the same year, aged 11, and later acquitted of attempted robbery. They said their rights under Article 8 (right to private life) and Article 14 (prohibition of discrimination) of the European Convention on Human Rights had been infringed. In its judgment, the court ruled:

> In conclusion, the Court finds that the blanket and indiscriminate nature of the powers of retention of the fingerprints, cellular samples and DNA profiles of persons suspected but not convicted of offences, as applied in the case of the present applicants, fails to strike a fair balance between the competing public and private interests and that the respondent State has overstepped any acceptable margin of appreciation in this regard. Accordingly, the

retention at issue constitutes a disproportionate interference with the applicants' right to respect for private life and cannot be regarded as necessary in a democratic society.[5]

In other words, holding the DNA of people not convicted of an offence on a criminal database is a breach of their human rights under the ECHR. If Lord Justice Sedley and his fellow judges had reached a similar conclusion in 2002, hundreds of thousands of innocent people would not now have their DNA retained; and nor would the government, in fulfilling the ruling of the European Court, be required to spend time and money erasing these profiles. It is hard to understand why the Appeal Court in 2002 did not think this was a human rights' breach whereas the European Court now says it is. What was especially peculiar about the UK government's case in the European Court is that it did not make out the case that ministers consistently give to a domestic audience – that the retention of the DNA from innocent people has been crucial to solving serious crime. In some of the most high profile murder cases, other evidence beyond DNA has been critical to securing a conviction

The Home Office has claimed that since April 2004 sampling people who have been arrested but not proceeded against has yielded a match with a crime scene in more than 3,000 offences. These include 37 murders, 16 attempted murders, 90 rapes and 1,136 burglary offences.[6] Yet according to Stephen Cragg, the barrister in the successful European Court case, 'The government did not have figures for the crimes solved by DNA data of unconvicted people on the database. The European court has said that if the UK government wants to be a pioneer of a DNA database it will have to make out a stronger case.' Cragg stressed: 'The majority of examples provided by the government involved matching suspects' DNA with crime scene stains. These cases did not involve samples retained from innocent people.'[7] That seems to demolish the government's justification for continuing with this practice and suggests that ministers have been at best somewhat flexible with their use of statistics. Why were they unable to make the same argument before the European Court that they have maintained in Home Office statements; or are the latter not to be believed?

The European Court ruling must have placed those on the so-called 'progressive' Left in something of a quandary since they support the EHRC and the Human Rights Act and yet see nothing wrong with retaining the DNA of innocent people. In that case, why did the Labour government never put a Bill to parliament to enact the first universal database of citizens in the world? The reason is obvious: the outcry would be enormous. The idea that the entire population should be treated as a pool of potential suspects is utterly grotesque.

There is also a school of thought that makes itself heard whenever these debates are held. They belong to the 'if you have nothing to hide you have nothing to fear' brigade, though there is not a great deal of evidence that many, or any, of them have volunteered to place their DNA on the database. However, there are myriad examples of the unfairness of the current system. Take the case of the motorist who was driving with his wife and child when their car was involved in a minor accident. He remonstrated with the driver of the other vehicle, one of two young men, whereupon he was punched in the face. He defended himself, suffered a few blows around the head, made it back to his car, bruised and bloodied, and drove home, where his wife phoned the police and passed on the registration number of the attackers' car. A week later, the police turned up on his doorstep. The two young men had made a counter-accusation that he had assaulted them. In the 'interests of fairness' he, too, was to be arrested and questioned. So he was taken to the station, his fingerprints and DNA were taken, a statement obtained and he was told to await a decision from the Crown Prosecution Service. This duly arrived a few weeks later: there was no case to answer and no further action would be taken.

This story was told to me as a correspondent on the *Daily Telegraph*, and while the individual concerned did not want to be identified I can vouch for its veracity. He asked the police to destroy the fingerprints and DNA sample since he did not see why he should be on a criminal database for the rest of his life but the request was declined. Until the European Court ruling forced the government to remove the profiles of young children, fewer than 1,000 had been erased as a result of requests to chief officers.

With such a large database you would have thought that we in the UK are more likely to obtain a match that could lead to the conviction of a murderer or, indeed, the exoneration of an innocent suspect, than in any other jurisdiction. Yet international figures do not bear this out. Furthermore, keeping the DNA profiles of innocent people on an almost random basis is not an efficient crime tool. For a detective looking for a needle in a haystack it just makes for a bigger haystack.

Britain is also a signatory to something called the Prum Treaty, an EU-wide agreement to share criminal data, including DNA, across the EU. Other EU police forces have access to the UK database on a 'hit, no hit' basis. In other words, the British authorities will inform their counterparts in, say, France whether a profile they have forwarded is retained on the British system. If it is, what would the police in France think? Let us imagine they are investigating the rape of a girl at a campsite and they take the DNA of all men staying there. Would they not be suspicious of a person whose DNA shows a positive match on the UK's criminal database, since their own one does not have a million innocent people on it? So you may have nothing to hide; but there may well be something to fear.

In response to the European Court judgment, the Home Office issued a White Paper setting out what it called 'a more proportionate, fair and commonsense approach' to DNA retention. But while there is greater flexibility with the profiles placed on the database, the samples themselves are not destroyed. More than that, the most recent Police and Crime Act gives the home secretary power to make new regulations about the retention of DNA, without further parliamentary scrutiny. In its response to the European Court judgment the Home Office told chief constables effectively to ignore the ruling and to continue adding to the DNA database the profiles of innocent people. Police chiefs were also 'strongly advised' to resist individual requests based on the Strasbourg ruling to remove DNA profiles from the national database in cases such as wrongful arrest, mistaken identity or where no crime has been committed. The Home Office has subsequently proposed that profiles of innocent people should be retained for six years. Some people, it appears, are more innocent than others.

The process of removing profiles is not due to begin until 2011 by which time hundreds of thousands more will have been added.

Simon Davies, director of Privacy International, said: 'The government has already stretched the limits of what should be permissible in a free society. Over the past decade, by deception and stealth, legislation and practice has allowed the collection and use of DNA in ways that would be entirely unacceptable in most democracies.'[8]

If it is the government's intention that the whole population should be on the database then legislation should be brought before parliament spelling out precisely what is proposed, rather than building it up through stealth, and a proper national debate should be held about it. It will not get very far.

SOME FACTS ABOUT DNA FROM GENEWATCH

- At the end of September 2008, the National DNA Database contained computerized DNA profiles and linked DNA samples from approximately 4.7 million individuals (more than 7 per cent of the UK population) (Hansard, 29 September 2008, col. 354W). This is a much higher proportion of the population than any other EU or G8 country.

- About a million people – an estimated 925,385 – had their DNA profiles added to the database when they were under 18. About 300,000 of these people are still children (under 18) (Hansard, 27 October 2008, col. 677W). About half a million people had their DNA profiles added to the NDNAD when they were under 16 years old (Hansard, 20 November 2008, col. 723W).

- About 30 per cent of the black population (aged over 10) have their DNA profile on the database. (Hansard, 10 November 2008, col. 800W, and can be compared with census population data). The proportion is much higher for young black men. In 2007, Baroness Scotland told the Commons home affairs select committee that three-quarters of the young black male population would soon be on the DNA database.

- It has been estimated that under current laws the database will expand to include 25 per cent of the adult male population, along with 7 per cent of adult women (R. Williams, P. Johnson, 'Inclusiveness, effectiveness and intrusiveness: issues in the developing uses of DNA profiling in support of criminal investigations', *Journal of Law, Medicine and Ethics*, 2005, no. 333, vol.545–58).

- DNA matches between crime scenes and individuals on the database include many matches with victims and innocent passers-by and false matches, so equating matches with criminals is misleading.

- Only some matches (called DNA detections) involve sufficient evidence to charge someone for a crime, and not all DNA detections lead to prosecutions or convictions. DNA detections increased significantly between 1998/99 and 2002/03, but the number of crime scene DNA profiles loaded on to the database each year also more than tripled during this time (from 19,233 in 1998/99 to 65,649 in 2002/03), as DNA began to be collected routinely from thefts and burglaries. The Home Office recognizes that the increased number of crime scene profiles added to the database drove the increase in DNA detections. Only about half the DNA detections can be attributed to the existence of the database. The majority of these are volume crimes, such as thefts and burglaries.

- Since 2002/03, the number of individuals with DNA profiles on the database has doubled from 2 million to 4.5 million, but there has been no corresponding increase in the number of crimes detected. The percentage of recorded crimes which involve a DNA detection has remained roughly constant at 0.36 per cent.

- About a million unconvicted people have their DNA profiles retained on the National DNA Database. At 31 March 2008, the total number of people with DNA profiles on the NDNAD but no police record of conviction, caution, formal warning or reprimand was estimated as 857,366. (Hansard, 15 September 2008, col. 2070W). This is lower than the 1 million figure given in 2006 (Hansard, 9 October 2006, col. 493W), because children given formal warnings or reprimands were not previously regarded as convicted. The system of final warnings was specifically devised to avoid children entering the criminal justice system unnecessarily.

- Based on Home Office arrest figures, GeneWatch has estimated that about 100,000 unconvicted under-18-year-olds have their DNA profiles retained on the National DNA Database. In September 2008, the Home Office estimated that only 39,095 under-18s had not been convicted, cautioned, received a final warning/reprimand and had no charge pending against them. However, this treats all children with charges pending or with final warnings or reprimands as if they were convicted. It is also calculated by assuming that 13.3 per cent of the NDNAD records are replicates, but that none of the Police National Computer (PNC) records are. This is unlikely to be true for under-18s because only older records (mostly adults) were kept on the NDNAD while PNC records were removed.

- Since 2004 there have been 1,643 requests from foreign countries from information from the NDNAD. Before 2004, such requests were rare (Hansard, 29 September 2008, col. 2345W).

Table 8 Percentage of total population on a police DNA database in 2005

Country	Percentage
Austria	1.04
Belgium	0.04
Croatia	0.23
Czech Republic	0.09
Denmark	0.07
Estonia	0.49
Finland	0.63
France	0.20
Germany	0.44
Hungary	0.28
Netherlands	0.09
Norway	0.15
Slovenia	0.29
Spain	0.01
Sweden	0.07
Switzerland	0.94
United Kingdom	5.23
USA	0.99
Canada	0.23

Source: GeneWatch.

CHAPTER 10

WHERE DO YOU THINK YOU'RE GOING? THE ABUSE OF COUNTER-TERROR LAWS

Counter-terrorist legislation is relatively new in the UK. The Prevention of Terrorism (Temporary Provisions) Act (PTA) was introduced in 1974 after the Birmingham and Guildford pub bombings by the IRA. Hitherto, there were no peacetime laws specifically tailored to dealing with terrorism. The Prevention of Violence Act, an emergency anti-sabotage measure introduced in 1939 was aimed at stopping the IRA disrupting the war effort, and expired in 1953. However, although a terrorist murder attracted the same penalty as any other murder – life imprisonment, though the minimum sentences may differ – the police needed special powers to investigate terrorist crimes. In particular, they required a longer period to detain a suspect without charge.

Before the PTA, the police could hold suspects for 48 hours for questioning before either charging or releasing them. The PTA allowed, in cases of terrorism, for a suspect to be held for seven days. This was hugely controversial. Since it contained additional powers, it was a temporary measure that required a positive vote of parliament every year in order to remain on the statute book. For many years, the Labour Party – despite introducing the Act – refused to support the measure under the Tories when it was brought before parliament for its annual renewal. Oddly enough, only when it began to emerge in the early 1990s that the IRA were prepared to sue for a peaceful settlement did Labour finally came around to supporting powers that would soon no longer be needed, or at any rate, not against the IRA.

Throughout the 1990s, it became apparent that the most significant terrorist threat to the UK no longer came from Ireland but from Islamist organizations that supported a jihad. To begin with, these were regarded as essentially foreign groups, based mainly in the Maghreb in North Africa and posing less of a threat to the UK than to countries such as France which had a colonial legacy in the region. However, the murder by terrorists of 63 tourists at Luxor in Egypt in November 1997, threats to passenger aircraft and the attacks on the American embassies in Kenya and Tanzania in 1998 in which more than 230 people died, convinced western policy makers that we were all vulnerable to terrorism.

In 1999, the government proposed to strengthen the existing powers in the PTA and put terrorism legislation on a permanent footing. The Terrorism Act 2000 was the product of this thinking. Like its predecessor it had special powers of detention, by now increased to 14 days. It put proscription of specified organizations on a statutory basis and allowed for the freezing of assets of suspected groups. Certain conspiratorial activities were outlawed. For the first time, a terrorism measure included specific additional policing powers, governing not what they could do after arresting a suspect but what they could do in their normal day-to-day activities.

Under the Police and Criminal Evidence Act (Pace) which governs the way police arrest and deal with suspects, they cannot just stop anyone and search or question them without having reasonable cause to believe they might be about to commit a crime or have committed one. However, where terrorism was concerned, the government wanted the police to have the power to stop and search anyone they chose to without reasonable cause to be suspicious of them. This provision was contained in Section 44 of the Terrorism Act – and, boy, did the police love using it, often to stifle perfectly lawful protest in the name of counter-terrorism. This was not a completely new measure. The power to stop and search without reasonable suspicion where it was considered expedient in order to prevent acts of terrorism was introduced by Section 81 of the Criminal Justice and Public Order Act 1994. Lord Lloyd, the former independent reviewer of terrorism legislation, observed that this power had been used with 'great discretion' and that it was 'reassuring' that a number of requests for authorizations had been turned down. On this basis he recommended its retention in the permanent anti-terrorism legislation that was eventually contained in the Terrorism Act 2000.[1]

Section 44 first came to public attention not long after the 9/11 attacks in the US in 2001. A group of anti-war protesters – many of them elderly veterans of 1960s ban-the-bomb marches – were stopped on their way to RAF Fairford, Gloucestershire, which was used by American B-52 bombers during the Iraq conflict. These people were quite clearly demonstrators. At the time, the government insisted that powers under this legislation were to be applied solely for the prevention and investigation of acts of terrorism. Yet among those stopped was an 11-year-old girl, who was required to empty her pockets, before being handed a notification slip under the Act – one of more than 1,000 issued to protesters.

In 2003, the section was again used against protesters, this time outside Europe's biggest arms fair at Excel in London's Docklands. When the legality of the use of Section 44 was tested by Liberty, the civil rights organization, the High Court said the police commander had been entitled to apply the powers because the arms fair was controversial, was happening near an airport and was close to the site of a previous terrorist incident at Canary Wharf. However, the Appeal Court said that if the police are to be given exceptional powers because of threats to public safety, they had to be used with the 'appropriate circumspection' and it was 'a fairly close call' as to whether they had been in this instance, though the police were given the benefit of the doubt.[2]

In 2005, a group of trainspotters were detained and searched under Section 44 at Basingstoke station, which was on a list of possible terrorist targets drawn up by the Home Office for the duration of the general election that year. By taking photographs of carriages and noting down serial numbers, the spotters were accused of behaving like a reconnaissance unit for a terrorist cell. They were forced to empty their pockets, explain their actions and prove their identity.

The best known misuse of Section 44 came at the Labour Party conference in 2005, when Walter Wolfgang, an 82-year-old German-Jewish émigré was ejected from the conference hall in Brighton for having the effrontery to heckle Jack Straw's foreign policy speech. As Mr Wolfgang tried to get back into the conference he was briefly detained by a police officer citing his powers under Section 44, because the whole of the conference area had designated by a chief officer as one that might be targeted by terrorists, and authorized as such by the home secretary. At the same Labour conference more than 600 people were stopped under Section 44.

Mark Wallace, a campaigner against ID cards, was stopped near the conference centre under Section 44 while collecting signatures for a petition. He was told by police that his details will be kept on file indefinitely and a video of his detention held for seven years, even though he had done nothing wrong. 'One minute I was peacefully collecting signatures, and the next I had five policemen around me, one with a video camera recording my every move and another taking my personal details, address and so on.' Mr Wallace said. 'It was bad enough that I was subjected to this unjustly, but why am I now registered for life as linked to anti-terrorist investigations, despite my innocence?' He added: 'It worries me that this could damage future travel plans or even attract suspicion in future cases, when all I have done is to use my freedom of speech. The fact that peaceful protest and petitioning is subject to police investigation is itself worrying, but a policy of keeping details of the innocent on file forever is an utter disgrace.'[3]

While Labour was in Brighton, the entire city was a designated area. As was discovered during the court hearings into the Excel stops, which predate the 7 July 2005 attacks in the capital, the whole of London has been given a blanket designation under Section 44, though this has to be renewed every 28 days. In view of the terrorist outrages that have taken place in London and elsewhere it is right that the police should have powers that improve their chances of intercepting potential bombers. But this is not what is happening. Section 44 is often deployed against people who would normally be regarded as protesters, not terrorists, or who have done nothing at all and do not fit the profile of anyone who is likely to be a terrorist, either. This is borne out by the official statistics. In the financial year the Act came into force – which included the period of the 9/11 attacks on New York and Washington – there were 10,200 stops and searches under the Act. The following year, there were 32,000 and for the financial year 2003–4, there were 33,800. By 2006–7 there were 42,000.[4]

Although these interceptions did lead to some arrests for terrorism-related offences (though not of terrorists themselves), people stopped under Section 44 powers were eight times more likely to be arrested for other offences, including motoring infractions. This suggests, at the very least, that the powers have been used in a pretty arbitrary way, despite assurances from the government that they would be deployed only when there is 'a good reason to believe that there is genuinely a terrorist threat'.

Table 9 shows that the vast majority of people stopped and searched under Section 44 and subsequently arrested were not charged with any terrorist offence.

Table 9 Searches of pedestrians, vehicles and occupants under Sections 44(1) and 44(2) of the Terrorism Act 2000 and resultant arrests, 1999–2000 to 2006–7, England and Wales

Year	Total searches	Total arrests	Arrests for terrorism offences	Arrests for other reasons
1999–2000	1,900	18	1	17
2000–01	6,400	45	1	44
2001–02	10,200	189	20	169
2002–03	32,100	380	19	361
2003–04	33,800	491	19	472
2004–05	37,000	468	64	404
2005–06	50,000	563	105	458
2006–07	41,900	480	28	452

Note: Sections 44(1) and 44(2) are formerly sections 13A and 13B of the Prevention of Terrorism (Temporary Provisions) Act 1989 which was repealed under the Terrorism Act 2000 (which came into force on 19 February 2001).

Source: Hansard.

In 2007–8, the stop-and-search figures almost trebled to 124,687 people yet only 1 per cent of searches led to an arrest. Nearly 90 per cent of the searches were carried out by the Metropolitan Police which recorded a 266 per cent increase in its use of the power. Officers in London used Section 44 to carry out stop and search between 8,000 and 10,000 times a month.

Every year, Lord Carlile QC, the Liberal Democrat peer who conducts an independent oversight of counter-terrorism legislation, voices his concern at the way Section 44 is used in England (though not in Scotland). In his 2005 review, Lord Carlile said the use of Section 44 'could be cut by at least 50 per cent without significant risk to the public or detriment to policing'.

His 2009 report made the same criticisms that he had urged the government to address in his previous reports, to no avail, it would seem. It showed that police were making unjustified searches of members of the public to provide 'racial balance' to stop-and-search statistics. Police were wasting money by carrying out 'self-evidently unmerited searches' which were an invasion of civil liberties and 'almost certainly unlawful'.[5]

As the terror threat against Britain is largely from Islamist extremists, there are disproportionately more Muslims stopped and therefore more Asians being searched than whites. However, Lord Carlile said the police should stop trying to balance the figures, and it may be that an 'ethnic imbalance' is a 'proportional consequence' of policing:

I have evidence of cases where the person stopped is so obviously far from any known terrorism profile that, realistically, there is not the slightest possibility of him/her being a terrorist, and no other feature to justify the stop. In one situation the basis of the stops was numerical only, which is almost certainly unlawful and in no way an intelligent use of the procedure. I believe it is totally wrong for any person to be stopped in order to produce a racial balance in the Section 44 statistics. There is ample anecdotal evidence this is happening.

Lord Carlile went on:

I can well understand the concerns of the police that they should be free from allegations of prejudice, but it is not a good use of precious resources if they waste them on self-evidently unmerited searches. It is also an invasion of the civil liberties of the person who has been stopped, simply to 'balance' the statistics. The criteria for section 44 stops should be objectively based, irrespective of racial considerations: if an objective basis happens to produce an ethnic imbalance, that may have to be regarded as a proportional consequence of operational policing.

Lord Carlile questioned why Section 44 powers are thought to be needed in some areas but not in others facing similar levels of risk. He criticized the Metropolitan Police for not limiting Section 44 use to parts of London, and said the number of searches being carried out by the force was 'alarming'. He said:

> I cannot see a justification for the whole of the Greater London area being covered permanently, and the intention of the section was not to place London under permanent special search powers. The figures, and a little analysis of them, show that section 44 is being used as an instrument to aid non-terrorism policing on some occasions, and this is unacceptable . . . I repeat my mantra that terrorism-related powers should be used only for terrorism-related purposes; otherwise their credibility is severely damaged.

Lord Carlile said the use of Section 44 had an 'undoubtedly negative' impact on community relations. He added: 'I am sure it could safely be used far less. There is little or no evidence that the use of Section 44 has the potential to prevent an act of terrorism as compared with other statutory powers of stop and search.'

The fact is that these powers are hardly used at all in Scotland; and while London is clearly a more prominent target, the Met did review its use of Section 44, stating that in future it would be restricted to policing 'iconic' or strategically important sites. Judging by Lord Carlile's continuing criticism, this is still not the case.

The Home Office defended the use of Section 44 powers thus:

> Stop and search under the Terrorism Act 2000 is an important tool in the on-going fight against terrorism. As

part of a structured anti-terrorist strategy, the powers help to deter terrorist activity by creating a hostile environment for would-be terrorists to operate [in]. Countering the terrorist threat and ensuring good community relations are interdependent and we are continuing to work with the police to ensure that the use of stop and search powers strikes the right balance.[6]

Typical of many statements from Whitehall, this misses the point. Nobody is suggesting there should not be a stop-and-search power, merely that it should be properly targeted for maximum impact against terrorists and not used as a catch-all. As Lord Carlile maintained, a good law would have ensured proper use of resources and the most effective use of police time: 'the intention of the section was not to place London under permanent special search powers.'[7]

Indeed it wasn't; but it happened because the law empowered the police to do this, even if parliament did not intend that they should. Of course, there is a balance to be struck between ensuring that the police have effective counter-terrorism powers and the freedom of the citizen to go about his daily business unmolested. There are times when exceptional measures are warranted to override the normal expectation that the police will intervene in our lives only if there is reasonable suspicion of a crime being committed. However, it is wrong to use them to stifle lawful protest.

In addition, many of those arrested under the Terrorism Act are never actually charged with anything. Home Office figures show that between 11 September 2001 and 31 March 2008, there were 1,471 arrests for terrorism in Britain. Of these, 521 resulted in a charge of some form, with 222 people charged with terror offences and 118 people charged with terror-related offences, such as conspiracy to murder. The Home Office said the number of those arrested who were charged is similar to that for other criminal offences. Of the 340 people charged in relation to terrorism, 196 were eventually convicted: 102 for terrorism offences under terror legislation and 94 for terrorism-related criminal offences. That means, out of 1,471 terrorism arrests, 102 were eventually convicted under terrorism legislation.[8]

The main offences for suspects charged under terrorism legislation were possession of an article for terrorist purposes, membership of a proscribed organization and fundraising.

The Home Office eventually acknowledged that there was something wrong with the way this law was being used by revising its operational guidance to the police in November 2008. In July 2009, the Met introduced what it called 'refined tactics' for the use of Section 44 powers which in future would only be deployed at pre-identified significant locations, such as iconic sites and crowded places, and when specific operations have been agreed for specific areas. Whether it has made any difference will only become apparent with Lord Carlile's next report.

SMILE PLEASE: YOU'RE NICKED

The Terrorism Act has since been updated by the Counter-Terrorism Act which came into force in the spring of 2009 and contains all the earlier powers and some more, including a new offence of taking pictures of police officers 'likely to be useful to a person committing or preparing an act of terrorism'. This was done by way of an amendment to Section 58 of the Terrorism Act 2000 and the addition of a new clause:

> 58A Eliciting, publishing or communicating information about members of armed forces etc
> (1) A person commits an offence who –
>   (a) elicits or attempts to elicit information about an individual who is or has been –
>   (i) a member of Her Majesty's forces,

        (ii) a member of any of the intelligence services, or
        (iii) a constable,
    which is of a kind likely to be useful to a person committing or preparing an act of terrorism, or
    (b) publishes or communicates any such information.
(2) It is a defence for a person charged with an offence under this section to prove that they had a reasonable excuse for their action.
(3) A person guilty of an offence under this section is liable –
    (a) on conviction on indictment, to imprisonment for a term not exceeding 10 years or to a fine, or to both.

This is such a catch-all measure that it can be used – and, in view of recent trends, will be used – to prevent photographs to which the police object merely by invoking counter-terrorist requirements. While it is important for officers involved in such operations to maintain anonymity, many photographers fear these powers are already being abused. Given the fact that photographs and video of police operations at the G20 summit in April 2009 uncovered allegedly brutal treatment that resulted in injury and even death, this is a particularly bad law. It is one that, as with Section 44 and the Regulation of Investigatory Powers Act (RIPA), is being used for purposes that parliament, surely, cannot have intended.

Before this law came in, many police officers already imagined that, somehow, they were exempt from being photographed; yet they were not. However, since the new terrorism legislation was passed, they are; or at least they are in a stronger position to claim that they are. When the Bill was going through parliament, many people warned that it could be misused and there were several stories to back them up. Andrew Carter, a plumber from Bedminster, near Bristol, took a photograph of an officer who had ignored a no-entry road sign while driving a police van. This might have appeared a somewhat petulant thing to do, but taking a photograph in a public place is not a crime. Yet the policeman smashed the camera from Mr Carter's hand, handcuffed him, put him in the back of the van and took him to the police station, where he was kept for five hours. When he returned to answer bail the following week, he was kept at the station for another five hours. He was released without charge, despite an attempt by the police to claim some spurious offence of 'assault with a camera'.[9]

In an article in the *British Journal of Photography*, Justin Tallis, a freelance photographer, recounted how he was threatened while covering a protest against the BBC's decision not to broadcast a fundraising film for Gaza. He was approached by an officer who had just been photographed. According to Tallis, the officer tried to take his camera away, but gave up as other photographers captured the incident.[10]

Early in 2009, an amateur photographer was stopped in Cleveland by officers when taking pictures of ships. The photographer was asked if he had any terrorism connections and told that his details would be kept on file. According to the government, while there are no legal restrictions on photography in public places, 'there may be situations in which the taking of photographs may cause or lead to public order situations or raise security considerations'.[11]

In March 2009, not long after the Act became law, Jamie Waylett, who played the character Vincent Crabbe in the Harry Potter film series, was arrested for taking a picture of police officers as he and a friend drove past them. The camera was seized; the police found no evidence of a terrorist conspiracy but they did find some pictures of cannabis plants that Waylett was growing in tents at the Kilburn home where his mother lives. Waylett, 20, was charged and ordered to do 120 hours of unpaid work by Westminster Magistrates Court after pleading guilty to the offence.[12] While he had clearly been breaking the law and was justifiably prosecuted for drugs offences, the reason for his arrest was a questionable use of the police powers to combat terrorism.

Gemma Atkinson, 27, was also detained after filming police officers conduct a routine stop-and-search on her boyfriend. She recorded part of the incident on her mobile phone at Aldgate East underground station on 25 March 2009, just one month after Section 58(a) came into force. Atkinson handed the footage, in which an officer can be heard telling her it is illegal to film police and demanding to see her phone, to the *Guardian* newspaper and said she was seeking to challenge the force in a judicial review. The incident was captured on CCTV. The opening part of the mobile phone clip shows two uniformed police officers searching her boyfriend, Fred Grace, 28, by a wall in the station. Atkinson said she felt that police had unfairly targeted Grace, who did not have drugs in his possession, and decided to film the officers in order to hold them to account. Seconds later, an undercover officer wearing jeans and a black jacket enters the shot, and asks Atkinson: 'Do you realize it is an offence under the Terrorism Act to film police officers?' He then adds: 'Can you show me what you just filmed?' Atkinson stopped filming and placed her phone in her pocket. According to her account of the incident, which was submitted to the Independent Police Complaints Commission that night, the officer tried several times to forcibly grab the phone from her pocket.[13]

Atkinson's solicitors, Bhatt Murphy, said faulty guidance to officers about how counter-terrorism laws apply to photography in public places may have contributed to her treatment. The Met guidance to its officers instructs them that when searching people under the Terrorism Act, they 'have the power to view digital images contained in mobile telephones'. It adds that the new offence relating to photographing officers does not apply in normal policing activities. The Met's guidance is different to that issued by the National Policing Improvement Agency, which specifically advises that 'officers do not have a legal power to delete images or destroy film' and suggests that, while digital images might be viewed during a search, officers 'should not normally attempt to examine them'.[14]

Why were these matters left up in the air by the counter-terrorism legislation? Parliament should have stopped this happening; more to the point, what was the government doing once again bringing forward such an illiberal measure?

This sort of legislation, invoked in the name of preventing terrorism, is an expansion of police powers that would not be allowed under any other guise; yet, as is seen from Table 9, terrorist powers are being used for non-terrorist reasons. Gradually people become inured to the whole panoply of legislation and surveillance that is justified in the name of defeating the terrorists and keeping us all safe, yet which is further incursion on individual freedoms. It leads the police to make demands that are totally unreasonable. Suffolk police, for instance, insisted that Facebook shut down a page dedicated to an over-zealous traffic warden because it contained 'hurtful criticisms'.[15] In addition, curbs were proposed on national security grounds on financial reporting during the banking crisis; students were prevented from filming an interview in Parliament Square; two evangelical preachers were threatened with arrest for committing a 'hate crime' by handing out Gospel leaflets in a predominantly Muslim area of Birmingham; and police have even reprimanded people for wearing T-shirts carrying the motif 'Bollocks to Blair'.

Andrew Pelling, the MP for Central Croydon, was stopped by officers under anti-terrorism laws after they found him taking photos of a cycle path in his area. He told them he was taking photos to highlight a 'long-neglected bicycle and pedestrian route', which had been of concern to his constituents and that he was intending on taking the photos to parliament 'to illustrate the dangers posed by the protracted maintenance works'. Yet the two officers insisted on searching him after they told him they thought he was taking photos of East Croydon train station. They searched his bag, but after finding nothing of interest they sent the MP on his way.

Mr Pelling said:

It is pleasing to see just how vigilant our police are at these times of heightened international political tension and the risk of terrorism here at home. I am glad my stop and search account as a white, middle-aged male shows that anyone can be suspected of, and questioned about, terrorism, regardless of race, creed or colour. This is another burden on the police when the key concern of combating knife killings is still an urgent call on local police resources.[16]

A police spokeswoman said: 'An officer stopped and searched a man's bag in Cherry Orchard Road on December 30, under section 44 of the Terrorism Act. The officer conducted a stop-and-search, taking into account the current terror threat, as he was taking pictures in the vicinity of a major transport hub.'[17]

Mr Pelling was unusual in being a white middle-aged man. Inevitably, Section 44 is used mostly to stop Muslims or people who look like they might be Muslims, including many young Asian men who are not. Asians are more than twice as likely to be searched as their white counterparts. Hazel Blears, then a Home Office minister, told MPs in 2005: 'Some of our counter-terrorism powers will be disproportionately experienced by people in the Muslim community. There is no getting away from the fact.' Ian Johnston, the chief constable of the British Transport Police, said in the same year: 'We should not waste time searching old white ladies.' So why do they?

HAVE YOU HEARD THE ONE ABOUT THE MUSLIM, THE JEW AND THE CHRISTIAN? WELL YOU CAN'T

Can you have a good law that makes it illegal to disapprove of someone, or of some form of activity or belief? Legislation already exists to prevent or punish people who assault or threaten an individual of whom they disapprove. But how can subjective emotions such as dislike be criminalized? If someone considers that Islam (or Christianity, for that matter) is a dangerous religion why should they not be allowed to say so? If they regard homosexuality to be offensive what is wrong with voicing that opinion provided there is no threat or overt discrimination involved? Yet laws have been devised to outlaw disapproval, probably for the first time in our history.

They may be couched in terms of hatred, but this does not of itself provide a justification. The government's decision to make incitement to religious hatred an offence triggered one of the most sustained revolts of Tony Blair's time in office. It began shortly after the 9/11 attacks in the US when David Blunkett, the home secretary, brought forward emergency counter-terrorism legislation. Clause 38 of the Anti-Terrorism, Crime and Security Bill would have extended existing legal provisions on incitement to racial hatred to cover incitement to religious hatred. However, in the Lords, the clause was removed by 240 votes to 141. Although it was reinstated by MPs, it was again blocked in the Lords, whereupon the government decided not to proceed with the proposal in order to get the rest of the legislation through. (That was also to prove controversial: this measure contained the powers to lock up suspected foreign terrorists without charge or trial, something later overturned by the Law Lords.)

Opposition came from an unexpected quarter: outside of parliament, comics, rallied by Rowan Atkinson, took up the cudgels. Atkinson had spent a substantial part of his career parodying religious figures from his own Christian background. His portrayal of a novice vicar haplessly conducting a marriage ceremony in the film *Four Weddings and a Funeral* was a masterpiece of timing and malapropisms. Atkinson feared that the new religious hatred law, introduced as a sop to Muslims because of the tough crackdown in the rest of the counter-terror legislation, would make any jocular or satirical references to religion illegal. For instance, would Monty Python's film *The Life of Brian* – which angered many Christians – be banned; or the television series *Father Ted* taken off the air?

In a letter to *The Times*, Atkinson voiced his 'great disquiet' about the proposed legislation, recalling a sketch in *Not the Nine O'Clock News* that showed Muslim worshippers in a mosque bowing to the ground with the voiceover: 'And the search goes on for the Ayatollah Khomeini's contact lens.' Atkinson added: 'Not respectful, but comedy takes no prisoners . . . I believe the reaction of the audience should decide the appropriateness of a joke, not the law.'[18]

Rory Bremner, the comedian and impressionist, shared his fellow performer's concerns: 'I think if there is a God it is very important He has a sense of humour – otherwise you are in for a very miserable afterlife.' Gerald Scarfe, the cartoonist, said: 'It is a very tricky area. Some people are hurt by any comment about it – not that we cartoonists care. But I am with Rowan Atkinson. I think anything is grist to the mill really.'[19]

Blunkett had stepped into the sort of legislative minefield that his predecessors had been careful to avoid. Jack Straw, when he was at the Home Office, ruled out just such an extension of the law when Muslim organizations called for the change during the passage of criminal justice legislation. Mr Straw correctly foresaw the difficulties of defining religiously motivated crimes, because there was a subjective test to be considered in addition to an objective one. He also doubted that more law was needed: 'In practice, almost all cases that appear to have a religious element will also have a racial element. When the perpetrators of these offences attack Muslims, they do not generally do so because of hostility to the tenets of Islam. They do so because of racist hostility.'[20]

Muslims had long regarded it as unfair that Jews and Sikhs, as distinct ethnic groups, were protected by race discrimination legislation and that there is an ancient law – that of blasphemy – that uniquely defends the Christian faith. However, the law of blasphemy did not protect the Church of England from criticism or derision. Moreover, there has been only one successful prosecution in the past 90 years (and that was a private one, against *Gay News* over the publication of a poem in 1977).

Atkinson was right to be alarmed by the home secretary's proposal. In the past, governments had always taken the view that freedom of speech and expression should only be curtailed when there is a likelihood and intention to produce a threat to public order. It had never been thought appropriate to punish those who merely offend other people's religious sensibilities. Because of the sectarianism in Northern Ireland, religious belief was brought within the scope of the Public Order Act in the province, though there have been very few, if any, prosecutions. There have also been laws against incitement to racial hatred since the mid-1970s. But while race is easily defined, religion is a matter of personal belief and assent. And the big problem with the legislation is that it did not define religion nor did it list the religions against which it would be illegal to incite hatred. There was also concern that a law on religious hatred could actually protect from criticism extremist cults that might legitimately attract opprobrium and prevent commentators attacking fundamentalists whose activities harm others.

In the House of Lords, the most vocal and high profile critic was Lord Mackay of Clashfern, a former lord chancellor and a strongly religious man who is a member of the Free Church of Scotland, known as the Wee Frees:

> Are people in our country to be prevented by the criminal law from ardently advocating their own faith when that faith may be in direct contradiction to the devoutly held tenets of others? Over the years, our country has witnessed serious divisions and much persecution has arisen from attempts to force people to abjure their dearly held views on such matters. I know from bitter personal experience how strongly even those who belong to the same community of faith may disapprove of one another's principles or conduct.

It is against this background that the proposal to make it a criminal offence to incite religious hatred has to be viewed. Ours would be a happier world if no hatred existed between any of us. There may therefore be much to commend in the idea of making it a criminal offence to incite hatred, although I doubt whether anyone would think this a practical proposition in the present state of our society. Where the intention is to make it a criminal offence to incite hatred of a particular description, great care is required. The existing law on such incitement has not proved itself easy to enforce. A good criminal law ought to be reasonably unambiguous in its definition, and also reasonably capable of being enforced when the description of conduct that it embodies occurs in practice.[21]

In many ways, Lord Mackay's objections to this law capture the wider problems with law-making in Britain: an attempt is made to establish something as a wrong that needs to be righted – in this case a view among some Muslims that they were not afforded the same protections for their religion as others. Despite the evident difficulties in framing the legislation, and in the teeth of opposition from many people who know better, the government nevertheless proceeded with the measure more to make a statement that it hoped would pay political dividends rather than to establish a workable legal foundation to the law of the land. Lord Mackay perfectly illustrated the dangers of this approach:

The words 'religion' or 'religious' are, to my mind, extremely vague terms to be used to define a statutory offence. Do they include, for example, satanic worship, atheism or agnosticism? Do they include matters of practice related to one's faith? Debates in the past have sometimes character-ised people with a certain viewpoint as Pharisees. Would it be a crime under the new law to refer to somebody as a

Pharisee, since, if it was done with sufficient earnestness, I think it might well amount to incitement to hate them? Bringing the criminal law into the area of religion in the way that is proposed is fraught with real difficulty. If such a law is brought in, I believe very difficult questions will confront the courts, as they have already done in relation to religion and charities. Where such difficulties arise in the courts, and the judges have to take decisions on them, the opprobrium from one side or the other in the dispute is directed not at those who introduced the law, but at the judges in their application of it.

For several years the protestations of the Lords won the day. The first attempt at a religious hatred law was withdrawn by David Blunkett who risked losing his anti-terror Bill entirely if he refused to back down. Furious, he blamed 'duplicitous and hypocritical' Tories and Liberal Democrats for the u-turn. He said in a statement:

The reason religious incitement was dropped was because the whole of the anti-terrorism Bill would have fallen because of the refusal of the House of Lords to accept the view of the Commons. This Parliamentary session was the opportunity to pass this into law, with other measures delayed and dropped because of the need to get anti-terrorist legislation passed.[22]

However, the government was not about to give up and, in 2004, the proposed new offence was included this time in the Serious Organised Crime and Police Bill. It defined religious hatred as 'hatred against a group of persons defined by reference to religious belief or lack of religious belief'. An offence would carry a maximum seven years in jail. Explanatory notes accompanying the Bill said the offence would apply: 'to the use of words or behaviour or display of written material, publishing or distributing written material, the public performance of a play, distributing, showing or playing a recording, broadcasting or including a programme in a programme service and the possession of written materials or recordings with a view to display, publication, distribution or inclusion in a programme service'. The note also explained: 'For each offence the words, behaviour, written material, recordings or programmes must be threatening, abusive or insulting and intended or likely to stir up racial hatred.'

In a column for the *Daily Telegraph*, Charles Moore, the newspaper's former editor, somewhat provocatively highlighted the restrictions that the proposed law would place on free speech by asking the question: 'Was the prophet Mohammed a paedophile? People are perfectly entitled – rude and mistaken though they may be – to say that Mohammed was a paedophile.'[23]

Certainly the juxtaposition of the Prophet's name and paedophilia was shocking and was intended to be; but why should it be a crime punishable by seven years in prison? In a response, Iqbal Sacranie, secretary-general of the Muslim Council of Britain, wrote:

> We seem to be revisiting the arguments that came to the fore during the Satanic Verses affair. Is freedom of expression without bounds? Muslims are not alone in saying 'No' and calling for safeguards against vilification of dearly cherished beliefs ... the incitement to religious hatred proposal is not a matter of advancing privileges for British Muslims. It's about establishing equality under the law. The current loophole in our legislation has resulted in far Right groups such as the BNP modifying their racist rhetoric of yesteryear – no doubt out of fear of prosecution – into a more explicitly and aggressively anti-Muslim invective, this time without fear of breaking the law. Stirring up hatred against people simply because of their religious

beliefs or lack of them ought to be regarded as a social evil. The BNP's ongoing Islamophobia can and has led to criminal acts, abuse, discrimination, fear and disorder. At the moment, there are laws against those who are stirred into committing these offences, but not against those that do the stirring. In opposing the incitement to religious hatred provision, Charles Moore, Rowan Atkinson and the National Secular Society are unwittingly strengthening the hand of those, such as the BNP, who peddle religious hatred . . . To be sure, proscribing legitimate free speech is not in the interest of any religion. The death of discussion, debate and robust criticism about a religion is the surest way of routing that religion itself. However, we can make a critical distinction between the substance and form of free speech. The law need not infringe on the substance but can assist to moderate the form, so that all people in this country, whatever their religion, may live in dignity, free from hatred and hostility.

Correspondents to the newspaper were alarmed by Moore's column. Once asked: 'Would he readily defend anybody who called Jews "Christ-killers"?' But even if the answer to that question is 'No' that is not the point. The issue here was whether it should be a crime punishable by up to seven years in jail, not whether the remarks were offensive, objectionable or defensible. As Bob Marshall-Andrews, Labour MP for Medway, said: 'I have very grave doubts as to whether it should be criminal – as opposed to merely socially unacceptable – to incite hatred against someone because of what we do; and religion is what we do and not what we are.'

While the law could apply to any religion, it was clear that it was aimed at meeting the objections of the Muslim community to the absence of any statutory protections for Islam. The timing of its resuscitation could hardly have been more cynical. A general election was expected the following year and Labour was desperate to regain the favour of Muslim voters after losing so much of their support because of the war in Iraq. Ministers knew there would be a backlash from the Lords that would make it difficult to get the legislation through ahead of the election – and this is precisely what happened. After raising the prospect once again of a law against religious hatred in order to remind everyone that it was an issue ministers felt strongly about, it was duly dropped so as to secure the passage of the Serious and Organised Crime Act before the 2005 general election.

This time, Labour included a promise in its manifesto to bring forward the measure in the next parliament, something that would make opposition in the Lords hard to sustain. The Salisbury Convention, introduced by Lord Salisbury, the Conservative leader of the House of Lords following Labour's landslide general election victory in 1945, holds that the House of Lords should not oppose legislation included in an election manifesto at the Second Reading. It is still permitted under the convention to propose reasoned amendments to the detail of a Bill, provided these amendments are not designed to destroy the Bill. Although not explicitly covered by the convention there is also an understanding that the House of Lords will not vote down Statutory Instruments. Since the Labour general election victory in 2005 both the Liberal Democrats and Conservatives have indicated that they do not feel bound by the Salisbury Convention because of decreasing voter turnout, the low share of the vote received by the government and the changes to the composition of the House of Lords introduced in 1999 by Labour.

Labour's 2005 manifesto said: 'It remains our firm intention to give people of all faiths the same protection against incitement to hatred on the basis of their religion. We will legislate to outlaw it and will continue the dialogue we have started with faith groups from all backgrounds about how best to balance protection, tolerance and free speech'.[24]

In late 2005, the proposal was duly brought back, this time as the Racial and Religious Hatred Bill, the third legislative vehicle used for the same measure. Wearily, the same coalition of opponents reassembled. Again, the government insisted it was not its intention to outlaw telling jokes about religion. Again, the fundamental flaw was the absence of any definition of religion and the threat to free speech.

And again, notwithstanding the Salisbury Convention, the Lords took a scalpel to the measure. This time, since it was a manifesto commitment, peers did not throw the whole thing out; instead they softened the proposed legislation to make it an offence to use threatening words or behaviour towards a religious group, but not statements and actions that were merely abusive or insulting. The amendments in the Lords also required prosecutors to show that a person intended his words or actions to be threatening, and would include a provision specifically safeguarding the right to free expression.

The government wanted to reverse these amendments when the Bill returned to the Commons in February 2006, but a head of steam against the measure had been building among Labour MPs. The government, despite a majority of more than 60, lost two crucial votes, only the second and third occasions that Tony Blair had been defeated since he took office in 1997. As a result, the government was forced to endure the humiliation of accepting unwanted changes to the Racial and Religious Hatred Bill that weakened its scope but reinforced the notion of freedom of speech.

No sooner had the religious hatred law been passed, albeit with safeguards, than Ministers introduced yet another law, this time to make 'homophobic' behaviour an offence. On this occasion those who feared they would be caught by the measure were Christian organizations preaching that homosexuality was wrong. The legislative vehicle was the Criminal Justice Bill 2007, which made it unlawful to use threatening words or behaviour on the grounds of sexual orientation. As with the religious hatred law, it was necessary to show that the offending words are intended to pose a threat and are not merely abusive, mocking or insulting.

Is this a good law? Do politicians have any business trying to ban 'hatred' in a free society? Surely, it is a requirement of liberty that you can hate anyone you want provided you do not act on it. Without the opposition of the Lords the Labour government would have imposed an extraordinary restriction on free speech. Ministers said it was not their intention to introduce what to all intents and purposes was a 'thoughtcrime'. Yet they tried three times to do just that only to be beaten back by the House of Lords which Labour (and the Tories, for that matter) wants to turn into another chamber of political hacks by making all its members stand for election. Had that already been the case when the religious hatred bills were going through, freedom of religion and freedom of conscience would probably be dead in Britain.

THE GRIM RIPA

It became known as the 'Snooper's Charter'. The Regulation of Investigatory Powers Act 2000, or RIPA, was used to spy on children to ensure that their parents were not lying about living within a school catchment area; it was deployed to stop householders putting recyclable refuse out with their normal rubbish; it allowed council officials to follow dog-owners to make sure their animals were not fouling the footpaths. Even though newspapers denounced the abuse of these powers and ministers told the agencies that possessed them to use them sparingly, those were precisely the functions for which it was brought into being.

It is often stated that RIPA was a counter-terror measure. It wasn't. Rather than bestowing new powers on a variety of state bodies, it was brought in to rationalize and regulate powers that already existed but which were used relatively sparingly. According to the Home Office: 'In fact, it did not create any new powers or techniques at all; nor did it permit any public authority to use powers which it could not have used prior to RIPA.'[25]

So why was it brought in at all, you may ask. The first time the government tried to introduce RIPA there was such a furore when people saw how many bodies either already had, or were about to be given, statutory snooping powers that it was withdrawn and then quietly reintroduced a year or so later.

The Home Office said that the new regulations merely gave statutory backing to agencies other than the police and MI5 that already carried out surveillance operations. For instance, local councils conduct undercover operations to check whether a shop is selling cigarettes or alcohol to children; food standards officers can recruit informants to ensure unfit meat is not being sold; and social security officers can follow individuals to check on whether they are working and claiming benefit.

But for the first time, the regulations exposed the full range of government bodies and quangos that can watch over people, check on what they are doing and monitor their communications. Many of these agencies are able to collect personal details about the use of phones and emails. In addition to the police, customs and the intelligence agencies, automatic access to communications data was extended to the ambulance service, fire authorities, HM Coastguard, hundreds of local councils, the Scottish Drugs Enforcement Agency and the UK Atomic Energy Authority Constabulary.

These bodies can obtain subscribers' names and addresses, details of telephone calls and emails made and received, mobile-phone locations accurate to within 100 yards, call waiting or call barring information, itemized call records and subscriber details. However, they cannot discover the contents of telephone conversations or emails: such interceptions still need a warrant signed by a minister. Nevertheless, limited access to communications details – such as the names and addresses of phone and internet subscribers – are available to hundreds of other bodies, including local councils.

When the RIPA legislation was going through parliament, ministers hotly denied that it would be abused or that councils would set up teams of agents to follow people walking dogs suspected of fouling the pavement. However, this is precisely what happened, as council chiefs themselves now acknowledge.

Yet they are also right to protest that they are caught between a rock and a hard place. For instance, if local councils are to uphold licensing laws by checking on pubs suspected of selling alcohol to underage children, how are they to do this if not in a covert way? The same could be said about keeping tabs on fly-tipping or other anti-social behaviour. It is all a question of proportion. The problem with RIPA is that there was no sense of proportion.

After the Act had been in operation a few years, there was clearly something amiss. This had nothing to do with counter-terrorism. After all, the police and MI5 can obtain warrants to intercept communications and carry out covert operations and have been doing so for decades. What was becoming apparent was the extent to which the RIPA powers were being taken up with alacrity by bodies that most people would not have considered covert organizations, like their local council.

The use of surveillance powers is monitored annually by the chief surveillance officer, usually a retired senior civil servant. In his annual report for the year to March 2009, Sir Christopher Rose said there had been 9,894 'directed surveillance authorizations' granted to public bodies, half of them local authorities.[26] A directed surveillance authorization is defined as 'covert surveillance of individuals while in a public place for the purposes of a specific investigation'.

Often authority for such activity is sought by a junior official, whereas the police and MI5 need the authority of a senior officer before making a request. Sir Christopher said some councils were guilty of using RIPA in a 'disproportionate' way. He specifically accused councils of 'a serious misunderstanding of the concept of proportionality' and threatened to strip them of their powers. He said, 'Many authorities do not recognize that they are vulnerable to criticism ... if activity is conducted without appropriate management or if activity is being conducted in a disproportionate manner. If authorities wish to retain the protection that RIPA affords, I encourage a greater attention to detail.'

He was particularly concerned that there was a risk of councils crossing the legal line into 'intrusive surveillance', which they are prohibited from doing: 'It is not acceptable to judge that because directed surveillance is being conducted from a public place this automatically renders the activity overt or to assert that an activity is proportionate because it is the only way to further an investigation.'[27]

As a result of the furore, Gordon Brown decided to review the laws. He told MPs: 'The Government is reviewing those public authorities that have access to these powers to ensure that they have a continuing and justifiable requirement for them. On completion the Government will list the authorities that can use each of the powers and the purposes for which they can use them, and set out revised codes of practice.'[28]

Requests to monitor communications are also scrutinized, this time by the interception of a communications commissioner. In his report for 2008, Sir Paul Kennedy showed that police, security services and other public bodies made 504,073 requests to 'communications providers' such as phone and internet firms for billing records and other information. The total was roughly the same as in 2007 but compared with an average of fewer than 350,000 requests a year in the two years before that. To a great extent this increase was to do with significantly enhanced counter-terrorist activity by the police and MI5, who still make the lion's share of requests for communications information. However, Sir Paul's report also disclosed that 123 local authorities made 1,553 requests for 'communications data' in the year to the end of March. Only a handful of the requests were for 'itemised call records', Sir Paul found, but 'quite a number of local authorities' had failed to comply with the commissioner's code of practice, usually because they were not properly trained. The report explained:

> Generally the trading standards services were the principal users of communications data within local authorities although the environmental health departments and housing benefit fraud investigators also occasionally make use of the powers. Local authorities enforce numerous statutes and Councils use communications data to identify criminals who persistently rip off consumers, cheat the taxpayer, deal in counterfeit goods, and prey on the elderly and vulnerable. The environmental health departments principally use communications data to identify fly-tippers whose activities cause damage to the environment and cost the taxpayers large sums to recover or otherwise deal with the waste.[29]

The controversy surrounding RIPA was an eye-opener for many people who had become used to having CCTV cameras everywhere and who were prepared to accept incursions by the state on their personal privacy if it made it easier to combat terrorism. But this was a different thing altogether. This felt alien; local officialdom snooping on people smacked of the Stasi in East Germany before the fall of the Berlin Wall.

Sir Simon Milton, then chairman of the Local Government Association, insisted that the powers were necessary to deal with legitimate concerns from local people about 'fly tippers, rogue traders and those defrauding the council tax or housing benefit system':

> Without these powers, councils would not be able to provide the level of reassurance and protection local people demand and deserve. Councils have been criticised for using the powers in relation to issues that can be portrayed

as trivial or not considered a crime by the public. By their nature, surveillance powers are never to be used lightly but it is important that councils don't lose the power to use them when appropriate.[30]

Councils increasingly began to use RIPA to investigate anything that can be classed as a criminal offence in cases which seemed to be petty and vindictive.

Gosport Borough Council in Hampshire used RIPA for an undercover investigation into dog-fouling, equipping officers with digital cameras and binoculars to spy on dog-walkers. Chris Davis, the council's head of internal audit, said: 'We have strategically placed members of our enforcement team to blend in with the natural environment and observe people walking dogs. They are using digital cameras to get hard evidence. Dog fouling is a real issue and in this case it is happening close to a leisure facility where children play.'[31] Stoke-on-Trent city council used RIPA to investigate 'illegal building work', while several councils have put cameras in tins and piles of twigs to catch fly-tippers.

By 2006, more than 1,000 applications per day were being made to use RIPA powers.

The most celebrated case, and the one that got this particularly bad law reformed, concerned the Joyce family of Poole, Dorset. Tim Joyce, 37, his girlfriend Jenny Paton, 39, and their three daughters were followed on school runs and watched at their home by Poole Borough Council to make sure they lived in the catchment area of the school their three-year-old daughter attended. Miss Paton described the council's actions as 'a grotesque invasion of privacy'. Mr Joyce said: 'It used to be that the Home Secretary had to talk to a judge to get surveillance through the police. Now it seems the world and his wife can carry out surveillance whenever they feel like it.'[32]

In June 2008, Sir Simon Milton sent a letter to the leaders

of every council in England, urging local governments not to use the new powers granted by RIPA 'for trivial matters', and suggested 'reviewing these powers annually by an appropriate scrutiny committee'.[33] But nothing much seemed to change.

In the autumn of 2008, an investigation by Chris Hastings of the *Sunday Telegraph* newspaper found that three-quarters of local authorities had used the Regulation of Investigatory Powers Act over the previous year. Of 115 councils that responded to a Freedom of Information request, 89 admitted that they had instigated investigations under the Act. The 82 councils that provided figures said that they authorized or carried out a total of 867 RIPA investigations during the year to August. Durham County Council emerged as the biggest user, with just over 100 surveillance operations launched during the period. Newcastle City Council used the powers 82 times, and Middlesbrough Council 70 times.

Derby Council made sound recordings of a property after a complaint about noisy children. Calderdale Council in West Yorkshire began 'direct covert surveillance' targeting one business. Bassetlaw, Easington, Bolsover and Darlington placed houses under video or photographic surveillance to tackle problems such as anti-social behaviour, unauthorized entry into gardens and benefit fraud. Others admitted using council staff to follow residents to determine whether they were working while claiming benefits. Dudley and County Durham used RIPA powers to send children into shops with secret video and audio equipment to see whether they could buy cigarettes and alcohol. Officials in Durham mounted 60 RIPA investigations against these kinds of businesses in the 12 months.[34]

Sir Jeremy Beecham of the Local Government Association denied councils used these powers to mount fishing expeditions: 'First and foremost it is about protecting the public, not intruding on privacy. Crime-busting powers are targeted at suspected criminals and used only when absolutely necessary.'[35]

Among other uses of RIPA were:

- Newcastle City Council used the Act to monitor noise levels from smoking shelters at two different licensed premises. The council has twice used the legislation to monitor noise from a vet's practice following a complaint about barking.
- Blaenau Gwent County Borough Council used it to deal with 16 complaints about barking dogs.
- Derby Council made sound recordings at a property following a complaint about noisy children.
- Peterborough Council investigated the operation of the blue badge scheme for disabled drivers.
- Poole Council used it to detect illegal fishing in Poole Harbour.
- Basingstoke Council used photographic surveillance against one of its own refuse collectors after allegations he was charging residents for a service that should be free. The operation was dropped when it was decided the allegation was false.
- Aberdeenshire Council admitted using the Scottish version of the Act to request the name and address of a mobile-phone user as part of an investigation into offences under the Weights and Measures Act.
- Easington Council put a resident's garden under camera surveillance after a complaint from neighbours about noise.
- Canterbury City Council used CCTV surveillance and an officer's observations to monitor illegal street-trading.
- Brighton and Hove council launched four operations against graffiti artists.
- Torbay Council accessed an employee's emails after an allegation that suspect material had been sent. A second employee was investigated over the 'use of council vehicle for personal gain'.
- Westminster City Council covertly filmed a locksmith following allegations of fraud.

- Durham County Council obtained authorization to monitor car-boot sales during an investigation into the sale of counterfeit goods.

By the spring of 2009, matters had not noticeably improved. Figures obtained by the Liberal Democrats, using the Freedom of Information Act, showed how it was possible for the most junior council officials to seek authorization for RIPA powers. One in five was below senior management grade, and few local authorities demonstrated they checked whether the powers were being used appropriately, something they had been warned about by the commissioner in his report the previous year.

Some councils used the powers to see if a staff member was 'working while off sick' or checked whether 'a claimant's partner is living at an address'. A survey of 400 councils in England and Wales by the Liberal Democrats found that many of them were using the powers to investigate trivial misdemeanours. In the study, 182 local authorities admitted employing 1,615 staff who had used the powers 10,133 times in the past five years. Less than 1 in 10 of these authorizations actually resulted in a prosecution, caution or even a fixed-penalty notice.

Across the 180 councils, the spying powers were mostly used to tackle benefit fraud (1,782 times), noise nuisance (942 times) and trading standards breaches (734 times). However, the powers were also used for 451 investigations into fly-tipping and 88 cases of unlawful dog-fouling. Other reasons included 'establishing the identities of those taking fairy lights from a Christmas tree', 'illegal sale of shellfish' and 'unauthorised internet access by staff'.

This is how the Home Office responded:

> Recent stories in the media have often misrepresented RIPA and what parliament agreed that local authorities can do under the legislation. Parliament gave permission to a range of public authorities to use covert investigatory

powers under RIPA, where they need them to carry out their statutory functions. Under RIPA, local authorities are able to use a far more restricted range of investigatory techniques than intelligence and law enforcement agencies. They are limited to using the least intrusive types of communications data; directed surveillance (which means covert surveillance in public places) and covert human intelligence sources (such as informants), and only for detecting or preventing crime and preventing disorder where it is necessary and proportionate for them to do so. There are strict rules to protect people from unnecessary or inappropriate intrusion and any use of the powers must be both necessary and proportionate to the crime being investigated.[36]

Yet by the spring of 2009, Jacqui Smith, then the home secretary, was proposing a thoroughgoing review of the powers and a consultation on how they might be reformed.

WHO CAN USE RIPA?

1. Any police force.
2. The National Criminal Intelligence Service.
3. The National Crime Squad.
4. The Serious Fraud Office.
5. Any of the intelligence services.
6. Any of Her Majesty's forces.
7. The Commissioners of Customs and Excise.
8. The Commissioners of Inland Revenue.
9. The Ministry of Agriculture, Fisheries and Food.
10. The Ministry of Defence.
11. The Department of the Environment, Transport and the Regions.
12. The Department of Health.

13. The Home Office.
14. The Department of Social Security.
15. The Department of Trade and Industry.
16. The National Assembly for Wales.
17. Any local authority (within the meaning of section 1 of the [1999 c. 27.] Local Government Act 1999).
18. The Environment Agency.
19. The Financial Services Authority.
20. The Food Standards Agency.
21. The Intervention Board for Agricultural Produce.
22. The Personal Investment Authority.
23. The Post Office.
24. The Health and Safety Executive.
25. A Health Authority established under section 8 of the [1977 c. 49.] National Health Service Act 1977.
26. A Special Health Authority established under section 11 of the [1977 c. 49.] National Health Service Act 1977.
27. A National Heath Service trust established under section 5 of the [1990 c. 19.] National Health Service and Community Care Act 1990.
28. The Royal Pharmaceutical Society of Great Britain.

CHAPTER 11

SLIPPERY WHEN WET: HEALTH AND SAFETY GONE MAD

Eco-warrior evicted from cave dwelling without fire exit

An eco-warrior has been evicted from the cave he lives in on his allotment patch in Brighton, East Sussex, because it doesn't have a fire exit. Hilaire Purbrick, 45, has inhabited the seven-foot cave he dug on his plot and dined off the land for the past 16 years. But after having the dwelling checked by the fire brigade, Brighton and Hove City Council decided it did not have enough exits and sought an injunction banning him from entering it.

Daily Telegraph, 18 June 2009

Are health and safety laws good laws or bad laws? Judging by the headlines they engender, it is easy to imagine they are malign. 'Elfnsafety' has become synonymous with petty bureaucracy, risk aversion, over-regulation and little Hitlerism. Richard Littlejohn, the *Daily Mail* columnist, has made a career often hilariously lampooning the idiocies that accompany the determination of officialdom to remove all risk from our lives. But how do we judge health and safety laws by our criteria of a bad law? If they keep us healthier and make us safer, are they not then good laws since they do what they set out to achieve? It is, though, possible to have a law that fulfils its purpose but is still a bad law. It is also moot whether health and safety legislation does make us safer. It can result in excessive caution that makes people make a wrong decision that causes more harm than good. Clearly on a construction site, the requirement by law to wear a hard hat or a safety-harness when working hundreds of feet above the ground must have made people safer. The prospect of a prosecution if an employer fails in this 'duty of care' under the 1974 Health and Safety at Work Act is an important constraint on dangerous procedures. But when fear of prosecution or a failure to undergo health and safety training prevents police officers disarming a gunman who subsequently kills the people he is holding hostage – then something has gone badly wrong.

Throughout history, health and safety laws have often been a response to appalling tragedies. In 1862, when the beam of a pumping engine at Hartley Colliery in Northumberland broke and blocked the only mineshaft and means of ventilation, 204 miners suffocated underground. Two years later new mining legislation required that every seam in a mine should have at least two shafts or outlets. Such laws continue to be passed to this day as specific dangers manifest themselves with the advance of technology. In 1974, the Flixborough disaster near Scunthorpe in which 28 people died was caused by a badly designed modification to a process plant releasing several tonnes of cyclohexane at high pressure and temperature, causing a massive explosion. After another disaster, this time at Seveso, in Italy, the Control of Industrial Major Accident Hazards (CIMAH) Regulations 1984 came into force. This obliged manufacturers who use certain dangerous substances to prepare a safety case – in which they have to demonstrate that the major hazard potentials of the activity have been identified and that adequate controls are provided – to be submitted to the Health and Safety Executive (HSE).

These two pieces of health and safety legislation a century apart demonstrate how the law has responded to specific threats to life and limb as they become apparent, often after the lives and limbs have been lost. By and large, the law has been applied in order to protect workers from employers who might put their lives in danger in order to cut costs or through negligence; or to address a safety issue that may only have come to light because of some terrible accident or appalling privation.

There were some workplace regulations in the eighteenth century, though they were more to do with wage bargaining. The 1788 Act for the Better Regulation of Chimney Sweepers and their Apprentices, intended to alleviate 'the misery of the said boys', was the first specific piece of legislation intended to make the lives of employees less onerous, albeit by standards that we would find appalling today. Apprentices had to be at least eight years old; each sweeper was limited to six apprentices; and, justices of the peace were to decide complaints. The intentions of the Act were largely ignored due to the lack of any means of enforcement.

As Britain became more industrialized in the nineteenth century, so parliament's interest in health and safety increased. In 1802, Sir Robert Peel's Health and Morals of Apprentices Act brought a 12-hour limit to the working day, a phased elimination of night work, separate sleeping apartments for boys and girls and no more than two to a bed. This Act was more an extension of the Poor Laws than safety legislation, however. It took philanthropic factory owners like Robert Owen to combine a Christian belief in a moral duty toward their employees with a hard-headed capitalist recognition that workers in safe surroundings might actually be more productive. Owen's efforts resulted in the 1819 Cotton Mills and Factories Act which prohibited children under the age of nine years from working in cotton mills, and restricted those over the age of nine to a 12-hour day.

The first genuine safety legislation was the Factory Act 1833, known as Althorp's Act after its sponsor Viscount Althorp, later 3rd Earl Spencer. It required younger children to attend school for at least two hours on six days of the week and introduced holidays for the children on Christmas Day and Good Friday, plus eight other half-days. The Act gave powers for the appointment of inspectors, because provisions of previous acts 'were not duly carried into execution who were empowered to enter any factory at any time and to examine therein the children and other young persons and to enquire about their condition, employment and education'.[1] Children under the age of 13 years had to be certified by a physician or surgeon as being 'of the ordinary strength and appearance' of a child of his/her stated age.

This heralded a cascade of similar Acts throughout the nineteenth century. The 1834 Chimney Sweeps Act forbade the apprenticing of any boy under the age of 10 years, extended to 16 in 1840. In 1842 the Mines and Collieries Act prohibited the employment underground of women and children under 10 and the 1872 Metalliferous Mines Regulation Act prohibited the employment in the mines of all girls, women and boys under the age of 12 years; introduced powers to appoint inspectors of mines; and set out rules regarding ventilation, blasting and machinery. The following year, the Agricultural Children's Act stated that children between the ages of 8 and 10 years could be employed in agriculture only if the parent signed a certificate stating that the child had completed 250 school attendances and, if the child was over 10, 150 attendances in the preceding 12 months. In 1901, the minimum working age was set at 12 and in 1937 workers under 16 were restricted to a 44-hour week.

And kids today complain about their lot.

The 1974 Health and Safety at Work Act is the guiding legislation for all modern health and safety law. It was introduced following recommendations of the Robens Committee which

reported in 1972. Lord Robens found that the existing legislation – there were then 30 Acts and 500 sets of regulations
– was defective. There was too much law, it was over-elaborate
and it was preoccupied with the physical circumstances in which
work was done as opposed to the workforce and the systems
of work. This was nothing new. As long ago as 1875, a Royal
Commission was appointed to deal with 'a perfect chaos of
regulations – all good in themselves when enacted – all having
a direct purpose, which most of the trades have outlived'.[2]
There were dozens of laws and regulations with no coherence,
as the Fabian Sidney Webb wrote in 1910: 'This century of
experiment in factory legislation affords a typical example
of English practical empiricism. We began with no abstract
theory of social justice or the rights of man. We seem always
to have been incapable of taking a general view of the subject
we were legislating upon. Each successive statute aimed at
remedying a single ascertained evil.'[3]

Robens recommended a new structure with an enabling
Act setting out the basic principles of safety responsibility and
providing a statutory base on which all future regulations could
be founded. New rules made under the Act would, if possible, be
confined to general statements of the objectives to be achieved.
He wanted greater reliance on standards and codes and for
no regulation to be made if a non-statutory alternative was
available. That way it might be possible to dispense with many
of the regulations which should, in any event, be made less
cumbersome and simpler: 'Safety and health at work is a matter
of efficient management. But it is not a management prerogative.
Workpeople must be encouraged to participate fully.'[4]

THE DEATH OF COMMONSENSE

But how did legislation which over the decades was directed at
protecting those seen as most vulnerable – women and children

– and which also helped to introduce safe practices for all workers become an all-encompassing regime that stops people who change clocks from climbing ladders, requires Christmas trees to be kept behind barriers and prevents pantomime performers from throwing sweets to children in the audience? As Bill Callaghan, former chairman of the Health and Safety Commission, said:

> Mention health and safety and the image is often more one of what I call 'elf'n'safety', 30-page risk assessments for the most trivial of activities, signs stating that a swimming pool has been closed for health and safety reasons, a jobsworth with a clipboard telling you not to do things. Safety experts are accused of fostering a nanny state and I have been called Britain's chief nanny.[5]

Callaghan was, understandably, a great fan of the 1974 Act, which he called 'a legislative landmark that has stood the test of time'. It certainly did what it said on the tin. Despite the plethora of health and safety laws there was no great improvement over the first half of the twentieth century in the rate of factory accidents. Indeed, by the end of the 1960s, around 1,000 employees died each year and the number of fatal and non-fatal accidents in factories, docks, warehouses and construction was over 300,000 in 1970 compared with 193,000 in 1961. After the 1974 Act safety improved markedly. In 2005–6, 160 employees and 52 self-employers were killed at work, the lowest on record.[6]
Callaghan said:

> Although compositional changes in the workforce can explain some of the improvement, the regulatory regime, proposed by the Commission and enforced by the Executive and local authorities, has been a major contributor. A cautious estimate is that over 5,000 lives have been saved by the health and safety improvements introduced following the 1974 Act. Construction remains a hazardous industry

but the number of deaths at work in that sector is a third of the late 1960s level despite the industry employing many more people.[7]

So why are Callaghan and those who have occupied his post since called the nation's chief nannies? Why do local councils, fearing an accident, prop up gravestones in cemeteries? Part of the problem lies in the scope of the 1974 Act. For the first time there was an attempt in law to unify safety legislation by provisions which were not confined to a particular type of workplace or work but applied in general. Not only were thousands of workers brought within the protection of the law, but it also applied to breaches committed when they were not at work. The Act laid down general duties that had not existed before, rather than specific obligations to deal with particular safety issues and modelled on duties under the common law.

The key element in the law is the general duty of every employer 'to ensure, so far as is reasonably practicable, the health, safety and welfare at work of all his employees'. As Lord Cullen observed: 'This went well beyond the scope of merely physical conditions ... These duties were clearly aimed at bringing home responsibility for accident prevention.'[8]

However, the 1974 Act went further still. It also imposed a duty on every employer 'to conduct his undertaking in such a way as to ensure, so far as is reasonably practicable, that persons not in his employment who may be affected thereby are not thereby exposed to risks to their health and safety'. This extended protection to the employees of others and to the general public. Here, then, is the source of 'elfnsafety madness'. The Act was clearly not meant to be overly prescriptive. Almost at every point, parliament inserted the words 'so far as is reasonably practicable'. The trouble is that what might have been considered reasonable in 1974 is seen as downright reckless in today's more risk averse society.

As Cullen said:

One of the fundamental questions which arises in the development of a safety regime is – How far should safety be regulated by legislation? Putting the matter the other way round, how far should those who conduct undertakings be free to manage safety for themselves? Society does not demand the total elimination of risk, so where is the line to be drawn? These are questions of policy for the regulator and, if necessary, the legislators to resolve as the regime develops . . . The benefits of state intervention in any matter of safety have to be weighed against the costs which it imposes. The pressures exerted by the public and various interests have to be taken into account without being allowed to dictate. All this assumes that there is room for choice. European directives on the other hand do not leave much room for manoeuvre.[9]

Has that balance been struck over the years? It is hard to make that case. Much of the confusion centres on the phrase 'so far as is reasonably practicable', wording that goes back at least as far as the mining legislation of the 1870s. From there the expression was brought into the Factories Act and then into the Health and Safety at Work Act 1974, and obtaining the status of a major principle in safety legislation. Over the years, the courts have tried to define it. Lord Justice Asquith said:

'Reasonably practicable' is a narrower term than 'physically possible' and seems to me to imply that a computation must be made by the owner, in which the quantum of risk is placed on one scale, and the sacrifice involved in the measures necessary for averting the risk (whether in money, time or trouble) is placed in the other; and that if it be shown that there is a gross disproportion between them – risk being insignificant in relation to the sacrifice – the defendants discharge the onus on them. Moreover, this

> computation falls to be made by the owner at a point of
> time anterior to the accident.[10]

This expression was intended to underpin the general
approach inherent in the 1974 Act, giving some latitude
where absolute safety standards were not obviously necessary
as they would be, say, in a nuclear power station. However, as
an example of how things can change, it is now forbidden to
carry out certain electrical tasks in your own home. Under the
regulations which came into force in January 2005, only simple
changes such as adding extra lights or sockets to an existing
circuit should be carried out without professional involvement
by a registered electrician. The alternative is to notify a local
building control body before starting any work and pay the
appropriate fee for an inspection and a certificate after work is
completed.[11]

How did we get from well-intentioned laws to stop children
being put up chimneys to a prohibition on installing a new
wiring system in your own house? It could be argued that this
is part of the same evolutionary process: it is about making us
all safer. There are many accidents each year involving people
trying to put in a new electrical circuit. But is it for the law to
impose restrictions on what people choose to do in their own
homes, however risky? If you stop someone fiddling with the
lights because they might kill themselves, why not prevent them
smoking in their own house, too? Or does that come next?
People who would consider that a preposterous suggestion
should ask themselves whether they thought they would see the
day when they were not allowed to install a breaker circuit in
their own bathroom.

It is the general duty in the 1974 law which makes all this
possible. Where does it stop? Where should it stop? Lord Justice
Asquith said: 'The computation falls to be made by the owner
at a point antecedent to the accident.' In other words, accident
prevention should be a matter of assessing and managing risk

rather than reaction to accidents. As a consequence, every public body (and private ones) have risk managers or health and
safety staff whose job is to assess the circumstances that might
lead to their employees taking legal action if they have not
taken all reasonably practicable steps to mitigate risk. Given the
difficulties of deciding what is reasonable and practicable, it is
better to seek to eliminate risk altogether by simply stopping the
activities that may give rise to it.

This has happened in the US whose approach to these matters
is now taking a grip here. In his book, *The Death of Common Sense
– How Law is Suffocating America*, Philip K. Howard describes how
the rationalist legal philosophy behind the modern regulatory
framework has largely supplanted the older common law
approach, which relies on the commonsense application of
general legal principles to particular cases. Howard says that
the general result of rationalist legislation is regulatory laws
which are both invasive and ineffective. In the US, and now
here in the UK, the excessive rigidity of modern regulatory law
makes it unable to adequately accommodate the special feature
of each individual case, and so it is at best ineffective, at worst
counter-productive.

Howard wrote: 'Modern law has not protected us from
stupidity and caprice, but has made stupidity and caprice dominant features of our society. Law must not promise to purge
people's souls. It cannot. Law can set up the conditions for
interaction and work toward changes over time. When it tries to
do more, it only drives us further apart.'[12]

This goes to the nub of the modern regulatory fetish. Whereas
common law evolved with the changing times and its truth was
relative, not absolute, nowadays statutes and regulations are
the dominant feature of the legal landscape. Centralized rules
are inimical to commonsense and to individual responsibility,
even though in health and safety laws there was an attempt to
keep a grip on it with the 'reasonable and practicable' concept.
With a regulatory approach, people argue not about right

and wrong, but about whether something was done the right way. Howard suggests that all this has contributed to another modern phenomenon: our loathing of government, caused not by its goals (which many share) but by its techniques. 'How law works, not what it aims to do, is what is driving us crazy.'[13]

Howard's point, and it is one we are missing in this country now, is that you cannot anticipate every possible contingency through a rule; to try to do so is the route to insanity. As Howard put it: 'Abandoning our commonsense and individual sense of responsibility, we live in terror of the law, in awe of procedure.' His book includes the story of how New York City refused to allow Mother Teresa to build a homeless shelter unless a $100,000 elevator was installed. Are we far away from this madness here; or are we there already?

RIP: HERE LIES . . . A GRAVESTONE PUSHED OVER BY A COUNCIL OFFICIAL

The journalist Quentin Letts endeavoured to find out whether health and safety really has gone mad in an entertaining documentary for *Panorama* (April 2009) entitled 'May Contain Nuts', an ironic reference to the warning carried on a packet of nuts in order to protect the manufacturer from being sued for failing to alert an allergic purchaser to the prospect of receiving an anaphylactic shock from eating the contents. He wanted to discover if it was really true that local authority inspectors had been propping up gravestones to ensure they did not fall over; or laying them on their sides to ensure they didn't, and then in some cases charging the families of the deceased for doing so.

The Labour MP for Bassetlaw, John Mann, had been campaigning against this activity, pointing out that no one had been killed by falling headstones in churchyards in the past ten years, though there had been a few instances of fatalities among children climbing on them.

Most cemeteries are owned by local authorities which take as their starting point the general duty provisions in the 1974 Act. Until recently, no one had considered the issue of gravestone-safety to be a problem, but guidelines to councils in England and Wales were issued in 2004 after the HSE warned that a falling gravestone can kill, despite a greater risk of being struck dead by lightning.[14]

Alan Bleasdale, the playwright, described how about 1,000 headstones were taken down in the Liverpool cemetery where his parents are buried. 'There was a three-year-old girl who had died in a car accident and her headstone with her picture on had been smashed to the ground. There's been absolute revulsion at this. It's officialdom run riot,' he said.[15]

An HSE document warned that the stability of headstones presents a threat to 'all cemetery users' and reported they have caused 10 accidents in recent years, including 3 deaths, though this was not supported by any evidence. The government said there had been 8 deaths over 30 years, though again without identifying the circumstances. Whatever the number of fatalities, if indeed there were any, this compares to about 3 people killed by lightning each year. The difference, of course, is that no one can be sued if someone is struck by lightning whereas with the gravestones even a 'general low level of risk may be called into question by the public following an incident or by operators when it comes to their assessment of the theoretical risk'. The HSE recommended every headstone be tested and suggested using a £700 topple-testing machine to apply a 50kg force. Most authorities reduced this to a 35kg force because so many memorials were failing the test.

Councils across the country began spending millions of pounds implementing this guidance, even though, as Mr Mann pointed out, 95 per cent of headstone staking was unnecessary (though even this is a classic example of the argument shifting from whether it should be done at all to whether it was being overdone).

Mann's perseverance paid off when the Ministry for Justice, which has responsibility for burials, issued new guidance in January 2009 advising that tampering with stones should be a last resort and that families must be contacted. In a 17-page document, fresh advice was issued to local councils. It stated:

> Over the past few years the issue of memorial safety has from time to time been the subject of adverse publicity and public distress – often because of over-zealous risk assessments or poor communication. In light of this burial ground operators have expressed concern about how to respond appropriately to the risks presented by unstable gravestones. Significant risks should of course be properly managed – but the risk of injury from a gravestone or other memorial which has become loose and unstable is very low. That is why we issued a joint letter to burial authorities in March 2007 to make clear that any action to manage risks in burial grounds needed to be sensible, proportionate, and undertaken in a sensitive way. The advice provided in this document is in response to the requests by burial ground managers for practical guidance to assist them in developing sensible, proportionate and sensitive arrangements for managing gravestones. It has been developed by relevant professional representative organizations from the Burial and Cemeteries Advisory Group. We are grateful to them for this work. This guidance sets out a sensible approach to assist burial ground operators to meet their legal responsibilities. By following this good practice burial ground operators can provide safe places to visit and work, and importantly make sure that remedial work to reduce any risk of serious injury does not cause unnecessary distress to bereaved families and others who value the great historical and environmental heritage of our cemeteries.[16]

In other words, let's have a bit of commonsense. Yet why should over-zealous council officials get the blame when they were only acting on advice issued by the HSE? Judith Hackitt, who took over from Bill Callaghan as head of the HSE in 2007, told Letts on the BBC: 'What we circulated is what we thought was commonsense guidance. Some people, not all by any means but some, over-interpreted, went over the top with the way they approached that and as a result of that we've withdrawn the guidance that was being misinterpreted.'[17] But is that true? Once the HSE sets out guidelines containing detailed information about the pressure to be applied to headstones it is a bit rich for those following it then to be accused of taking it too far.

This is by no means the only example of egregious health and safety nonsense. A survey by Keele University researcher Sarah Thomson showed some schools (not many, it is true, but more are joining in) have banned conkers because they fear the horse chestnuts could be used as 'offensive weapons' and this caution had extended to other games enjoyed by children for generations. Thomson found a school where an ancient playground tree, worn smooth by generations of village children climbing on it, was felled before an Office for Standards in Education inspection. The head-teacher admitted that no child had fallen off the tree and been injured in the seven years she had been at the school, but a local education authority adviser had warned her that inspectors would 'have you for that'. So the tree went.[18]

Thomson found that the British Bulldog game has been banned from most schools and one school had forbidden skipping because some girls had wrapped the ropes around their necks or had fallen over after tying their legs together for three-legged races. After studying the playtimes of 1,000 children in three counties (Staffordshire, Shropshire and Lancashire), Thomson concluded that excessive restraints were being placed on play and many school playgrounds are 'barren, sterile and unimaginative'.

Concerns about school safety were heightened by the 1996 Dunblane shootings and the 1997 Wolverhampton school machete attack; but fears that inspectors will mark a school down is another cause. The Health and Safety Act protects school visitors and contractors, but the regulations do not apply to pupils. This means that decisions on health and safety issues and the burden of ensuring pupils' safety are often passed to individual heads. Schools are where common sense really has parted company with reality. Teachers are frightened to apply a plaster to a child's graze in case it leads to an allergic reaction. One teacher told Thomson: 'Wet paper towels are the answer to everything now we are no longer allowed to put on a plaster.' Thomson noted:

> All the schools I visited saw playtime as a time that could not be left entirely to the children's wishes. Furthermore, it seemed that many of the children's attempts to play were extinguished by the same supervising adults who complained that children 'did not play'. I observed quite organized games prevented for a variety of reasons. For instance, at the beginning of one summer lunch hour when there was a brief absence of staff, a number of children had made two teams for a game of rounders. As staff appeared this game of rounders was stopped because the very action of throwing the rounders' bat backwards after a hit was considered dangerous to the rest of the team. It seems that the search for a safe, disciplined playground is as real a constraint to freedom as the iron railings and wooden fencing that prevent the children leaving the premises.[19]

HIT OR MYTH?

But is this behaviour the result of health and safety laws? Those directly involved in applying them or who have campaigned for them resent these laws getting a bad press and being blamed for over-zealous and irrational attitudes. The TUC, in an exercise similar to that carried out by the EU when it wearied of stories blaming it for banning curly cucumbers and the like, sought to test some of the more outlandish examples carried in the newspapers in recent years:

> [We] found that some are just not true, and many others are misrepresentations of the truth. This does not mean that every health and safety story we read about is made up. In some cases regulations have been wrongly interpreted. However that is different from saying that health and safety regulations, or their enforcement have been wrong. In none of the stories we looked at did we find that was the case. In other examples employers have used health and safety as an excuse for not doing something which they did not want to do anyway, or as an excuse for saving money.[20]

The first 'myth' looked at by the TUC was that health and safety regulations ban the use of ladders. 'This story reappears regularly. In fact there is no ban on ladders so long as they are used safely.' But in trying to debunk the 'myth' the TUC report simply confirmed its truth. To say there is no ban on ladders 'provided they are used safely' goes to the heart of the matter: the attempted eradication of all risk. Nobody ever suggested there was a ban on using ladders. Instead there is an excessive caution attached to their use that seems to go beyond commonsense. It is never going to be 100 per cent safe to climb up a ladder, though in the vast majority of cases it will be. A sensible aim must be to ensure that when someone does climb a ladder it is as safe as is 'reasonably practicable', though an accident can never be entirely ruled out. Each year 13 people on average die falling off ladders and 12,000 are seriously injured.

The HSE issues guidelines that, 'Every employer shall ensure that ... work equipment ... is not used after installation or assembly in any position unless it has been inspected in that position.' Is that 'reasonably practicable'? Given the concerns employers have of facing legal action by the HSE, they inevitably err on the side of caution and insist employees sign up for ladder awareness courses. The 'health and safety' culture has led to the creation of special ladder awareness courses which employees likely to use ladders are expected to attend. The course costs over £200, which falls on the taxpayer or the consumer depending on whether it is for the public or private sector. Meanwhile, there is an army of inspectors who carry out checks to ensure ladders are safe, notes of the inspection have to be documented and the paperwork has to be kept for three months after the job is done. Something that had been commonsensical has morphed into something bureaucratic, expensive and time-consuming that treats grown-ups like children.

Another 'myth' tackled by the TUC study was that employers are overly cautious because of the fear of health and safety regulations. It said the truth was the opposite because 'over a million workers get injured every year and 25,000 people are forced to give up work because of injury or illness caused by work'. According to the TUC, this shows that 'employers are very much taking risks with their workers' health'. All it shows, however, is that life is risky and that accidents happen; the implication is that all accidents are the result of bad employers.[21]

Judith Hackitt wearily observed that health and safety laws were often confused in people's mind, and on the front pages of the newspapers, with excessive concern over health and safety, when the two were not connected. On the other hand, while the kerfuffle over topple-testing gravestones was 'a mistake', Hackitt was unrepentant about one or two-day ladder-use courses:

> For people who are using them all day, every day it's probably not a bad thing. And the best ladder courses will not just go through the basics but will show the consequences of bad practice. This guy fell off a ladder – that's what happens if you don't do it properly. People need to get past the 'I'm fireproof' argument. 'It won't happen to me'.[22]

Organizations like the HSE, which employs thousands of staff, have an interest in trying to eliminate all risk often to the detriment of the commonsense that they say they would like to see people exercise. This even turned into a plot line in *The Archers* radio show at Christmas 2008 when the annual Ambridge pantomime was almost called off because of the danger posed by a falling beanstalk.

However much Hackitt may hate her staff being dubbed the 'Health and Safety Taliban', she considers it a worthwhile job because so many people make so many mistakes. In 2008, 229 people were killed in workplace accidents, 2,000 died prematurely because they had been exposed to asbestos and 100,000 people have been injured at work, 28,000 with amputations. She says, 'Let's focus on the real problems. If I find all of this rubbish demoralising, imagine what it's like for our inspectors.'[23]

The problem with risk aversion is that it results in over-regulation and excessive caution. Another of the TUC myths is that there are fewer rules and health and safety laws now than there used to be because of the consolidation in the 1974 Act. There are fewer rules than there were when they were activity specific, but there has been a growth in recent years. Certainly, regulation has accelerated in this field with 31 pieces of law between 1956 and 1996 and 53 since 1997. Yet it is the general duty in the 1974 legislation – or at least the way it is interpreted – which is the central issue. The people who drafted the law knew such a sweeping obligation could cause difficulties, which is why they went out of their way to include the key phrase 'as far as is reasonably practicable'; but we have moved a long way from applying that caveat in the way it was intended.

Hackitt says that 'a significant proportion of the population don't yet seem to be capable of making commonsense decisions'. This may well be true; but at what point in our history did the state decide this was a matter for its involvement? It is also undoubtedly the case that the excessive regulation in this area prevents people taking commonsense decisions that might be the safer option.

In 2004, when police officers were called to a house at Highmoor Cross, near Henley-on-Thames, after reports of shots being fired during a barbecue on the premises, they remained at a distance while they carried out an 'assessment'. At the house, Stuart Horgan had shot his estranged wife Vicky Horgan, her sister Emma Walton and their mother Jacqueline Bailey. Two of the women died but at least one of his victims was still alive when the police were first called. Thames Valley Police refused to allow their own officers or paramedics anywhere near the crime scene for over an hour, while they carried out a risk assessment of the area in order to 'safeguard any members of the public who could be at risk, as well as officers and other emergency service personnel at the scene'.

Roy Gibson, a neighbour who went into the garden to help the victims, called the police six times in total, 'begging' them to come and help. 'I told them it was deadly serious. I told them these women were dying.' But Thames Valley Police says that its policy on firearm incidents is to risk-assess whether the vicinity is safe before entering, or before allowing paramedics to enter. The police despatched a helicopter within 10 minutes of receiving Gibson's first call to try to ascertain whether the gunman was still present and whether he still posed a threat. An ambulance crew arrived at the police rendezvous within three minutes of being called, but were prevented from proceeding to the flat by police awaiting the results of the risk assessment. The assessment took over an hour even though Mr Gibson told them repeatedly that the gunman had fled. Had he still been there, it was still the job of the police to do something. As Mr Gibson said: 'That's their job, isn't it?' In the event, it was left to Gibson's wife to try to comfort the victims while Gibson stood guard outside:

> My wife's inside the house; I'm outside the house with a lump of wood in my hand just in case he did come back.

But it didn't matter to me if he had come back. We weren't scared. We did what human beings are supposed to do. There's three people lying in that house bleeding to death. These are neighbours, friends; you're supposed to help.[24]

After Mr Gibson's furious outburst, the police carried out an internal review overseen by the Independent Police Complaints Commission, which concluded that there was no justification for the delay. Peter Neyroud, Thames Valley chief constable, apologized to the victims' family and local people, including Mr Gibson and his wife Georgina. He said: 'We could have and should have been faster to the scene to protect the wounded and the public of Highmoor Cross. I regret very much the distress which the additional delay caused to the victims and witnesses.'

But Peter Neyroud and Detective Superintendent Mick Tighe, author of the review, said no individual officer was to blame. Instead, they claimed the fiasco was due to failings in training and national policy, which emphasizes locating the perpetrator rather than getting to the victims: 'The weaknesses identified . . . are fundamental issues for Thames Valley police and possibly the police service nationally'.[25]

While the country was shocked by the way the police responded it was by no means a unique occurrence. The actions of Thames Valley police that day fit a broader pattern of risk-averse policing, where forces around the country increasingly tend to take a step back from heated incidents in order to assess the dangers before acting.

In 1995, Lorraine Whiting was shot by her husband before he shot and killed himself. She spent almost an hour on the phone asking to be taken to hospital while the police stood outside assessing whether the gunman was still present. According to reports, Whiting told the police 25 times that the gunman (her husband) was dead, but the police said that he might be pressuring her to say that and refused to storm the house.

Whiting bled to death. In November 2003, Alan Pemberton shot his wife Julia and their 17-year-old son William at their home in Berkshire, before turning the gun on himself. Reportedly, at 7.10 p.m. on the evening of the killings, a woman called police in great distress saying that her husband had a gun. At 7.45 p.m., neighbours reported hearing gunshots. It wasn't until 1.45 a.m. that the police entered the house and discovered the three bodies, six-and-a-half hours after the woman's distress call. In January 2003 police spent 15 days and £1million outside an east London flat occupied by a gunman. Halfway through the siege a man being held hostage by the gunman had to escape by his own devices, by jumping out of a window. The gunman was later found dead in the flat. In 2008 in Wigan, Jordon Lyon, 10, drowned trying to rescue his younger sister. Community support officers on the scene were held back from helping by rules and regulations, defined by a spurious idea of health and safety. The inquest into his death heard they did not rescue him as they were not trained to deal with the incident.[26]

The most bizarre aspect of this is that we rarely see the police on routine patrols any more and if we do they are always in pairs because of security concerns even in the leafiest of avenues in the safest of places. The one time you would want the police around is when there is a gunman on the loose, shooting people, or threatening to shoot people, or holding someone hostage – yet this is when they hold back. They have adopted a safety-first approach: that is, putting their own safety, and apparently the safety of the public, before the welfare of those who are in great danger. Whatever the health and safety industry may claim about 'myths' the fact is that a baleful culture has taken a grip and it will be the devil's own job to loosen it.

Judith Hackitt may try to uncouple this attitude from the law itself, but the two are inextricably linked. It may not have been the intention of parliament when the Act was passed; but it is the consequence of the way it was drafted. Was it envisaged then that an actor playing Nelson during the Battle of Trafalgar commemoration should wear a life-jacket over his costume; or that organizers of the Lleni fancy dress festival in Powys would have to cancel because they would have to employ an extra 60 stewards on health and safety grounds? Will anything be done about this? The Conservatives have voiced the concerns raised by most people but will they change matters? David Davis, when he was shadow home secretary, said:

> Too often right-minded officers are weighed down by the suffocating welter of form-filling, box-ticking and bureaucracy. Red tape and regulation are holding the police back. This has fed a health and safety culture that makes the police less healthy, and the public less safe. In some areas, officers can't throw out a lifebelt in an emergency without first conducting an assessment of the risk to themselves. This nonsense has got to stop.

He added: 'A Conservative government will change the law to ensure that, when officers respond to an emergency, they put public protection above all other considerations.'[27] Let us hope that was not just hot air.

Another Tory, Boris Johnson, who was MP for Henley at the time of the Highmoor Cross fiasco, said there was a fundamental ideological gulf that explained the different approaches:

> Lefties tend to believe above all in the role of the state in ironing out human imperfection. That is why it appeals to them to ban hunting, smoking, smacking, snacking, and to swaddle everyone in the public and private sector with a great choking duvet of risk assessments. Conservatives tend to think that of the crooked timber of humanity was no straight thing ever made, and that it is no business of the state to be endlessly sawing and sandpapering us all into shape. If you try to exterminate all risk, you impose

rules that squeeze out individual responsibility, and deprive everyone in the public services of the flexibility they need to deliver the results they want.[28]

YULE BE SORRY

Could it have been imagined by those who campaigned to stop children being forced up chimneys or mill-workers losing limbs that the government would consider it necessary, as it did in 2008, to issue a special health and safety leaflet for the Christmas festivities?

Entitled '*Tis the Season to be Careful*, it was produced by the Children's Department and contained such staggering insights as a warning that hot fat spitting from cooking roast potatoes can hurt and that, if a glass bauble falls off the tree and smashes on the floor, the pieces of glass should be avoided, especially by people with bare feet. The government produced 150,000 leaflets to be distributed at shopping centres and nurseries 'to help make Christmas safe'. Among other perils, they alerted families to the dangers of tinsel: a thousand people each year, the leaflets solemnly intoned, are 'hurt by trimmings or when decorating their homes'.

For all the HSE's and the TUC's rage against health and safety mythology, it is a depressing fact that health and safety hectoring has become a substitute for actually doing the things that government and state agencies should be doing, such as protecting the truly vulnerable. An insidious culture of petty control and intrusiveness has taken a grip on every aspect of our lives. True enough, people do things at Christmas they would not do normally, such as standing precariously on a stool to put up decorations or placing lighted candles beneath a ceiling festooned with highly inflammable streamers. Yet previous generations of officialdom did not think it necessary to offer advice to those unable to grasp that teetering on the top rung of the step ladder in a heroic attempt to fix the star on the tree does carry a modicum of risk. Why does ours?

And this is not, as some people aver, because we live in a risk-averse world; if anything, people today are even more adventurous than their forefathers, hurling themselves off bridges attached to elasticated rope, jumping off mountain-tops with a parachute, snowboarding down vertical snow-faces and backpacking through hazardous places. My son on a trip to Bolivia cycled along a 35-mile road nicknamed the 'Trail of Death', often just a few feet from a 5,000-foot sheer drop, something I would never have dreamt of doing as a student in the 1970s, even if we could have afforded to get to South America in those days.

This is less about a modern terror of derring-do than a function of too much government – an assumption that local councils and other state agencies should interfere in small things because they no longer know what to do about the big things. There is something grotesque about a system in which the country's social services fail to ensure the safety of a baby known to be at risk yet feel obliged to tell the rest of us to avoid falling over a drunken houseguest on Christmas Eve. Health and safety is not something that exists apart; it is of a piece with all those other agencies, including the Criminal Records Bureau, whose rationale has been lost in a fog of senseless activity carried out by a growing army of jobsworths who need to justify their own existence.

This is rarely more in evidence than at Christmas. What went through the mind of the local council bureaucrat who decided that Kevin Simpson, a school patrolman in Hampshire, must remove the tinsel from his lollipop? 'It is just a fun, goodwill gesture and on these miserable winter mornings it does light up the children's faces,' said Mr Simpson.[29]

How is tinsel on a lollipop hazardous? Who makes these decisions, and why? Panto performers across the country have been told not to throw sweets into the audience unless they are soft and chewy. Environmental health officials have introduced training courses for Father Christmases to help them avoid backache during their present-giving duties. A traditional Christmas Day charity swim in the North Sea off Southwold, Suffolk, has been cancelled because of the prohibitive cost of public liability insurance, police and a lifeboat. In addition, the presence of lifeguards was required but none could be found. Swimming in the sea in December will carry two obvious risks: of getting cold and of getting wet. There is always a remote possibility that someone might drown. But if people want to take the plunge – and for charity as well – why should they have to worry about insurance and lifeguards?

Health and safety concerns were cited by shopping-centre managers in Hemel Hempstead, Hertfordshire, when they chose not to invite Brownies and Guides to a carol-singing event for the first time in 20 years in 2008. Gill Oxtoby, divisional commissioner of the West Herts Guides, said: 'It's such a shame because it's been a long tradition and has allowed the girls to give some service to the community.'[30] In Llandovery, Carmarthenshire, a tradition of erecting trees on ledges over shop fronts came to an end because the town councillors who normally install them have been told they cannot climb ladders without ensuring they had been on a course which none of them had time for; nor could they afford to pay for scaffolding, or hire a cherry-picker to conform to the requirements. So, no trees.

When Heather Welsh, of York, attempted to buy a box of Christmas crackers in Marks & Spencer staff refused to sell them to her before seeing her ID; it was illegal, they said, to sell them to children. A spokesman for M & S said: 'The signage in-store is to alert customers to age-restricted products. It is in compliance with the Explosives Act 1875 and Fireworks Safety Regulations 1997.'[31] Miss Welsh was 22 at the time; the amount of gunpowder in a cracker is minuscule.

In Wimborne, Dorset, organizers of a performance of Handel's *Messiah* by the Collegium Vocale at the Church of St Stephen had to cancel the event because members of the audience could be injured in the dark if there was a power cut. Ian Davis, the choirmaster, was obliged to carry out a risk assessment under what he called 'absurd' regulations. These suggested there was a possibility of litigation, even if unlikely, so the concert was scrapped. Mr Davis said, 'The law states that a dark church is dangerous if it does not have relevant health and safety procedures in place. The walk up to the building is in darkness at night and the law states that we need lighting outside in case there are potholes and rocks and we can't afford it.'[32]

LIONS LED BY DONKEYS

One of the oddest manifestations of this health and safety madness is the horse passport. Since 2004, it has been a requirement for owners of all equines, including horses, donkeys and ponies, to be in possession of a passport, whether they are travelling or not. It is, effectively, a form of ID introduced so that if you eat a horse you can be sure it is OK.

A new body, the Horse Passport Agency, has been created to administer this regulation and there is a fine of up to £5,000 and, for a second offence, one month's imprisonment for failing to register. Imagine it. You could go to jail because you forgot, or declined, to get the Shetland pony at the bottom of your garden an ID card. Racehorses and competition horses have long required some sort of identity document to travel overseas. But why all horses? This story begins in Brussels, where regulations were introduced in the mid-1990s to ensure that horses treated with certain drugs do not enter the human food chain. European Commission decision 93/623 required registered horses born after 1998 to be accompanied by a passport when they are moved. The intention was to simplify the trade in pure-bred horses. Commission decision 2000/68 amended this to ensure horses that have been treated with drugs are not later served up on the plate of a Belgian diner. Since the British do not eat horsemeat, the UK obtained a 'derogation' (i.e. it did not have to enforce the requirement) that ran out in 2003. But instead of demanding another, the government said it was legally bound to introduce compulsory passports for all equines. Horse Passports (England) Regulations 2004 require all owners to obtain a passport for each horse they own. This includes ponies, donkeys and other equidae. Owners cannot sell, export, slaughter for human consumption or use for the purposes of competition or breeding a horse which does not have a passport.

So every owner, whether of the oldest nag in the farthest field or the proudest hunter in the stable yard, needs to obtain a silhouette or sketch of their animal, which must be produced by an expert such as a vet, and then send it the agency. The cost may not be exorbitant to an individual owner but will be significant to a stables or a donkey sanctuary. Why is it necessary at all in Britain?

The regulations are enforced by trading standards officers with the power to enter stables and fields to see whether the horse matches the description on the passport. It is backed by a database which Alun Michael, the former 'minister for the horse' at the Department for the Environment, Farming and Rural Affairs (Defra), who introduced the measure, said 'would be to the advantage of the horse industry in the event of horse diseases becoming a problem in this country'. Asked in the Commons to identify what disease he had in mind, he failed to offer an example.[33] Some in the industry say there are spin-off advantages, such as allowing potential buyers to check whether an animal has been stolen and discovering how many horses and ponies there are in the country.

However, the principle reason was set out on Defra's own website: 'It will satisfy the European Commission that the UK has a viable method of identifying horses that have been treated with medicines that must not be administered to food producing animals.' Since only a few thousand horses are slaughtered in this country and exported to Europe for food, why not limit the requirement to them? Why do a million owners have to go through this rigmarole because other countries have a taste for horsemeat?

As Mr Bumble said in *Oliver Twist*, the law is a ass. Only nowadays, it needs a passport to identify it as one.

CHAPTER 12

CAN WE HAVE OUR COMMONSENSE BACK NOW, PLEASE?

> Doing less of the wrong thing is not doing the right thing.
>
> John Seddon, *Systems Thinking in the Public Sector*

Why do modern governments make such a pig's ear of most things they touch? They appear to be devoid of commonsense and judgment. They respond disproportionately to perceived wrongs, grievances, injustices or faults, introducing new laws to try to mould human behaviour in a way that a few not very clever ministers or officials with a particular axe to grind see fit. The net result of this constant interference is a sullen people that spends much of its time wondering what happened to the country of which it was once proud; an over-taxed private sector; a poorly educated underclass dependent upon benefit handouts that militate against bettering oneself; and a demoralized public sector which has grown in size yet diminished in effectiveness. The upshot of this excessive and obsessive state tinkering has been a huge increase in public spending – often merely to fulfil the requirements of unnecessary laws, not to improve the fabric of the land.

Since 1997, annual public spending has doubled to £674 billion with little obvious to show in the way of improvements in schools, hospitals or infrastructure. Bad.laws are responsible for much of this, though the bad laws are merely a reflection of a flawed ethos of what makes things work and a warped political culture. Labour's 'reforms' of the public sector were accompanied by a complete misunderstanding about how they could be made to work better, more effectively and more cheaply. They were all required, often by statute, to hit centrally decided targets. Ministers were persuaded that this would be a way of measuring that the amount of money invested was matched by an improvement in outputs. This was a massive – and massively expensive – mistake from which it will take the public sector many years to recover. It has also guaranteed that the serious retrenchment in public spending that is now required will be far more painful in terms of lost jobs than would otherwise have been the case had the services been leaner and fitter in the first place.

Yet the Labour government was completely deaf to any criticism of its target fetishism and wilfully ignored all well-intentioned suggestions for running public services in a way that would benefit them, the people who work in them and the rest of us.

Nobody listened to those who pointed out the inefficiencies of the system because a self-serving cadre of tick-box inspectors, backed by officials in Whitehall who established the standards and targets that underpinned the system, were not prepared to admit they were wrong, not least because it would put them out of a job. Despite mounting evidence that the target culture was perverse in its outcomes, expensive to administer and ultimately harmful, those who benefited from its existence continued to promote it and no minister had the guts to call a halt. The government even adopted the language of the private sector to justify its approach, referring to 'customers' and 'clients'; yet it ran the public services on behalf of the producers, not the consumers. It designed failure into almost everything it has done on our behalf. Essentially, the whole edifice of public-service delivery is rotten from top to bottom and needs a fundamental redesign.

This was spotted very early on by John Seddon, an occupational psychologist who worked for Toyota and specialized in systems management thinking. For years he advised ministers and Whitehall officials that there was a far better approach that would produce outcomes commensurate with the investment. He recognized that simply throwing more money at public-sector failure, which was Gordon Brown's favourite, and ultimately disastrous, approach, simply compounded their failure. He wrote:

> If investment in the UK public sector has not been matched by improvements, it is because we have invested in the wrong things. We think inspection drives improvement, we believe in the notion of economies of scale, we think choice and quasi-markets are levers for improvement, we believe people can be motivated with incentives, we think leaders need visions, managers need targets and that information technology is a driver of change. These are all wrong-headed ideas. But they have been the foundation of public-sector 'reform'.[1]

Seddon said that public services had requirements placed on them by a whole series of bodies that were all based on opinion rather than knowledge. Many were burdened with specifications, targets, regulations and the like which made matters worse.

The really scary thing is that the government continued to dig a deeper and deeper pit into which to pour our money. New management approaches and further 'reform' that were pursued through Labour's term in office simply compounded previous mistakes. Seddon wrote, 'At the heart of the problems with public-sector reform is the regime's incapacity to do the right thing. It is focused on doing the wrong things and assumes compliance to be evidence of success. The inability to act is systemic.'[2]

What people want from public services is for them to work properly, rather than being given the power to pick a healthcare model, vote on a local education policy or elect a chief constable. Waste can be eradicated if the systems are properly designed against demand rather than phoney outcomes. As Seddon put it: 'As soon as you create a split between front and back office, you also create waste. To do the same on a larger scale is to mass-produce it.' The same failures are built into all public services, and to address the problems by reducing the number of targets is pointless: 'Doing less of the wrong thing is not doing the right thing.'[3]

Waste on the scale we have seen demoralizes people working in the public sector and angers those who pay for or use services. It is also stupefyingly costly. Cumulative public spending since 1997 stands at £4,500 billion – double the total for the preceding ten years. How much of this is wasted? The public sector employs 800,000 more people than in 1997, many of them engaged in developing specifications, writing guidance, drawing-up standards, devising targets, enforcing inspections – all in the name of a reform programme that does not work properly. Interestingly, this view is not confined to academics like John Seddon, but is felt right across the public sector itself.

The great irony is that in July 2009, at the last knockings of its time in office, the Labour government published a policy document acknowledging (though not in so many words) that the target culture had suffocated initiative and its continuance was unlikely to deliver the reforms that the Labour Party wanted to see. The new approach, laughably called 'Building Britain's Future', proposed that the various parts of the public sector that deliver services directly to us as taxpayers, such as the police, doctors and teachers, should be allowed to make more of their own judgments based on what is needed locally. A prime minister who for years defended a system – indeed, was its architect – that had shown itself to be wasteful, inefficient and even perverse in its outcomes, suddenly stood up and said, whoops, that didn't work after all, so here is Plan B.

Why were targets introduced? The government would have you believe it was to drive up standards, but in reality they were a means of showing that Labour 'cared'. They were a political device. Whenever ministers were challenged about high levels of offending or poor levels of literacy they could say: 'But we have a target to reduce it/increase it/scrap it, so we must be good.' Targets were ostensibly introduced to hold the government to account, but were used as a means of deflecting criticism. The benchmarks were set not by you or me but by the very people who sought to obtain political capital from their attainment; those who had to operate within this straitjacket found themselves unable to use their experience and discretion to do things a different way.

On what did we spend all the money that pushed public spending up to levels not seen since wartime? Labour's education policy, a top-down fiasco, has left hundreds of thousands of children lacking in basic numeracy and literacy skills. The target approach did not cut crime; it made it worse. While offences such as burglary and car-theft fell because of better security, the streets became less safe. Police chiefs were under pressure to ensure their officers were at a crime scene within a fixed time period because this was measurable, unlike the deterrent nature of local bobbies doing their community rounds. Soon, fewer police officers were seen in public; instead, they were either waiting around for something to happen or filling out the voluminous paperwork that was considered necessary to push up standards. In the NHS, targets showed themselves to be dangerous. An inquiry into 'appalling standards of care' at Mid Staffordshire Hospitals Trust found that patients were being moved from A&E units before they were properly assessed because of pressure to hit a government-set target to treat them within four hours.[4]

TAX CREDIT FIASCO

Consider what happened with tax credits, which began to be introduced in 1999. Here was an apparently well-intentioned idea to help the poorest in society yet it turned into a nightmare of indebtedness for myriad families (some of whom even had to rely upon Salvation Army food parcels to survive), wasted vast sums of taxpayers' money, elicited a prime ministerial apology (that rarest of commodities) in the House of Commons, raised a host of questions about the competence of the public servants tasked with administering the scheme and resulted in the biggest liability payout ever made by a private contractor. Tax credits were meant to subsidize poorly paid work through the tax system, remove the stigma of benefits and 'make work pay'. Yet within months of their introduction, they were the subject of more complaints to MPs, the Inland Revenue, the Ombudsman and citizens' advice centres than any public policy in history. Years later, the system is still in chaos. The Parliamentary Ombudsman and the Citizens Advice Bureaux (CAB) continue to report an inundation of complaints. It is a system in chaos; yet this is something Labour ministers seemed unwilling to acknowledge.

When he became chancellor in 1997, Gordon Brown could have retained the existing Family Credit and made it more generous if he wanted to help poorer families. But he had a far grander scheme in mind, though you would not have guessed it from the passing reference in Labour's 1997 election manifesto: 'We will keep under continuous review all aspects of the tax and benefits systems to ensure that they are supportive of families and children.' Why did he not just improve what was already in place? Frank Field, who was minister for welfare reform in the first Labour government, believes he wanted to be seen as a great reformer in the tradition of David Lloyd George:

> The background can be found in that half sentence in the 1997 manifesto. Gordon took that as his mandate to reform

the whole system. Departments have cultures and the DSS as it then was, now the DWP, has a culture of paying out money. The Revenue has a culture of collecting money. Partly because Gordon wanted to change the welfare state so it was in his image, like Lloyd George, that level of reform, that means you have to do spectacular things. It doesn't lend to incremental reform in which you hold many of the issues constant. It means you throw the whole thing up in the air.[5]

The problems were compounded by an incessant, almost compulsive, tinkering. From 1999 onwards, the government abolished family credit, introduced working families' tax credit, introduced the disabled person's tax credit, introduced a childcare tax credit, introduced an employment credit, abolished the married couple's tax allowance, introduced the children's tax credit, introduced a baby tax credit, abolished the working families' tax credit, abolished the disabled person's tax credit, abolished the children's tax credit, abolished the baby tax credit, introduced a child tax credit, abolished the employment credit and introduced a working tax credit. As Field said: 'It was like gardeners going round pulling up their plants all the time to see whether the roots are still there.'

GOING ROUND IN CIRCLES

There are occasions where the government has simply gone around in circles to general confusion. The classic example of this was the reclassification of cannabis. The law controlling cannabis was set down in the Misuse of Drugs Act which when it went through parliament in 1971 had three categorizations: Class A containing the most dangerous substances like heroin and cocaine; Class B, with lesser drugs like cannabis and amphetamines; and Class C with controlled drugs like tranquillizers and painkillers. The ostensible point about this classification was to provide a matrix of potential and relative harms linked to a penalty scale. So Class A drugs carried the toughest punishments, with up to 7 years in prison for possession and a maximum of life for trafficking. Class B drugs attracted lesser, though still severe, penalties of 5 years and 14 years; and Class C had penalties of 2 years and 14 years. And that is where the law stood for 30 years until one afternoon in October 2001 David Blunkett, the home secretary, stunned MPs with a surprise announcement that he wanted to change the law and lower the categorization of cannabis to a Class C substance.

Mr Blunkett wanted to make the change in the law in the interests of 'consistency and credibility'. By the time the government had finished making a pig's ear of it, few would have used those epithets to describe a policy that had become utterly bewildering. You have to wonder whether they were smoking the stuff themselves and passing the spliffs around their ministerial committees. Eight years and three home secretaries later (and despite receiving consistent advice from the government's own specialist team, the Advisory Council on the Misuse of Drugs, that, actually, Mr Blunkett was right to lower the classification), it was moved back to Class B.

After all the shenanigans with the drugs laws, the government was back where it started. What had been the point of the exercise?

RIGHTING THE WRONGS

Why does modern British government make so many big and costly mistakes and why does it continue to do so? Does it not learn from its mistakes? There is something deeply and systemically wrong with administration in this country. Too much public policy either fails to achieve its stated objectives; or it does so at exorbitant cost; or it makes bad situations worse; or it has undesirable and unforeseen consequences. A civil service which was once the envy of the world has had its reputation tarnished by years of politicization and impossible demands placed upon it; laws are introduced almost weekly that merely serve to inconvenience people and drive them to distraction, not help them; bad decisions are routinely arrived at; and public projects that are simply unnecessary are introduced, vastly over-budget, while those that are needed are incompetently delivered, or not delivered at all.

Anthony King, professor of government at Essex University, has spent many years wondering why this is so and endeavouring to find out what might be done to put things right. He says:

> The high incidence of policy failure in Britain undoubtedly has a number of sources. Incompetent, unimaginative and blinkered ministers – and ministers who have been in their jobs for only weeks or months rather than years – must certainly be counted among them. So must hyper-ambitious ministers – the majority? – who care more for their careers and their media image than for developing policy that will serve the public interest and stand the test of time.[6]

King identified a litany of problems: restless ministers more concerned with simply leaving a mark and attracting attention to themselves ('I make an announcement therefore I am') than with doing anything of lasting benefit; ill-trained and inexperienced civil servants; excessive reliance upon IT systems that cannot deliver what is demanded of them within budget; the Treasury's reluctance to fund capital projects; and Britain's culture of adversarial politics 'which encourages leaders of all political parties to make policy promises for the purpose of differentiating themselves from their opponents irrespective of their promises' intrinsic merits'.[7]

King argued that nothing less than a fundamental change in political culture is required, with far greater emphasis on deliberation and less on the sort of posturing that has led to the promulgation of so much bad law and so many failed policies.

We have all known for several years that something has gone badly awry, without being wholly clear what it was and lacking something specific on which to vent our anger. The great expenses scandal of 2009 provided an outlet; but it was only a symptom, not a cause. The real culprit was a steady succession of bad laws and the imposition of a target culture that stifled local decision-making, removed discretion, cost the earth and gradually suffocated the life out of the great tradition of British commonsense.

It is not too late to reverse this but it requires the government to trust people more to run their own lives. It needs to loosen its grip and to give greater discretion to professionals to get on with what they have been trained to do without always looking over their shoulders for the man with the clipboard. Teachers whose jobs are made harder, not easier, by the imminent arrival of the Ofsted inspectors, like the outriders of the Spanish Inquisition, should be allowed to do their jobs; police officers must be allowed to bring order back to the streets and to use their experience and judgment in dealing with crimes, without constant worry about whether they are hitting the right target or ticking the right box. Politicians must understand that although advances in data-storing technology enable them to gather information about us all, this does not mean that they should.

Most of all, what is needed is a complete change of culture in the upper reaches of government. The perpetual legislative tinkering, the endless interference, the intrusiveness, the micro-management, the nannying, the hectoring, the belief that Whitehall knows best: it has all got to stop. Our commonsense has been stolen. We want it back.

NOTES

CHAPTER 1

1   Labour Party election manifesto, 1997.
2   Nick Clegg, '3,000 new criminal offences created since Tony Blair came to power', *Daily Mail*, 16 August 2006.
3   John Stuart Mill, *On Liberty*.
4   Edward Gibbon, *Decline and Fall of the Roman Empire, Vol. 4*, 1788, Chapter XLIV: Idea Of The Roman Jurisprudence. Part II.
5   A.V. Dicey, *An Introduction to the Study of the Law of the Constitution* (1885).
6   A.J.P. Taylor, *English History: 1914–1945, The Oxford History of England*, Oxford, 1965.
7   Harry Snook, *Crossing the Threshold: 266 ways the state can enter your home*, Centre for Policy Studies, London, 2007.
8   Joint Committee on Human Rights, 19th report, UK Parliament, September 2004.
9   ibid.
10 'Minister Announces Taskforce For Electronic Records', Department of Health press release, 22 July 2006.
11 Charles Clarke's speech on the media and civil liberties, LSE, 24 April 2006.
12 *Perspectives on a Changing Society*, British Social Attitudes, 23rd Report, 24 January 2007.
13 ibid.

CHAPTER 2

1   David Halpern and Clive Bates with Greg Beales and Adam Heathfield, *Personal Responsibility and Changing Behaviour: The state of knowledge and its implications for public policy*, Prime Minister's Strategy Unit, London, February 2004.
2   ibid.

3   Steve Doughty, 'Quangos spend more than £1bn on spin in a year', *Daily Mail*, 16 January 2009.

4   David Cameron, interview in the *Financial Times*, 13 January 2009.

5   Lord Jones of Birmingham evidence to the House of Commons Select Committee on public administration, 15 January 2009.

6   George Bridges, 'David Cameron should slash the public payroll', *Daily Telegraph*, 27 June 2008.

7   Daniel Finkelstein, 'If you thought this was bad, just you wait', *The Times*, 13 May 2009.

8   ibid.

9   Gordon Brown, speech on liberty, University of Westminster, 29 October 2007.

10   Tony McNulty, House of Commons, 23 October 2006.

11   Inspector Gadget, *Perverting the Course of Justice: The Hilarious and Shocking Inside Story of British Policing*, Monday Books, 2008.

12   Ian Johnston, President's Speech, National Conference of the Police Superintendents' Association for England and Wales, 16 September 2008.

13   Sir Ronnie Flanagan, Independent Review of Policing HMIC, February 2008.

14   Gordon Brown, House of Commons, 30 January 2008.

15   House of Lords Merits of Statutory Instruments Committee, 13 December 2007.

16   'Legislative Scrutiny: Health Bill; Marine and Coastal Access Bill', Joint Committee on Human Rights, Eleventh Report, April 2009.

17   *Sunday Telegraph*, 24 October 2009.

18   Jonathan Petre, 'Home for retired missionaries loses grant – because it won't ask residents if they are lesbians', *Mail on Sunday*, 28 December 2008.

CHAPTER 3

1   Kenneth Baker, House of Commons, 22 May 1991, Hansard vol. 191, cols 945–58.

2   Dangerous Dogs Bill Second Reading, 19 June 1991, Hansard vol. 192, cols 644–99.

3   The Pet Owners Parliament, Dangerous Dogs Act Watch website, www.petparliament.com, December 2008.

4   Kennel Club, 'New Bill Could Reduce Dangerous Dog Attacks', 27 April 2009.

5   House of Lords, Dog Control Bill Second Reading, 24 April 2009, Hansard col. 1689.

6   Jon Silverman, *History Today*, November 2000.

7   House of Commons debates, 25 June 1991, Hansard vol. 193.

8   ibid.

9   ibid.

10   *Daily Telegraph*, 2 May 1991.

11   Jon Silverman, ibid.

12   *The Public Inquiry into the Shootings at Dunblane Primary School on 13 March 1996*, The Stationery Office, London.

13   *Independent*, 16 October 1996.

14   House of Commons, 4 December 1996, Hansard col. 1166.

15   *Daily Mail*, 18 February 2009.

16   ibid.

17   ibid.

18   Hansard, 13 January 2009, col. 713W.

19   Stephen Moss, 'The banned rode on', *Guardian*, 7 November 2006.

20   Countryside Alliance News Release, 10 March 2009.

CHAPTER 4

1   This was as near to an accurate count as could be managed by going back through a variety of sources, mainly the parliamentary website and the National Archives.

2   Tony Blair speech to the Metropolitan Police conference in London on modernizing criminal justice. The title 'Re-balancing the criminal justice system' would be used time and again by Mr Blair, including in another set-piece policy address in Bristol in June 2006, suggesting that all the laws introduced between the two speeches had failed.

3   Helena Kennedy, *Just Law: The Changing Face of Justice and Why It Matters to Us All*, Chatto and Windus, London, 2004.

4   Blair, ibid.

5   'Lord Phillips of Worth Matravers Lord Chief Justice of England and Wales annual report of the Appeal Court's Criminal Division', 19 January 2009.

6   House of Commons select committee on home affairs, fifth report session, 2003–4).

7   Tessa Mayes, 'A law that could make stalkers of us all', *Spectator*, 15 November 2006.

8   Henry Porter, 'Blair laid bare: the article that may get you arrested', *Observer*, 29 June 2006.

9   Terri Dowty, quoted in BBC News Online magazine, 30 April 2004.

10   Nicola Lacey, ibid.

11   The Home Office, ibid.

12 R v A, [2005] EWCA Crim 3533; (2006) 1 Cr App R 28; *The Times*, 5 January 2006.

13 Draft Criminal Justice and Police Act 2001 (Amendment) and Police Reform Act 2002 (Modification) Order 2004. Fourth Standing Committee on Delegated Legislation, 14 September 2004.

14 The Right Honourable Lord Justice Leveson, Senior Presiding Judge, 'New developments in criminal justice: the approach to summary justice both in and out of court', lecture at the Centre for Crime and Justice Studies, King's College, London, 12 December 2007.

15 Richard Ford and Frances Gibb, 'Spot fines and cautions make criminal law a farce, says judge', *The Times*, 24 December 2007.

16 ibid.

17 'Woman accused of breaching noisy sex Asbo', Press Association, 27 April 2009.

18 Jack Straw, House of Commons, 8 April 1998, Hansard, col. 370.

19 Alexander Deane, *The Great Abdication: Why Britain's Decline Is the Fault of the Middle Class*, Imprint Academic, Exeter, 2005.

20 Straw, (see note 18).

21 Decca Aitkenhead, 'When home's a prison', *Guardian* (Society section), 24 July 2004.

22 Downing Street press conference, 12 May 2005.

CHAPTER 5

1   Interview with the author.

2   Letter to the *Daily Telegraph*, 7 June 2005.

3   Debate on Licensing Act, 8 June 2005, Hansard, col. 146WH.

4   ibid.

5   ibid.

6   DCMS, 'New streamlined rules to help pubs, village halls and other licensed premises', Press Notice 110/09, 29 July 2009.

7   House of Commons written answers, 14 Jun 2005, Hansard, col. 235W.

8   Interview with the author.

9   ibid.

10 'Circus fans face silent comedy after ban on clowns' trumpets', *The Times*, 23 September 2008.

11 Martin Burton, Evidence to the House of Commons Culture, Media and Sport Committee, Examination of Witnesses (Questions 146–59), 28 October 2008.

12 *The Times*, ibid.

13 Evidence to the Culture Media and Sport committee, ibid.

14 Burton, ibid.

15 DCMS Regulated Entertainment Guidelines, June 2007.

16 Interview with the author.

17 Letter from Chris Fox, president of the Association of Chief Police Officers, to Tessa Jowell, 2 July 2003.

18 House of Commons Culture Media and Sport Committee, Examination of Witnesses (Questions 200–219), 11 November 2008.

19 Robert Hardman, '"Roll over Beethoven". How I see it', *Daily Mail*, 23 June 2009.

20 Lord Clement-Jones, letter to the *Guardian*, 15 June 2009.

21 House of Commons Culture, Media and Sport Committee, Evidence, 11 November 2008.

22 ibid.

23 ibid.

24 Submission to committee, 29 September 2008.

25 Terence Blacker, 'Where are the guitar riots and accordion assaults?', *Independent*, 21 July 2009.

26 House of Commons Office of Deputy Prime Minister Select Committee, 2005, Memorandum by the British Beer and Pub Association (BBPA) (RL 16).

27 House of Commons Office of Deputy Prime Minister Select Committee, 2005, Memorandum from the Federation of Small Businesses (FSB) (RL 01).

28 ibid.

29 'Hairdressers face jail for offering customers mulled wine', *Daily Telegraph*, 29 November 2008.

30 House of Commons Culture, Media and Sport Committee, Evidence, 28 October 2008.

31 House of Commons Culture, Media and Sport Committee, Sixth Report Session 2008–9 HC 492.

32 Government Response to the House of Commons Culture, Media and Sport Committee Report on the Licensing Act 2003 Session 2008–9 Cm 7684.

33 ibid.

34 UK Music statement, 14 July 2009.

CHAPTER 6

1 Seymane's Case, King's Bench Opinion by Sir Edward Coke, 1604: 'The house of every one is to him as his castle and fortress, as well for his defence against injury and violence as for his repose.'

2   William Pitt, Earl of Chatham, speech on the Excise Bill, House of Lords, 1763.

3   Domestic Violence, Crime and Victims Bill [Lords], New clause 42 – Powers of authorised officers executing warrants, Public Bill Committees, 6 July 2004.

4   ibid.

5   'Bailiffs get power to use force on debtors', *Sunday Times*, 21 December 2008.

6   House of Commons, 8 March 1989, Hansard, col. 895.

7   Home Office, letter to Geert Wilders, 10 February 2009.

8   Serious Organized Crime and Police Act 2005 (Designated Area) Order 2005, Second Standing Committee on Delegated Legislation, 12 October 2005.

9   Constitutional and Governance Bill Explanatory Notes, July 2009

10   DCI Mick Neville, Security Document World Conference, London, 6 May 2008.

11   Cited on Channel 4 News Factcheck, 18 June 2008.

12   Neville, (see note 10).

13   BBC News website, 2008.

14   Brandon C. Welsh and David P. Farrington, *Home Office Research Study 252: Crime Prevention Effects of Closed Circuit Television: A Systematic Review*, Home Office Research, Development and Statistics Directorate, London, 2002.

15   Brandon C. Welsh and David P. Farrington, *Effects of Improved Street Lighting on Crime*, The Campbell Collaboration, Oslo, 2008.

16   'To CCTV or not to CCTV', Nacro, June 2002.

17   ibid.

18   'Lampposts beat CCTV at cutting crime', *Daily Telegraph*, 29 June 2002.

19   ibid.

20   Martin Gill and Angela Spriggs, *Home Office Research Study 292: Assessing the Impact of CCTV*, Home Office Research, Development and Statistics Directorate, London, 2005.

21   Henry Porter, 'There's no escape from these snoops', *Observer*, 3 December 2006.

22   Brendan O'Neill, 'Watching you watching me', *New Statesman*, 2 October 2006.

23   Peter Lilley, House of Commons, 29 November 2004, Hansard, col. 413.

24   The Identity Cards Act 2006 (Information and Code of Practice on Penalties Order 2009).

25   The Identity Cards Act 2006 (Prescribed Information) Regulations 2009.

26   Tony Mansfield and Marek Rejman-Greene, *Feasibility Study on the Use of Biometrics in an Entitlement Scheme*, National Physical Laboratory, Teddington, 2003.

27   Privacy International, 'The UK Identity Card proposals', November 2004.

28   Justice, 'Information Resource on Identity Cards', December 2004.
29   House of Commons, 24 February 2009, Hansard, col. 544W.
30   Labour Party Election Manifesto, 2005.

CHAPTER 7

1   Action for Children, 'As long as it takes: a new politics for children', September 2008.
2   *Daily Telegraph*, 17 September 2008.
3   ibid.
4   *Every Child Matters – The Next Steps*, DFES, March 2004.
5   Statutory Instruments 2007 No 2182 Children and Young Persons. The Children Act 2004 Information Database (England).
6   Joint Committee on Human Rights, 19th Report, September 2004.
7   ibid.
8   ibid.
9   'Child database will pry into family life', *Sunday Times*, 6 April 2008.
10   House of Lords, Hansard, 20 March 2006, col. 87.
11   Sarah Womack, 'Celebrity children will get database privacy', *Daily Telegraph*, 31 August 2006.
12   On the Channel 4 programme *Your Kids Under Surveillance*, September 2006.
13   'Director of "nappy curriculum" quits', *Daily Telegraph*, 8 November 2008.
14   'Early learning policies should not be imposed', Open EYE Campaign Steering Group letter, *The Times*, 24 July 2008 .
15   http://petitions.pm.gov.uk/OpenEYE.
16   'Toddler "assaulted" using "Supernanny" naughty chair', *Independent*, 16 September 2006.
17   'At the mercy of the anti-discipline police', *Sunday Times*, 1 October 2006.
18   Jennie Bristow, *Spiked*, 11 October 2006.
19   Interview with the author.
20   Police Research Group, *Phoenix Data Quality, Special Interest Series: Paper 11*, Home Office, London, 1998.
21   National Centre for Policing Excellence, *The Police National Computer Code of Practice*, Home Office, London, 2005.
22   *The Bichard Inquiry Report*, 22 June 2004, HC 653. Questions 1.252 to 1.264.
23   Frank Furedi and Jennie Bristow, *Licensed to Hug*, Civitas, London, 2008.
24   ibid p.xi.
25   ibid p.48.
26   ibid p.10.
27   House of Commons Home Affairs Select Committee, Evidence, 17 June 2008.

28 'CRB wastes money and alienates volunteers', letter, *Daily Telegraph*, 27 June 2008.

CHAPTER 8

1 'All eyes on Ireland's smoking ban', *BBC News*, 29 March 2004.
2 Letters to the Editor, *Daily Telegraph*, 2 June 2009.
3 'Smoking out the truth on the ban – two years on', *Publican*, 25 June 2009.
4 BBPA, 26 June 2009.
5 *Publican*, 26 June 2009.
6 'Pub in Hanley "killed" by smoking ban', *Sentinel*, 10 June 2008.
7 'We've lost it all. This has bankrupted us', *Huddersfield Daily Examiner*, 17 May 2005.
8 'Lincoln pub will close', *Lincolnshire Echo*, 9 April 2008.
9 *BBC News*, 4 April 2008.
10 'Scottish pubs suffering two years since ban', *Publican*, 26 March 2008.
11 'Smoking ban closes only cinema on the island', *BBC News*, 2 April 2008.
12 'Forest re-ignites calls for smoking ban reform', *Publican*, 1 July 2009.
13 Blog on the Conservative Home website, June 2009.
14 *Daily Telegraph*, 1 July 2009.
15 *Daily Mail*, 8 August 2006.
16 House of Commons Third Delegated Legislation Committee, Hansard, 21 June 2007.
17 ibid.
18 ibid.

CHAPTER 9

1 'Put young children on DNA list, urge police', *Observer*, 16 March 2008.
2 GeneWatch, www.genewatch.org/sub-537968. Accessed 4 December 2009.
3 House of Commons, Criminal Justice and Public Order Bill. Second Reading, 11 January 1994.
4 Lord Justice Sedley, BBC Radio Four News, 5 September 2007.
5 S. and Marper v. The United Kingdom (2008) European Court of Human Rights.
6 Home Office. *DNA Cracks Crime*. 4 January 2006.
7 'Government plans to keep DNA samples of innocent', *Guardian*, 27 February 2009.
8 Privacy International press release, 4 December 2008.

CHAPTER 10

1   Lord Lloyd, *Inquiry into Legislation Against Terrorism*, Stationery Office, London, 1996.

2   Court Of Appeal Judgement On Authorisation And Use Of Section 44 Of The Terrorism Act 2000, 29 July 2004.

3   Interview with the author, 2005.

4   Home Office figures.

5   Lord Carlile, *Report on the Operation in 2008 of the Terrorism Act 2000 and Part 1 of the Terrorism Act 2006*, The Stationery Office, London, June 2009.

6   Home Office statement, June 2009.

7   Carlile, op.cit.

8   Home Office press notice, 13 May 2009.

9   'Man arrested and locked up for five hours after taking photo of police van ignoring "no entry" sign', *Daily Mail*, 20 August 2008.

10 'Jail for photographing police?', *British Journal of Photography*, 28 January 2009.

11 ibid.

12 'Harry Potter actor Jamie Waylett guilty of growing cannabis', *The Times*, 16 July 2009.

13 'Woman "detained" for filming police search launches high court challenge', *Guardian*, 22 July 2009.

14 ibid.

15 'Police shut down Facebook page after angry drivers post hate comments about "Terminator" traffic warden', *Daily Mail*, 15 January 2009.

16 'Andrew Pelling MP stopped by cops for taking pictures of East Croydon cycle path', *Croydon Guardian*, 7 January 2009.

17 ibid.

18 Letters to the Editor, *The Times*, 16 October 2001.

19 *Daily Telegraph*, 18 October 2001.

20 House of Commons, Hansard, 23 June 1998, col. 894.

21 *Daily Telegraph*, 21 October 2001.

22 'Religious hatred law abandoned after Bill retreat, *Daily Telegraph*, 15 December 2001.

23 *Daily Telegraph*, 11 December 2004.

24 Labour Party Manifesto, *Forward not back*, 2005, pp 111–12.

25 *Misconceptions about RIPA*, Office for Security and Counter-terrorism, Home Office, London.

26 Sir Christopher Rose, *Annual Report of the Chief Surveillance Officer*, The Stationery Office, London, 2009.

27 ibid (2008).

28 House of Commons, Hansard, 22 July 2008, col. 111WS.

29   Sir Paul Kennedy, *Report of the Interception of Communications Commissioner*, The Stationery Office, London, 2008.

30   Local Government Association for England, letter to all council leaders, 23 June 2008.

31   'Council spy cases hit 1,000 a month', *Daily Telegraph*, 12 April 2008.

32   *Daily Mail*, 11 April 2008.

33   Local Government Association for England, (see note 30).

34   Chris Hastings, 'Anti-terrorism laws used to spy on noisy children', *Sunday Telegraph*, 6 September 2008.

35   Local Government Association for England (see note 30).

36   Office for Security and Counter-terrorism, *Misconceptions about RIPA*, Home Office, 2008.

CHAPTER 11

1   Key dates in the sociological history and development of Great Britain. Education resources.

2   Royal Commission of the Working of the Factory and Workshop Act 1875.

3   Sidney Webb, preface to B.L. Hutchins and A. Harrison, *A History of Factory Legislation*, London, 1910.

4   Lord Robens, *Report of the Committee on Safety and Health at Work*, The Stationery Office, London, 1972.

5   Bill Callaghan, chairman, Health and Safety Commission, the Annual ACAS and University of Warwick Lecture in memory of Sir Pat Lowry, 20 March 2007.

6   HSE figures.

7   Callaghan, (see note 5).

8   Lord Cullen, 'The Development of Safety Legislation', Royal Academy of Engineering and Royal Society of Edinburgh Lecture, 1996.

9   ibid.

10   King's Bench Division, Edwards v. NCB, 1949.

11   Building (Amendment) (No.3) Regulations 2004 (SI 2004/3210).

12   Philip K. Howard, *The Death of Commonsense: How Law is Suffocating America*, Random House, New York, 1994.

13   ibid.

14   John Ungoed-Thomas, *Sunday Times*, 16 May 2004.

15   ibid.

16   *Managing the safety of Burial Ground Memorials: Practical advice for dealing with unstable memorials*, Ministry of Justice, January 2009.

17   BBC *Panorama*, 'May Contain Nuts', 26 April 2009.

18   S.J. Thomson, 'Do's and Don'ts: children's experiences of the primary

school playground', *Environmental Education Research*, Special issue: vol.13, no.4, 2007.

19 Sarah Thomson, 'Playground or Playpound: the contested terrain of the primary school playground', Department of Education, Keele University, paper to the British Educational Research Association.

20 *Health and Safety Myths: Looking at the truth behind the headlines*, TUC Report, TUC, London, October 2006.

21 ibid.

22 Hugo Rifkind, 'Health and Safety – a grave error of judgment', *The Times*, 21 April 2009.

23 ibid.

24 'Police accused of waiting too long over barbecue shootings', *Daily Telegraph*, 8 June 2004.

25 'Police apologise for murder scene delay', *Guardian*, 7 October 2004.

26 *BBC News*, 21 September 2007.

27 David Davis, speech during campaigning for Crewe and Nantwich by-election, 15 May 2008.

28 Boris Johnson, 'Safety phobia isn't funny – it can be fatal', *Daily Telegraph*, 7 October 2004.

29 'Council "Scrooges" ban lollipop man's tinsel', *Daily Mail*, 10 December 2008.

30 'Young carol singers in safety ban', *BBC News*, 27 November 2008.

31 'University student, 22, refused M&S Christmas crackers under Explosives Act', *Daily Telegraph*, 17 December 2008.

32 'Christmas concert cancelled over fears audience member might "fall over in the dark"', *Daily Mail*, 17 December 2008.

33 House of Commons, Hansard, 5 February 2003, cols 408–16.

CHAPTER 12

1 John Seddon, *Systems Thinking in the Public Sector*, Triarchy Press, Axminster, 2008.

2 ibid.

3 ibid.

4 'Patients "being hurried though casualty departments"', *Daily Telegraph*, 14 July 2009.

5 Interview with the author.

6 Anthony King, 'Deliberation and the making of British public policy', University of Essex conference paper, May 2004.

7 ibid.

INDEX

NB. Page references for tables are in **bold**.